D0068775

POOREST OF AMERICANS
THE MEXICAN AMERICANS OF THE
LOWER RIO GRANDE VALLEY OF TEXAS

ROBERT LEE MARIL

UNIVERSITY OF NOTRE DAME PRESS
NOTRE DAME, INDIANA

Library of Congress Cataloging-in-Publication Data

Maril, Robert Lee.
    Poorest of Americans: the Mexican Americans of the lower
Rio Grande Valley of Texas / Robert Lee Maril.
        p.   cm.
    Bibliography: p.
    Includes index.
    ISBN 0-268-01580-5
    1. Mexican Americans—Rio Grande Valley—Economic
conditions.   2. Mexican Americans—Texas—Economic conditions.   3. Mexican Americans—Rio Grande Valley—Social
conditions.   4. Mexican Americans—Texas—Social conditions.
5. Rio Grande Valley—Economic conditions.   6. Rio Grande
Valley—Social conditions.   I. Title.
F392.R5M37   1989
305.8'687207644—dc20   89-40015

Manufactured in the United States of America

In memory of

MEREA SENTER MARIL

CONTENTS

PREFACE

I have used several different methods to collect and analyze the data in this study. I have closely scrutinized pertinent census data as far back as the records will allow, and have collected other kinds of relevant data from different local, state, and federal agencies. I have reviewed numerous studies from a variety of disciplines which touch on the Valley, however tangentially—there have been relatively few efforts by social scientists which have focused directly on the Valley and its people. I have relied heavily on secondary historical sources of the region; at the same time I have interviewed, when possible, particular residents about important historical events and processes.

In 1985 and 1986 I also interviewed seventy-five Valley businessmen, social workers, police officers, doctors, migrant farm workers, growers, bankers, ranchers, lawyers, priests and nuns, educators, college students, politicians and political activists. Certainly this was not a representative survey, but it provided additional insights into the data already collected.

This study is based upon thirteen years of professional experience in the Valley. My own previous research projects have focused upon health issues among poor Valley Hispanics, the peculiar nature of the Valley economy, and social problems common to this border region. I have been particularly involved in the study of the multiple uses of marine resources in this area by both industry and the poor, resources which include the Valley's commercial shrimp industry, minerals, and coastal lands.

This book is also based upon what I have learned about the Valley and its people from working in this region. In 1975 I taught reading to migrant farm workers at Texas State Technical Institute in Harlingen. For twelve years I was an instructor and researcher in the Department of Behavioral Sciences at Texas

Southmost College in Brownsville. I also taught college courses in Port Isabel, San Benito, and Harlingen. The vast majority of these students were low-income Mexican Americans; they were a constant source of information about the social processes which predominate in the Valley.

I also learned much about the Valley from serving as a consultant to a number of Valley educational institutions, city, county, and state programs and agencies designed to serve the poor, and the legal community. For seven years I was a board member, then vice-president and president of the board, of a health clinic which served low-income Mexican-American women. In 1982 I started a private junior high school in Brownsville; this involvement led to close contact and knowledge of middle- and upper-class families in Brownsville, Matamoros, and the surrounding area.

The methodological strength of this study is that it employs several different methods of data collection and analysis which are buttressed by firsthand experiences over an extended period of time. I have made every attempt to guard against the bias of personal observation and experience. A continual dialogue with other colleagues in sociology, anthropology, history, and economics has helped me to maintain a balanced perspective. I have endeavored to be as fair and objective as possible in this study; if I have erred in this, it has been on the side of caution and restraint.

I owe much to the intellectual contributions of Michael V. Miller; without him this project would not have been initiated. I would also like to thank Ellwyn Stoddard, Oscar Martinez, Noel Parsons, Paul Durrenberger, Michael B. Katz, José Hinojosa, Jim Copp, David Gartman, Amy Bushnell, and two anonymous reviewers, all of whom commented on various drafts of the manuscript. At Texas Southmost College Jim Sullivan, Manuel Medrano and his students, Antonio Zavaleta, Ginger Woods, and Juliet Garcia were very generous in their support. Cheryl Shirley and Alice Gonzalez both served as typists; I also have Ms. Shirley to thank for the map. Mike Jepson was an able research assistant in the final stage of research. William B. Davis, Dean of the Graduate School at the University of South Alabama, and Robert Shipp, Director of the Coastal Research and Development Institute, were particularly supportive of my research. As always, Andrea Fisher Maril provided the emotional support during the difficult times so that this book could reach completion.

I would also like to thank those individuals who served as informants, particularly those who work in Valley public school systems, health clinics, hospitals, and local poverty agencies and programs.

A timely grant from the Catholic Diocese of Brownsville and Texas Southmost College facilitated the final research for this book.

Any faults, of course, remain my own and not those of either individuals who helped me or institutions which provided funds for the research.

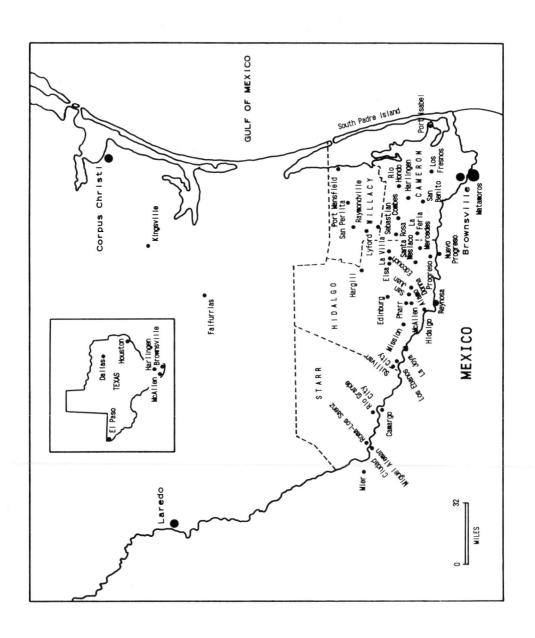

INTRODUCTION

The Lower Rio Grande Valley of Texas, the Valley as it is called, lies at the extreme southern tip of Texas on the border with Mexico. The Valley covers a large area, some 4,200 square miles, and is divided into the four counties of Cameron, Hidalgo, Starr, and Willacy. This region is home to more than 600,000 Americans, approximately 80 percent of whom call themselves Mexican-American, the remainder identifying themselves as Anglo.

The Valley does not visually replicate the stereotypical landscapes of urban poverty. There are no block-long, high-rise slums. There are no overt signs of urban blight—the vacant lots, concrete shells of buildings, the glass-covered playgrounds.

There are, instead, Mexican-American *barrios,* residential Mexican-American neighborhoods, which appear far different from their urban counterparts in the north. The *barrios* are filled with single-family dwellings, often several to a small lot, the newest facing the back alley, all surrounded by a homemade wooden or wire fence. Most houses are painted in bright colors. Many of the yards are carefully tended, with an abundance of flowers and gardens in bloom. This vegetation sometimes completely covers the tiny two- and three-room houses.

As one walks down a *barrio* street on a summer afternoon, there are the sounds of children playing, dogs barking, birds singing, doors slamming, and an occasional car racing up the street. Hibiscus, acacia, poinsettia, and other flowering plants and trees, including citrus, provide a tropical lusciousness to the neighborhood. In the spring the sweet aroma of orange and grapefruit blossoms blankets these same streets.

It is not unusual to see a home owned by a middle-class Mexican-American family amid the homes of the poor. Almost always this dwelling is constructed of brick; rooms have been

1

added on as the family's needs and wealth increased over the years.

The Valley countryside is dotted with *colonias*, rural subdivisions which house some of the poorest of the Valley Hispanics. It is estimated that there are over one hundred *colonias* in Hidalgo County alone. Here the poverty is more visibly acute, from the one-room wooden shacks to the rusting oil drums which residents use to store drinking water hauled from nearby irrigation ditches. There are few paved streets, street lights, sewers, or drains. When it rains, many *colonias* quickly flood. Outhouses and septic systems fill the streets and yards with raw sewage.

Nevertheless, it is quite possible to visit the Valley and never really see a *colonia*. *Colonias* remain relatively invisible; many lie far from the major highways and roads, squeezed between enormous fields of cotton, sorghum, and corn, or hugging the edges of irrigation canals and citrus groves.

At first glance the downtown area of Valley towns seems no different than those in other parts of Texas or the Southwest. Across the tracks, in the poorer sections, the small furniture stores, bars, clothing stores, and car repair shops are similar to those in Dallas, Houston, St. Louis, or Los Angeles.

Mexican Americans in restaurants, grocery stores, and urban malls dress well in light clothing that is suited to the climate; bright tropical colors predominate. Small children appear especially well dressed and groomed and receive much attention from their parents. Yet in the Valley it is not just female heads of families, nor the young, nor those who are unemployed who are poor. Nor is it those who fall into poverty for the first time. Poverty is the norm among Valley Mexican Americans. To live in the Valley and to be Hispanic is almost by definition to be in or close to poverty.

Each year hundreds of thousands of American tourists flock to the beaches of South Padre Island and to the mercados, restaurants, and cantinas of nearby Mexico. It is quite possible for these occasional visitors to focus on the pleasures of the Valley's subtropical climate, the miles of beaches, the sunsets over the Laguna Madre, and the bright lights of Matamoros and Reynosa on the southern banks of the Rio Grande. It is quite possible to accept the pleasant physical appearance of the Valley barrios at face value and to never see a Valley *colonia*. But although the poverty is not at once apparent, it is very real. The brightly painted exteriors of the small Valley homes belie the lack of financial security, adequate health care, educational opportunities, even the availability of food from one week to the next.

It is no exaggeration to observe that the ultimate burden of poverty is the degree to which it scars the soul. My wife and I had the good fortune to be foster parents for three Mexican-American teenagers. The personal poverty of our foster children was not just a lack of material goods, food, a roof over their heads. It was a poverty in which their self-esteem and worth had been daily questioned. They rarely had the luxury of taking their emotional security for granted. No census data can measure this impact on our three foster children or upon the hundreds of thousands of Valley poor. Some are able to carry the burden and heal with time; others are not.

Valley poverty is systematically perpetuated by political and social institutions which justify and maintain a social order premised on inequality. Having observed the system firsthand for more than a decade, I have had sufficient time to note how it reacts to demands for social change and how it continues to thrive. This study not only describes the current conditions in the Valley and their historical development, but offers a blueprint for the changes that must take place if poverty is to cease as a way of life for the majority of people in the Valley.

1. HOW POOR?

The Mexican Americans of the Lower Rio Grande Valley of Texas are among the poorest people in the United States. By almost every quantifiable measure which describes poverty or correlates of poverty, Valley Mexican Americans are much poorer than those who live in other cities and regions of this country.[1] This is not to minimize the poverty of other Americans, but to assert the existence of this neglected population of Mexican-American poor.

Social scientists and policy-makers have argued for many years over exact definitions of who is poor and who is not. Indeed, there is a surprisingly large literature focused on this issue, yet a clear definition of poverty is not easy to come by.[2] The most commonly accepted indicator of poverty is annual income, but it is also important to consider other measures which relate to the quality of life. These include unemployment rates, educational levels, health status, housing conditions, and the tax base. Other characteristics of the economic infrastructure are also important, such as the quality of water, sewage and sanitation, the availability of police and fire protection, and Emergency Medical Services (EMS).

Statistics, while relatively easy to collect and commonly accepted as useful, have a tendency to oversimplify, even dehumanize, that which they describe. Lists of numbers can easily numb the minds of even the most sensitive observers. For this reason, qualitative data are of equal importance. Such data not only lend depth and credence to the statistics, they provide the necessary background from which to interpret the statistics. Qualitative data will be used extensively in the following chapters.

ANNUAL INCOME

Based on a study of food consumption by the Department of Agriculture in 1955, the Social Security Administration of the federal government devised a definition of poverty which is now the standard.[3] This definition was developed in 1964, revised in 1969, and again in 1982, but the core of the definition has not changed. In 1955 families of three or more persons spent approximately one-third of their income on food. The poverty level for Americans was set at three times the cost of a food plan as devised by the Department of Agriculture. This food plan was an emergency plan that provided minimal sustenance. Other considerations are also taken into account in the definition, including family size and sex of the head of the household. Inflation is considered, as are other contingencies such as reliance on federal subsidies that might theoretically mask the real buying power of an average family.

Thus annual income is the crucial variable in determining who is poor and who is not, according to the government. Census statistics describing both median family incomes and per capita incomes for Valley families and individuals demonstrate the large percentages of the Valley's population who are poor or near poverty.

A comparison of median family incomes (table 1) indicates the lack of improvement in Valley incomes over the past three decades.[4] Valley median incomes are a fraction of the median family incomes for non-border counties of Texas and the rest of the United States.[5] In 1960 the median family income in Cameron County, for example, was just $3,326, or 56.8 percent of the

TABLE 1

Median Family Income, 1960, 1970, 1980

	1960		1970		1980	
	Median	% of U.S. Median	Median	% of U.S. Median	Median	% of U.S. Median
United States	$5,620	100	$9,867	100	$19,661	100
Texas	4,880	86.2	8,490	88.5	19,619	99.7
Cameron	3,216	56.8	5,068	52.8	11,731	59.6
Hidalgo	2,780	49.1	4,776	49.8	12,083	61.4
Starr	1,700	30.2	3,593	36.4	8,627	43.8
Willacy	2,902	51.6	4,156	42.1	11,443	58.2

Source: U.S. Census

TABLE 2

Per Capita Incomes for Selected Years

	1959 INCOME	% OF U.S. MEDIAN	1969 INCOME	% OF U.S. MEDIAN	1979 INCOME	% OF U.S. MEDIAN	1983 INCOME	% OF U.S. MEDIAN	% CHANGE IN 24 YEARS
United States	$1,836	100	$3,139	100	$9,494	100	$11,687	100	—
Texas	1,713	93.3	2,950	94.0	9,439	99.4	11,686	99.9	6.6
Cameron	1,007	54.8	1,580	50.3	5,506	57.9	6,654	56.9	2.1
Hidalgo	867	48.3	1,523	48.5	4,939	52.0	6,012	51.4	3.1
Starr	525	28.5	1,072	34.1	3,178	33.4	3,734	31.9	3.4
Willacy	946	51.5	1,232	39.2	4,596	48.4	5,862	50.1	-1.4

Source: U.S. Census.

national median. Twenty years later, in 1980, median family income in Cameron County had increased to 59.6 percent of the national median, a gain of only 2.8 percent.

Per capita income figures for the four counties in the Valley show the same trend (table 2).[6] Per capita income in Hidalgo County in 1959 was less than one-half as much as the national median. Twenty-four years later, in 1983, per capita income had increased by only 3.1 percent in Hidalgo County. Moreover, as with median family incomes, per capita income figures for Valley counties were very different from other Texas counties. Families and individuals in Texas showed significant increases in income over this twenty-year period, while Valley residents did not. The most recent survey by the Department of Commerce placed the McAllen-Edinburg-Mission and the Brownsville-Harlingen Metropolitan Statistical Areas (MSA) as the lowest and third lowest, respectively, in personal annual income in the United States.[7]

Median and per capita income figures of Valley residents place many families and individuals well below or close to the government's definition of poverty (table 3). In 1980, 26.0%, 29.0%, 50.6%, and 29.6% of all families in Cameron, Hidalgo, Starr, and Willacy Counties, respectively, were below the poverty line.[8] A similar trend is evident in all four counties for individuals.

TABLE 3

Poverty Status of Valley Counties, 1970, 1980

	1970				1980			
	Persons below Poverty Line		Families below Poverty Line		Persons below Poverty Line		Families below Poverty Line	
	#	%	#	%	#	%	#	%
United States	27,208,583	13.7	5,481,149	10.7	27,392,580	12.4	5,670,000	9.6
Texas	2,038,025	18.7	413,804	14.7	2,035,873	14.7	412,076	11.1
Cameron	64,009	46.0	11,686	38.5	66,046	31.8	12,813	26.0
Hidalgo	89,938	49.8	15,995	42.0	99,081	35.2	18,920	29.0
Starr	9,713	54.9	1,896	51.9	13,698	50.6	2,684	50.6
Willacy	8,865	57.2	1,556	46.1	6,065	34.8	1,200	29.6

Sources: U.S. Census, Texas Employment Commission

The percentages of Valley families and persons in poverty are two and one-half to three times that of all Texas families and persons. However, it is important to note that there were substantial declines in individual and family poverty from 1970 to 1980 in the Valley. The reasons for this apparent trend will be discussed in detail below.

One problem with using a definition of poverty which emphasizes annual income is that those individuals very close to poverty are by definition excluded from consideration. A family of four, for example, which earned even a few dollars more than $8,414 in 1980 would not have been counted among the poor, although certainly their situation could be considered little better than those earning $8,414. For this reason the Census also tabulates those whose earnings are 125 percent of a poverty income, and when these families are included we get a more accurate statistical picture of the extent of Valley poverty.

In 1980 the number of families in this expanded category was close to one-half the total number of all families in the towns of Pharr, Edcouch, Elsa, La Feria, Raymondville, Rio Grande City, Donna, Mercedes, and Weslaco (table 4). Several Valley cities have more than one-half of their families in poverty.[9] Among these are Alamo (50.6%), Roma and Los Saenz (62.2%), Las Milpas and Hidalgo Park (62.9%), and Alton (71.2%). Eleven percent of all Valley residents live in *colonias,* unincorporated housing developments where the poorest of the poor reside. Unfortunately separate annual income figures for families and individuals who live in *colonias* are not available.

Since 1970 the actual numbers of Valley poor have increased, but the percentage of the poor who compose the total Valley population has in fact declined. In Hidalgo County, for example, there were 9,413 more individuals (2,925 families) who were poor in 1980 than in the previous decade even though the percentage of those who were poor declined. Similarly, in Cameron County there were 2,040 (1,127 families) new to poverty but the percentage of the population who were poor declined. Only in Willacy County was there a decline in the number of people who were poor as well as in the percentage who were poor. From 1970 to 1980 there was a total increase of 8,383 (3,696 families) in poverty in the Valley.

TABLE 4

Valley Cities by Families in Poverty, 1980

	All Families	Families in Poverty	Families in 125% Poverty	% of Families in 125% Poverty	Rank by % in 125% Poverty	Rank by # of Families in Poverty
Alamo	1,332	537	675	50.6	4	13
Alton	533	303	380	71.2	1	17
Brownsville	19,243	5,338	6,875	35.7	15	1
Donna	2,187	887	1,084	49.5	6	10
Edcouch	676	268	312	46.1	8	20
Edinburg	5,476	1,233	1,744	31.8	18	7
Elsa	1,090	424	546	50.0	5	15
Harlingen	10,577	2,195	3,206	30.3	19	3
La Feria	888	301	356	40.0	13	19
Las Milpas/ Hidalgo Park	561	308	353	62.9	2	18
McAllen	15,929	3,316	4,333	27.2	21	2
Mercedes	2,752	1,049	1,357	49.3	7	9
Mission	5,494	1,370	1,812	32.9	17	6
Pharr	4,843	1,569	2,070	42.7	11	4
Port Isabel	887	195	251	28.2	20	21
Raymondville	2,137	723	965	45.1	9	11
Rio Grande City	1,952	671	839	42.9	10	12
Roma/ Los Saenz	740	382	461	62.2	3	16
San Benito	4,223	1,057	1,445	34.4	16	8
San Juan	1,739	442	647	37.2	14	14
Weslaco	4,433	1,357	1,865	42.0	12	5

Source: U.S. Census

One might be tempted to ignore the gross increase in numbers of newly Valley poor and, instead, to focus on the positive, the drop in the percentage of those in poverty. This view would attribute the lower percentage to the creation of new jobs, largely arising out of the relocation of cut-and-sew and electronics plants to the Valley. However, there are some strong data to suggest an influx of better educated and more highly skilled personnel to the Valley during the 1970s to take the best of these new jobs. These new professionals and managers helped to contribute to the decline in the percentage of the Valley population who are poor, while the status of those in poverty changed little. Miller documents the lack of improved income among long-term poor residents in Brownsville in the 1970s in spite of increases in manufacturing jobs.[10] All that is left after the manager and supervisor's positions are taken in these plants, and in the new businesses which these industries stimulate, are minimum wage jobs that provide few benefits, little job security, and no future.

It would be misleading to ignore this decrease in the percentage of those who were poor during the 1970s as compared to the present decade. On the other hand, the short- and long-term impact of apparent advances among the poor must be closely scrutinized. My argument here is that increases in minimum wage jobs as the result of cut-and-sew operations, electronic plants, and the newer twin-plants of the 1980s, "maquiladoras," are far from an economic panacea and have resulted in very limited opportunities to the Valley poor.

This extreme Valley poverty is far from equally shared between the majority of Mexican Americans in the Valley and the Anglo minority (table 5).[11] Of the Valley poverty population in 1987, there were an estimated 201,245 Hispanics compared to 6,747 Anglos. Since Valley Hispanics outnumber Anglos at a rate of five to one, one would expect there to be more Valley Hispanics who are poor than Valley Anglos. However, the percentage of all Valley whites who were poor is 6.2 percent as compared to 39.7 percent of all Valley Hispanics. Valley Hispanics are six and one-half times more likely to be poor than are Valley Anglos.

This earnings differential is explained in part by the distribution of occupations between Mexican Americans and Anglos.[12] Mexican Americans are underrepresented in executive, professional, and technical occupations, all of which are traditionally higher-paying jobs, and are overrepresented in service occupations, agricultural work, precision products, machine operations, transportation, and handlers—all jobs which pay at the low end of the wage scale (table 6).[13]

Although only 16 percent of the total Valley population is Anglo, Anglos are employed in 46.6 percent of all executive jobs, 45.5 percent of all professional jobs, and 30.7 percent of all technical jobs. Anglos are outnumbered in the Valley five to one,

TABLE 5

*Valley Poverty Population by Age, Sex, and Race, 1987**

	TOTAL	BLACK	HISPANIC	ANGLO
Total Population	616,200	1,548	506,372	108,280
Poverty Population				
Total	208,467	475	201,245	6,747
Under 16	94,254	147	93,755	352
16-21	24,672	73	24,048	551
22-54	62,857	188	60,651	2,018
55-64	10,970	32	9,559	1,379
65 and Over	15,714	35	13,232	2,447
Female Poverty Population				
Total	112,168	286	107,899	3,983
Under 16	47,112	74	46,785	253
16-21	12,831	41	12,530	260
22-54	26,274	62	25,291	921
55-64	4,881	10	4,301	570
65 and Over	6,161	12	5,266	883
Male Poverty Population				
Total	96,299	189	93,346	2,764
Under 16	47,142	73	46,970	99
16-21	11,841	32	11,518	291
22-54	26,274	62	25,291	921
55-64	4,881	10	4,301	570
65 and Over	6,161	12	5,266	883

*Figures do not include Starr County.
Source: Texas Employment Commission

but there are almost as many Anglo executives as there are Mexican-American executives: 6,593 to 6,909. On the other hand, Mexican Americans who work as handlers, cleaners, or helpers outnumber Anglos in the same jobs 9,205 to 847.

Poverty figures for Hispanics throughout the United States have always been disproportionately high. In 1980, the percentage of Hispanic poor outnumbered Anglos who were poor by 25.7 to 13.0 percent, almost two to one.[14] However, poverty rates for Valley Mexican Americans are twice as high as the rates for Hispanics nationwide—Valley Mexican Americans are not poor simply because they are susceptible to the various factors which influence Hispanic poverty throughout the United States. There is something unique about Valley poverty.

Poverty along the U.S.-Mexico border is far worse than in any other regions of the United States.[15] Valley Mexican Americans, however, are considerably less well-off than other border

TABLE 6

Valley Employment by Occupation and Race, 1980*

	HISPANIC		ANGLO		BLACK		
	#	%	#	%	#	%	TOTAL
Exec., Admin. Managerial	6,909	50.9	6,593	48.6	63	.4	13,565
Professional Specialty	9,704	53.7	8,218	45.5	118	.6	18,040
Technicians & Related	2,373	69.2	1,056	30.7	0	.0	3,429
Sales Occupations	14,312	71.9	5,568	27.9	20	.1	19,900
Administrative Support	17,875	71.5	7,071	28.2	46	.1	24,992
Service Occupations	19,358	85.7	3,084	13.6	146	.6	22,588
Farming, Forestry, & Fishing	12,092	84.5	2,193	15.3	15	.1	14,300
Precision Production, etc.	16,853	75.9	5,307	23.9	25	.1	22,185
Machine Operator, etc.	14,339	94.2	855	5.6	21	.1	15,215
Transportation, Moving Material	7,464	87.1	1,078	12.5	26	.3	8,568
Handlers, Cleaners, Helpers	9,205	91.4	847	8.4	12	.1	10,064

*Figures do not include Starr County.
Source: Texas Employment Commission

peoples in California, Arizona, and New Mexico. The five sparsely populated Texas border counties of Dimmit, Kinney, Maverick, Presidio, and Zapata are the only border counties which have populations poorer than the Valley.[16] However, these counties have a combined total population of less than 45,000, or 7.5 percent of the Valley's growing population, and are predominately rural compared to the Valley's urban population. Laredo in Webb County is the Texas border city which comes closest to approximating the depth of poverty found in the Valley's cities and colonias.

The extent of Valley poverty is, nevertheless, far worse than all of these income figures would suggest. A variety of other quantitative measures, correlates of poverty, help to further document the degree of poverty in this region.

OTHER INDICATORS OF EXTREME POVERTY

Unemployment rates of the more than 300 MSAs are regularly gathered by the Department of Labor. In 1976 the McAllen-Pharr-Edinburg MSA ranked 305th out of 305, having the highest unemployment in the nation. That same year the Brownsville-Harlingen-San Benito MSA ranked 303rd. By 1986 the two Valley MSAs still ranked among the five MSAs with the highest unemployment in the United States.

Unemployment trends over the last decade in the Valley have been quite unlike the rest of Texas or the United States.[17] While Texas has enjoyed boom years and subsequent very low unemployment rates for a time (table 7), unemployment in the Valley over these same years has steadily increased.[18] The average unemployment rate for all four counties has risen from 12.5 percent in 1978 to 20.5 percent in 1986. Rates for similar time periods in Texas and the United States were two and one-half times lower than those in the Valley.

Because of the rapid decrease in oil prices in 1986, Texas is suffering through an economic "bust." Unemployment in Houston in the spring of 1988, for example, was at 9 percent. At the same time that Houstonians and a majority of others throughout the state of Texas complained very loudly about their run-away unemployment rates and the hard economic times they faced, Valley unemployment was almost double that of the hardest hit regions in the rest of Texas.[19]

Subemployment rates include not only the unemployed but also the underemployed, the working poor, those discouraged from seeking work, and the subemployed themselves, those who work but are receiving food stamps. Conservative estimates of subemployment rates in 1974 were at approximately 25 percent.

TABLE 7

Unemployment Rates for Selected Years

	1978	1980	1983	1985	1986
United States	6.1	7.1	9.6	7.1	6.9
Texas	4.8	5.2	8.0	7.0	8.0
Cameron County	10.1	9.6	15.3	14.5	15.9
Hidalgo County	12.8	12.8	19.5	19.1	19.6
Starr County	31.4	36.7	40.5	33.8	37.1
Willacy County	10.2	13.4	14.5	12.8	13.3
Average of the Four Counties	12.5	12.6	17.5	20.5	21.5

Source: Texas Employment Commission

Based on interviews with local and state economic experts, I estimate that subemployment rates easily exceed 35 percent of the total work force.

A majority of poor Mexican Americans work full or part time in the Valley but fall, nevertheless, into poverty. In Cameron County 32.4 percent of all poverty householders work full time and 31.0 percent part time, while in Hidalgo and Willacy Counties the figures are 30.5 and 36.8 percent.

Poverty in the Valley falls most heavily on the young and on women.[20] Of the 208,467 Valley citizens who are defined as poor, nearly half are under age sixteen (see table 5). Women between the ages of 22 and 54 are much more likely to be poor than men of the same age.

One-third of all Valley residents received food stamps in 1986.[21] More than 200,000 Valley poor received food coupons valued at $114,600,298, and more qualify but choose not to receive food stamps.[22] Valley fishermen are very reluctant to accept what they consider to be government handouts; only in the very worst of economic circumstances, when all other financial resources were exhausted, would they ask for help.[23] Only 27.3 percent of all poverty families in Hidalgo and Willacy Counties and 27.2 percent in Cameron chose to accept any form of public assistance in 1980.[24] A vast majority of Valley poor only seek out public assistance when there are no other alternatives available.[25]

The number of Valley recipients of the Women's, Infants', and Children's Nutrition Program (WIC) is far lower than one would expect, although certainly not insignificant—35,853 Valley poor, or about 6 percent of the population.[26] Workers in this program believe that increased publicity and education about the program would attract more Valley residents. Similarly, the number of those who receive benefits from Aid to Families with Dependent Children (AFDC) is much lower than expected.[27] In 1985, 35,031 adults and children received $1,742,786 per month.

The lack of formal education as well as the quality of education are both serious impediments to economic success in the Valley. There are tremendous differences in levels of educational attainment in the adult population in the Valley as compared to all Texans (table 8).[28] In 1980, 25.6 percent of all residents of

TABLE 8

Educational Attainment by Race in Cameron and Hidalgo Counties, 1970 and 1980

EDUCATION	1970						1980						
	TOTAL		HISPANIC		NON-HISPANIC		TOTAL		HISPANIC		NON-HISPANIC		TEXAS (% ALL RACES)
	#	%	#	%	#	%	#	%	#	%	#	%	
Elementary & Junior High													
0 - 4 Yrs.	49,259	34.0	46,507	47.2	2,752	5.9	64,735	26.6	60,097	35.9	1,421	1.9	6.5
5 - 8 Yrs.	32,641	22.5	25,645	26.0	6,996	15.1	49,601	20.3	41,916	25.0	7,685	10.5	14.1
High School													
1 -3 Yrs.	16,121	11.1	8,489	8.6	7,632	16.5	26,061	10.7	15,797	9.4	10,319	14.1	16.7
4 Yrs.	24,306	16.8	10,731	10.9	13,575	29.3	47,649	19.5	25,585	15.3	22,064	30.3	28.8
Some College	11,920	8.2	3,895	4.0	8,025	17.3	29,025	12.5	14,137	8.4	14,892	20.4	17.0
College Graduate or More	10,641	7.3	3,321	3.4	7,320	15.8	25,839	10.6	9,470	5.6	16,369	22.5	16.9
Total	144,888	99.9	98,588	100.1	46,300	99.9	243,180	100.2	167,002	99.6	72,750	99.7	100.0

Source: U.S. Census

Cameron and Hidalgo Counties had fourth-grade educations or less, compared to 6.5 percent of all Texas residents. The percentage of all adult Texans who did not graduate from high school was 37.3 percent, while in the Valley 57 percent, more than half the population, failed to receive a high school degree. Moreover, when the educational attainment of Valley adults is controlled by race, staggering differences between Mexican Americans and Anglos emerge.[29] Anglos in the Valley closely approximate statewide levels of educational attainment, while Valley Mexican Americans are among the worst-educated in the United States.

According to the census figures presented in table 8, 35.9 percent of all Mexican-American adults in the Valley had less than five years of schooling, compared to 1.9 percent of all Anglo adults. Of the Mexican Americans living in Cameron and Hidalgo Counties, 70.3 percent did not have a high school degree, as compared to 26.5 percent of Valley Anglos. Finally, only 5.6 percent of the Mexican Americans achieved college or professional education as compared to 22.5 percent of Valley Anglos.

While years of schooling is closely tied to eventual income, the quality of the schooling is extremely important. A high school or college degree only has economic worth if the student can translate his skills into a satisfactory job. While somewhat larger percentages of Mexican Americans in the Valley are staying in school longer, the quality of the education that they are receiving is suspect. Standardized test scores, drop-out rates, teacher-student ratios, evaluation of administrators, and more subjective interpretations of students, teachers, administrators, and parents will be closely examined in chapter 6.

Housing in the Valley is another correlate of acute poverty. More than one third (36.5%) of all Valley housing is substandard.[30] Almost 7 percent of the housing that is in use is characterized as "deteriorated, no longer suitable for habitation." The 1980 Census data show that 8 percent of all Cameron County houses lacked complete indoor plumbing, while Starr County had 14.7 percent, more than seven times that of the Texas average of 1.9 percent.[31] Outdoor privies are still a common health hazard in the Valley despite vast improvements as a result of federal monies. Housing conditions in the Valley's colonias are among the worst in the nation.[32] Overcrowding, operationally defined as more than one person living in a room in a given house, is a serious problem. The rate of overcrowding in the Valley for all four counties is 31 percent—more than four times the state average of 7.2 percent. While Valley housing is often in a poor state of repair and lacks many basic necessities, it is, nevertheless, very expensive relative to the incomes of the general population. Housing in McAllen and Brownsville in 1985 was rated the least affordable; only Laredo was ranked below the Valley in all of Texas.[33] Forty-four percent of all renters in the Valley pay excessive rents for their apartments or homes.[34] Excessive payment is operationally defined as a monthly payment which exceeds one-fourth of the family's income. Of all homeowners in the Valley, 20.8 percent pay excessive mortgage payments.

Even these dismal figures underestimate the housing conditions of those Valley residents, 11 percent of the population, who live in the 435 Valley colonias.[35] Housing in these developments is particularly inadequate as measured by several studies in Hidalgo and Cameron Counties. One study of a sample of colonias in Hidalgo County found that 3,098 out of 5,193 units were in sound condition, but 1,445 were in deteriorating condition and 642 were in dilapidated condition.[36]

The poor have limited housing choices. Colonia residents buy lots which they can afford on their limited incomes. The lots may be purchased for small down payments, but the long payment period totals, in the end, not much less than land for a middle-income family. Having purchased their own land, the poor then build their own houses. These houses are limited by the finances and skills of the owners. The developer rarely furnishes the infrastructure that middle-income Americans take for granted: roads are rarely paved; water, electricity, and sewage are often promised but seldom delivered; police and fire protection are sporadic; garbage service nonexistent. One Valley economist estimated that it would require $100 million just to provide the existing colonias with paved roads, water and electric lines, sewage, and adequate drainage to prevent flooding.[37]

The magnitude of poverty in the Valley limits the ability of municipalities and county governments to provide basic services. City taxes are a significant part of city revenues, property taxes on the average composing more than one-half of these tax re-

venues. Even though property taxes in Brownsville are the highest
in the state, actual revenues based on assessed values are inor-
dinately low.[38] Residents in Brownsville paid on the average
$52.87 in property tax in 1985, the lowest in the state. McAllen
property owners paid just a little more, $71.94. There are, as a
result, limited funds available for police and fire protection, street
repair and maintenance, sewage, sanitation, health care including
ambulance service, and parks and recreation.

Valley beaches and parks are a state and nationwide tourist
attraction, but residents of the Valley, because of their poverty,
can only afford to pay $14.87 per capita to support city parks
and recreational programs. (In Dallas, for instance, per capita
taxes are $84.01.) The direct result is that residents in Valley
cities have proportionately fewer city parks per population and
only a handful of recreational programs for full-time residents,
including programs designed for the young during their summer
vacation.

County governments face a similar dilemma; it is very difficult to provide basic services when the revenues are not forthcoming. A serious problem in recent years has been finding the
monies to fund police and fire services to the more rural areas
of the counties; EMS is not now available to some areas of the
Valley.

Given the conditions of poverty, crime in the Valley is in
general much lower than one might expect.[39] The reported number of crimes in the Valley is close to the Texas state average of
5,826 per 100,000. However, the number of murders, rapes, rob-
beries, aggravated assaults, burglaries, and thefts have increased
dramatically. The increase in murders, according to local police,
is the result of expanded organized drug trafficking in Cameron
and Hidalgo Counties. Vehicle theft has become a particularly
significant problem in Valley cities adjacent to Mexico over the
past decade.[40] However, crime rates include only those incidents
that are reported to the authorities. Among the poor in the Valley
there are a variety of reasons not to report crimes to the police.

The grim poverty which all these figures describe is the result
of larger historical forces. The economic, political, and social
systems which have predominated over the last two centuries in
the Lower Rio Grande Valley of Texas have created a poverty
without comparison in the United States.

2. BLOOD AND CASTE:
FROM SPANISH COLONIZATION TO
THE TWENTIETH CENTURY

Boca Chica Boulevard runs straight east through Brownsville, out past the airport and the *maquiladoras,* out past the shotgun dwellings that border the road as it turns into a two-lane and becomes Highway 4. Where the land is irrigated by the river, only a few miles to the south, it is lush with cotton, sorghum, and occasional citrus groves. Here, the vegetation quickly gives way to mesquite and brush. On either side, the road is bordered by rusty barbed wire fence. A lone steer feeds off what little it can find.

The paved highway abruptly ends amid signs announcing a major new resort development, *Playa del Rio,* "River Beach." Litter and garbage are everywhere: charred logs from old campfires, broken bottles and beer cans, and flotsam from the Gulf of Mexico. Unlike the beaches of South Padre Island, just to the north, Boca Chica is not maintained by county clean-up crews. So far it has been kept free of development, but not of weekend trash.

Farther down the beach, due south, a freshwater river ambles by, emptying its modest contents into the Gulf. At most, this river is perhaps thirty yards across, from one bank to another. The waters are dark and muddy; their color stains the Gulf's waters a darker hue. A federal water quality study in the mid-1970s revealed that the water and its fish are contaminated.

Hundreds of miles upstream, the Rio Grande is still truly a great river. Over eons of time, the river's broad and clear waters have cut a breathtaking gorge into the land just south of Taos, New Mexico. From its source in the southeastern mountains of Colorado, the Rio Grande runs fast and turbulent, passes the

19

twin cities of El Paso, Texas, and Juarez, Mexico, disappears, then fed by Mexican watersheds, rumbles through the immense canyons of Big Bend.

North of Del Rio, the river is slowed by a massive dam which forms Lake Amistad. Falcon Dam, near Zapata, does the final injustice, so that by the time the river rolls under the new bridge that crosses from Brownsville to Matamoros, it is little more than a trickle. As I look at the mouth of this once mighty river, which draws its strength from the waters that drain thousands of square miles of Colorado, New Mexico, Texas, and Mexico, I find it difficult to imagine what the Spanish must have seen four hundred years earlier as they set off from its banks to explore a new world.

INDIGENOUS PEOPLES

At the Sabal Palm Grove Sanctuary, maintained by the National Audubon Society, native palms grow thick and close, shutting out the sun with their broad fronds. Unlike the palms planted by developers in the twentieth century, these trees are native to the region. Their shelter has created a unique microenvironment that provides cover for small animals and a great diversity of birds.

When the first Spaniards arrived, both banks of the river were lined with such palm forests. Beyond the palms were short grasslands, an extension of the taller prairies that existed all the way to the Canadian border. The Spaniards named the river *Rios de las Palmas,* "River of Palms." From behind these palms the Indians slowly emerged—curious, cautious. These hunters and gatherers were composed of a variety of different tribal groups called Coahuiltecans, who inhabited the region for several thousands of years before the Spanish explorers came.[1] These Indians built temporary shelters along the banks of the Rio Grande during certain seasons of the year. Their survival depended on various edible plants and game, including snakes, rodents, snails, and insects.

At the mouth of the Rio Grande is the so-called Brownsville Complex, site of shell middens that reveal hints of these indigenous cultures. Artifacts have been discovered which demonstrate that these Indians actively traded with other tribal groups in the interior of Mexico and much further to the south.[2] Certain sites excavated within Hidalgo and Willacy Counties suggest that the Indians faced a harsh and desolate existence—water was in short supply, game limited and seasonal.[3] In Starr County prehistoric sites have revealed a similar limitation of resources.[4]

The lands in Cameron and Willacy Counties which border the coast and the Rio Grande may have provided the Indians with a somewhat easier existence. The extreme tip of South Texas and the bordering lands of Tamaulipas still have a climate with a mean temperature in the mid-seventies.[5] Fish then were more plentiful; small game, deer, and seasonal migrations of waterfowl could have provided an adequate source of meat along with the rich abundance of plant life. Sources of fresh water away from the river would have been problematic, however, for the rainfall here averages only twenty-seven inches a year.

SPANISH COLONIZATION

The Spanish first came seeking gold, land, peoples, political and economic power.[6] Alonzo Alvarez de Pineda appeared at the mouth of the Rio Grande in 1519. Other explorers followed irregularly for the next one hundred years: the expeditions of Camargo, de Auz and Ramirez, Garay, and Caniedo each met with failure.

In 1748 José de Escandon set out from Querétaro with 755 soldiers and 2,515 citizens to form the new colony of Nuevo Santander.[7] During the long period between Pineda and Escandon, various explorers crisscrossed the Rio Grande, but none considered the desolate and isolated area along the lower Rio Grande of much importance. Escandon, in contrast, was determined that the new Spanish colony would help counter the growing influence of the French in Louisiana and also halt the Indian uprisings that constantly threatened Nuevo Leon, Coahuila, and parts of Texas. His final objective was to bring Christianity to the region.

Of the new colonists, the majority came from Coahuila and Nuevo Leon. These seven hundred families were mustered by offers of free land, no taxes for ten years, free food until their first crops were harvested, and expenses for travel. After founding in quick succession Santa María de Llera, Güemes, Padilla, and Jiménez, several small communities were settled along the Rio Grande. Camargo was laid out in 1749, followed by Revilla (now Guerrero) and Reynosa. In the next few years a total of fourteen towns and missions, three north of the river, were constructed.

The colonists who came to live along the Rio Grande in the northern portion of Nuevo Santander intended to farm the new lands and graze their livestock on the virgin prairie grasses. Land was allotted to each settler to raise beans, corn, and other vegetables and to pasture his sheep, goats, and cattle. At first there was no particular need to found communities on the north side of the river. However, within a few decades, the virgin grasses on the south side were overgrazed and livestock were being driven regularly across the Rio Grande where the lands remained, for a time at least, very productive.

Laredo, on the north side of the Rio Grande, was settled by the Spanish in 1755. Rio Grande City, the first Valley town, was founded by Escandon's colonists soon after, in 1757. Dolores, on the southern bank, was laid out in 1761, followed by Matamoros in 1765. Roma, on the northern bank, was founded in 1767. Brownsville, directly across the Rio Grande from Matamoros, did not become a town until the 1840s; for many years it was a tiny trading community dependent on its sister city of Matamoros.

By 1757 a census of the area, which included the lands from Laredo south to the mouth of the Rio Grande, listed twenty-four settlements and missions with a total population of 8,993. There were 3,473 Indians in the missions, the majority of whom farmed small plots, hunted, and helped in the construction of new buildings.[8]

This same census showed that farming in the region was far less successful than raising goats, sheep, and cattle. Mier's population of 274 lived in primitive mud huts called *jacales,* farmed small plots of bottom land, and looked after 44,000 head of stock. In Guerrero there were 357 Spaniards, mestizos, and mulattoes who tended 51,000 head. One powerful family supported twenty-three families of laborers living in *jacales* in tiny Dolores.

In contrast Camargo, the largest settlement in Nuevo Santander, had 678 inhabitants who lived in attractive adobe houses, farmed plots by the river, and looked after more than 80,000 head of livestock.[9]

The land was surveyed in 1767 and land grants which fronted both sides of the Rio Grande were given to the colonists by the Spanish Royal Commission. Those who received grants of land can be divided into three groups. The first is composed of colonists who had lived in the area the longest; each received approximately 9,000 acres of land for ranching and just over 1,200 acres for farming. These were the so-called *primitivos*. Those who had lived less than two years as colonists were awarded the same amount of ranch land, but no land for crops. The second group of grantees were members of the elite who received large tracts of land between 1767 and 1810 for the grazing of livestock. Lands that were vacant were assigned to a third group between 1770 and 1810. With a few exceptions these lands came to belong to the relatively rich ranchers of the region.[10]

The original land grants of the *primitivos* bordered on the river to provide the owner with the necessary access to water for his crops and herds. These original land grants, then, resulted in very long and narrow strips so that as many grantees as possible could take advantage of the river. On the northern side of the Rio Grande, some distance from the banks of the river, grantees received more traditional squarish blocks of land for grazing their growing herds.

The economic, political, and social relationships which developed among the new colonists of Nuevo Santander's northern frontier were shaped to a great degree by the physical constraints of the environment and the violence which permeated the region. The new settlements were geographically isolated from their homeland; it took months for goods to arrive from Mexico City. As the land was overgrazed, mesquite and brush quickly overtook the region. The thick vegetation made travel even more difficult, further isolating the small communities and ranches from each other and from New Spain. The diaries of one well-known French priest graphically describe the difficulty of reaching the ranches and towns.[11] To this day, the Lower Rio Grande Valley of South Texas and the Mexican state of Tamaulipas remain isolated from both Mexican and American economic, political, and cultural centers.

Colonists who had come to farm the region were soon faced with the harsh realities of life along the Rio Grande. Annual rainfall is not only very limited, it is inconsistent. It may rain six inches in one afternoon, then not another drop for four months. The best farming lands, those which bordered the Rio Grande, were subject to irregular flooding. Despite the hard work of the colonists, the lands around Mier were found to be unsuitable for any kind of cultivation. In spite of these difficulties, colonists struggled to plant their crops of beans, corn, squash, and other vegetables on small patches of land which fronted the Rio Grande or the creeks which fed into it. The colonists also sought out low-lying lands which were more likely to retain the irregular rainfall. In many places the rich delta soil offered great potential for bountiful harvests. Considerable efforts were made to irrigate these lands, but all such attempts met with failure.[12] Colonists did not possess either the knowledge or the adequate technology for successful irrigation.

Distinctions premised upon class were of relatively minimal importance among the first colonists; a notable exception was the very small community of Dolores. However, the failure of agriculture and the primacy of the ranching system created a social structure which consisted of a small number of families with relatively modest wealth (Reynosa's wealthy Hinojosa family was one of the notable exceptions), who presided over a much larger number of ranch workers. Gradually some of these ranch workers fell into a condition resembling peonage; their servitude was premised upon their debt to the ranch owners.[13] In contrast, in the small towns there remained a tiny, nascent class of skilled and semi-skilled workers who avoided the caste-like system which developed on many of the ranches. Some subsistence farming also continued along the most fertile banks of the Rio Grande.

The constant threat of violence increased the workers' dependence on the ranch owners and the affluent in the small towns along the river. From 1792 until more than a century later the colonists were continually harassed by roaming bands of Apaches, Comanches, Mescaleros, and Kickapoos, each tribe displaced by increasing population pressures on their traditional hunting grounds.[14] From 1812 to 1830 the attacks became so ferocious that the ranches north of the Rio Grande were abandoned so that the colonists could seek safety behind the walls of the new towns and larger ranches.

FRONTIER CONFLICT

The hybrid system of land and class relationships was further strained by bloody violence that went far beyond the initial Indian wars. This frontier became a focal point for wars of independence, American and Mexican civil wars, and wars fanned by those interested in promoting trade. In addition, banditry and smuggling plagued the river, their violence affecting the security of every household.[15]

Brownsville was founded as a fort by Major Jacob Brown in 1846 on the site of a small trading community directly across the river from Matamoros.[16] Brown was ostensibly sent to the area by General Zachary Taylor to keep an eye on the Mexican soldiers in Matamoros; Taylor remained with his main forces at tiny Port Isabel. Texas was an independent republic (1836–1845), awaiting admission to statehood. The Mexican government still claimed as its own the lands between the Rio Grande and the Nueces River, lands which included all the Valley. President Polk dispatched General Taylor to the border to establish the hegemony of the United States over these contested lands. Polk used Taylor's forces to inflame the Mexican citizenry and soldiers in Matamoros.

During the Mexican War which followed, Brownsville, Matamoros, Bagdad at the mouth of the Rio Grande, and Rio Grande City became the staging area for American troops who were preparing to invade Mexico. The original towns on the southern banks became a battlefield. By all accounts, the American troops were poorly trained, undisciplined men who found, upon arriving at the mouth of the Rio Grande, wretched housing, mealy food, and a water supply that quickly led to serious outbreaks of dysentery.[17]

In these wretched living conditions, under a torrid sun, tempers quickly exploded and American soldiers, predominantly from the Southern states, fought and killed each other and the Mexicans in Matamoros. Livestock was stolen, and women were attacked. More than five hundred American soldiers died from disease and murder, including those who were executed, before the planned invasion of Mexico ever took place.

The original settlements of Mier, Camargo, and Guerrero became battlegrounds for the Mexican War. The battles of Resaca de Palmas and Palo Alto were fought during this time on the outskirts of Brownsville, but were insignificant compared to the carnage and destruction of communities that occurred south of the river.

The Treaty of Guadalupe Hidalgo was signed at the end of the war in 1848, and the disputed territory between the two rivers was taken by the United States as part of the spoils of victory, but this did not bring peace to the region. Failed revolutions in Mexico increased the problem of banditry along the border. The remnants of armies, marginal men both Mexican and American, who did not return to their homes after the war, plagued the area. Neither the safety of the citizens nor of the livestock could be assured; murder and theft of stock were the background of daily life.

Health care along this new frontier was problematic and limited by the knowledge of the day. Rapid increases in the density of the population because of wars and revolutions compounded the health problems. Recorded cholera epidemics broke out in Brownsville in 1843, 1858, and 1866, while yellow fever killed many Brownsville citizens in 1867 and 1882.[18]

Nature remained unkind. Major recorded hurricanes devastated the coastal areas of the Valley in 1858, 1867, and 1880. Settlements at the mouth of the Rio Grande were particularly vulnerable to tropical storms.[19]

ANGLO SETTLEMENT

The Treaty of Guadalupe Hidalgo provided for Mexican landowners to retain the titles to their land north of the Rio Grande and to be granted American citizenship, but few of the Mexican elite were actually able to do so. Anglos descended on the Valley after the signing of the treaty and, through the court system, quickly came into control of the lands originally deeded to the Spanish colonists. Fehrenbach emphasizes that:

> There is some truth that many Mexican landowners, especially the small ones, were robbed in south Texas by force, intimidation, or chicanery. But what is usually ignored is the fact that the hacendado class, as a class, was stripped of property perfectly legally, according to the highest traditions of U.S. law.[20]

The city of Brownsville is a case in point. The land for the city, not the fort, was purchased by Charles Stillman under an unclear title. The Mexican heirs to the original grant title contested Stillman's purchase all the way to the Supreme Court. In the process an American law firm wound up with the 1500 acres upon which Stillman had laid out the town. They then sold this land to Stillman for a very low price.[21]

A portion of the lands that were claimed by Anglos who flocked to the Valley belonged to the heirs of the Espiritu Santo Grant to Don José Salvador de las Garza in 1782. Much of their original 260,000 acres, another example of land grabbing, soon fell into Anglo hands.

Cameron County was founded in 1848. It was named for Ewen Cameron who had led an attack on Mier during the war with Mexico. Hidalgo County was carved out of Cameron County in 1852. It was named, in order to draw support from Mexicans who lived within its boundaries, for the famous Mexican priest Father Miguel Hidalgo who had started the Mexican Revolution at the turn of the century. Founded in 1894, Starr was named for Dr. James Harper Starr, former Secretary of Treasury of the Republic of Texas. Willacy County was carved out of Cameron and Hidalgo in 1911 and named for a local farmer and member of the Texas State Legislature, John G. Willacy.

Horgan best captures the flavor of these times in his description of Brownsville around 1850:

> Bankrupts, escaped criminals, deserters from the armies of the recent wars, gamblers and swindlers set the tone. The barrooms were fighting pits. Pistol duels added style to mur-

der. Murderers and other offenders were lynched at the town shambles by hanging from the timbers on which beeves were butchered. . . . The sheriff—a huge man of great strength and a brutal force—usually killed the men he set out to arrest. Bloodhounds guarded the gate to his jail.[22]

The case of Juan Nepomuceno Cortina is an excellent example of the degree of violence that pervaded the area and continually threatened the social stability of the region.[23] Son of a well-to-do rancher, he was involved in an incident on a downtown Brownsville street. A deputy sheriff was beating a poor Mexican ranch hand when Cortina intervened and, in the struggle, shot the deputy sheriff. Thus began the extralegal life of Cortina and what some historians have referred to as the Cortina Wars, 1859–1860.

Cortina returned to his ranch, rallied around himself a small band of men, and seized all of Brownsville by force; he did not give it up until federal troops arrived. He is seen by historians as either a bandit or a Robin Hood-like figure, fighting on both sides of the river on behalf of poor Mexicans and Mexican Americans. He is accused of killing Mexicans, but placing the blame, on the south side of the river, on Anglos, while on the north side of the river blaming the Mexicans. Today, his supporters view him otherwise, arguing that he should be seen as a defender of his people against the land-hungry and racist Texas invaders.[24]

Whatever one's view of Cortina, the nature of his exploits is typical of the times. Striking from either side of the border, he played havoc with those who maintained order. Federal troops finally chased him into Mexico where, eventually, he was caught by the Mexican government in its attempt to clamp down on frontier banditry. But Cortina soon returned, this time as the governor of the State of Tamaulipas. From outlaw to the highest official of the region, Cortina exemplifies the extremely conflictual nature of U.S.-Mexico border relations.

TRADE AND ANGLO ELITES

The American Civil War brought boom times to Brownsville, Matamoros, Bagdad, Reynosa, Rio Grande City and the other river settlements, but at a great cost in social turmoil. The war, when coupled with the internal problems that Mexico herself was facing as the French landed under Maximilian, again provided a backdrop of blood and violence. Mexico was technically a neutral power during the war, allowing her ports to escape the blockade by the North. In practice that meant that the frontier river ports served as primary exporters of the South's agricultural products, mainly Texas cotton, in its vain attempt to raise capital to sustain the war. The populations of Matamoros and Brownsville exploded in response, to 40,000 and 25,000 respectively.

Ranching along the river suffered in the nineteenth century. While the region did manage to develop external markets for its livestock and their by-products, internal markets were equally important. Farming remained extremely marginal. Valley farm products could barely feed the local population, and corn and wheat were imported into the Valley. Ranchers traded their cattle for these grains along with salt from operations like those at Sal del Ray. Vegetables and fruits were imported from New Orleans. Graf summarizes,

> The story of agriculture in the lower Valley is principally a story of great expectations, which at best came to moderate realization and at worst were dismally unsuccessful.[25]

It was trade, not ranching or farming, that flourished on this river frontier and quickly became the single most important industry. During the nineteenth century it was the banker, the merchant, and border entrepreneur who best represented the strength of the modest economy of the area. The Mexican merchant and his cross-river counterpart sustained the small towns and the ranches, supplying the necessary goods, exporting ranch products, and increasingly transporting goods between the two emerging nations, Mexico and the United States.

These merchants were not above meddling in international politics if it could improve their business. Some Brownsville and Matamoros merchants, for example, joined together to provide the region on both sides of the river with a permanent free trade zone which, they hoped, would stimulate the local economy. Tired of the Mexican federal government's imposition of tariffs on goods imported and exported across the river, these local entrepreneurs helped to organize a revolution in Tamaulipas.

The merchants contributed heavily to the campaign of the Mexican General José María Carvajal, encouraging him to do battle with Mexican federal troops in the hope that he would, upon victory, establish an independent Republic of the Rio Grande that supported free commerce across the border. When Carvajal lost a series of important battles to Mexican troops stationed at Matamoros, the businessmen quickly withdrew their support.[26]

From the 1870s to the turn of the century, armed banditry continued to plague the area.[27] The ranches resembled small fortresses and the towns never transcended the frontier mentality of law and order. For some thirty years after Carvajal, various Mexican generals attempted to construct a Republic of the Sierra Madre. The continued conflicts contributed to the rigidity of the two social systems which developed in the Lower Rio Grande Valley, the town system and the ranch system.

The new Anglo merchant class, composed of families from New York, Pennsylvania, and several European countries, sought control over regional trade after the Treaty of Guadalupe Hidalgo. Every attempt was made to control the politics, economy, and social structure of the small American border towns as well. In Brownsville, for example, the new elite quickly reshaped the town's 2,000 Mexican inhabitants into a political machine manipulated by Anglo leaders representing the interests of the new merchant families.[28]

The Mexicans who lived in Brownsville had little notion of democratic values. They were corralled into two political parties, the Reds and the Blues, and told for whom to vote. For the most part illiterate, owning no land, employed at subsistence wages like the workers on the ranches which surrounded them, they were easily persuaded through intimidation and/or trivial favors. Elections were times of parties and fiestas, of sky-high promises made to illiterate Mexican peasants who had become, because of the vagaries of international politics and boundaries, citizens of the United States.

The wealth of this small merchant class was tightly held and did not "trickle down" to those below them. The small town elites saw their fortunes grow in their entrepreneurial ventures, but the majority of the population benefited little by their economic success.

Considerable fortunes were made by merchants who cornered the steamboat traffic along the Rio Grande during the Civil War. These moneys were then used by families such as the Stillmans and Kenedys to purchase enormous tracts of land north of the Valley and also in Cameron and Hidalgo Counties. These lands were purchased from small landowners who held the small *porciones* (or remnants of the *porciones* which they had inherited) of the original land grants or who still held larger parcels of land. By 1890 the Kenedy and King families, in addition to their vast holdings outside of the Valley which formed the King Ranch, owned over 600,000 acres in Cameron County. Ninety ranchers in 1890 owned 97 percent of all Cameron County lands.[29]

BOSSISM

Political bossism was spawned in the 1850s by this new merchant class.[30] Machine politics in the Valley provided the promise of political and social stability, a genuine alternative to the previous violence. In exchange for the vote of the majority composed of poor Mexican Americans, Valley bosses could offer protection from the lawlessness and a limited system of patronage. To the ranchers, the bosses could provide legal titles to suspect land claims, low property evaluations, and a necessary legal friend should disputes arise.

From the beginning, this political patronage was quite modest. It took the form in Cameron County of jobs in public education, law enforcement, city and county government, and the customs house. A large number of these jobs went to Mexican Americans. The small Mexican-American middle class acquiesced to the bossism, finding the small favors and the occasional job far better than any other of the limited alternatives. Bossism dovetailed nicely with the quasi-feudalistic relations that had existed in the Valley and on the south side of the Rio Grande since Spanish colonization. Valley bosses provided small favors, paid their share for weddings and funerals, and settled, outside the legitimate court process, disputes among the poor.

Judge James B. Wells was the prototypical Valley boss. For four decades, roughly from 1880 to 1920, he ruled Cameron County with an iron hand. He brought in the Texas Rangers to control the banditry and lawlessness. When Catarino Garza, a Mexican who had settled in Rio Grande City, staged abortive raids into Mexico in 1891, Wells again called the Rangers in and they were successful in capturing most of Garza's men. The so-called Garza Revolution was symptomatic of the political instability of the Valley and south of the river at the turn of the century. However, the Rangers often did not distinguish between Mexican bandits and poor Mexican Americans.

In Starr County Manuel Guerra established a similar political machine that ran the county well into the twentieth century. Similar men or combinations of men held sway in Hidalgo and Willacy Counties.

During the 1880s the ranch owners began the tedious process of fencing their properties, at least in part to control the stealing of stock.[31] The fencing of the land also reinforced the existing class structure. One either worked for the patron on his ranch or struggled to make a living in the small towns. There were very few small farm or ranch operations.

There were, however, a small class of semi-skilled and skilled workers in the towns. The 1860 and 1870 censuses mention a small number of men who worked as silversmiths and wheelwrights, as well as those who were employed in other crafts in Valley towns. These individuals were able to buy city lots upon which they constructed small homes, but this precursor of a Valley middle class held little political power.

The wealthy maintained their social ties through elaborate parties, dances, and other ritual celebrations which served to strengthen relationships of class.[32] Those who were not rich did likewise, especially on the ranches, where religious holidays and other occasions were annually celebrated as a break from the monotonous and grueling daily routine. Often the peons from other ranches would travel many miles in order to share with their neighbors the brief days and nights of celebration.

Intermarriage among Mexican, Mexican-American, and Anglo members of the small upper class was common along the Rio Grande as recorded in Brownsville, Mier, Rio Grande City, Reynosa, and Camargo. Families of the rich associated with one another, based upon the common ties of vested self-interest. Not a few of the wealthiest families in Rio Grande City, for instance, were composed of Southern white males who had married Mexican or Mexican-American women and were raising bi-racial families.

Racism, however, did not disappear from the Valley—it simply accommodated the rich. Members of the upper class were treated well by the rest of society, regardless of racial or ethnic heritage, because their status in a ruling elite demanded it. Racism and its supporting beliefs and values thrived throughout the Valley, periodically reinforced by new Anglos moving to the region, the use of law enforcers such as the Texas Rangers, and the influence of Mexican culture.

The Valley's population grew very slowly in the latter half of the nineteenth century (see table 9). Cameron County, in spite of Brownsville's temporary boom years during the Civil War, had only about 11,000 people in 1870. Starr had little more than 4,000; Hidalgo about half that number. While the population of all three counties increased from the 1880s to the turn of the century, gains were very modest. Cameron County was still the most populated of the three, with a population of approximately

TABLE 9

Population of Valley Counties
1850–1980

	CAMERON	HIDALGO	STARR	WILLACY
1850	8,541	—	—	—
1860	6,028	1,182	2,406	—
1870	10,999	2,387	4,154	—
1880	14,959	4,347	8,304	—
1890	14,424	6,534	10,749	—
1900	16,095	6,837	11,469	—
1910	27,158	13,728	13,151	—
1920	36,662	38,110	11,089	—
1930	77,540	77,004	11,409	10,499
1940	83,202	106,059	13,312	13,230
1950	125,170	106,446	13,948	20,920
1960	151,098	180,904	17,137	20,084
1970	140,368	181,535	17,707	15,570
1980	209,727	283,229	27,266	17,495

Sources: Texas Almanac and U.S. Census

16,000 by 1900. Starr grew to about 11,000 and Hidalgo was the least populated with almost 7,000. By the turn of the century approximately 34,000 American citizens called the Valley their home.

The rigid class system in the Valley towns and on the ranches, enforced in part by an ideology of racism, was well suited to the particular demands of life along the Rio Grande. It was neither truly Spanish, Mexican, nor American, but a hybrid system which endured many years of violence and great suffering.

3. ECONOMIC DEVELOPMENT, RACISM, AND THE GROWTH OF POVERTY

In less than three decades, from the turn of the century to the 1920s, the Valley was transformed into one of the most productive agricultural regions in Texas. This transformation required the capital of opportunistic land developers and Midwestern farmers as well as the sweat of thousands of Mexican and Mexican-American laborers. As the land changed hands from the Anglo ranchers and the few who could trace their ownership to the original Spanish land grants to the Anglo farmers from Kansas and Illinois, this vast area of mesquite, cactus, and brush was painstakingly cleared for the plow and the grove. Laborers constructed earthen ditches which carried Rio Grande water to parched lands some distance from the river. For the first time in the history of the region, it was possible to plant and harvest crops with the knowledge that a steady supply of water would provide the necessary nourishment. This land of scattered ranches and small river towns became, almost overnight, a fertile agricultural oasis which boomed with new crops, new farm towns, and new poverty.

New sources of political power and expanded sources of subordination developed from this economic transformation. Racism, new neither to the Valley nor to the rest of the United States and Mexico, was a vessel of this subordination. This racism was grounded in economic convenience and fed, in part, by the traditions and values already in place. Political bossism continued to provide the machinery by which new members of the Valley's elite could maintain control well into the 1980s. Poverty was not invented by this new agricultural elite, but it was both a requirement of the economic system which they established and a by-product of that same system. Those in poverty sought ways to escape it and a nascent Mexican-American middle class developed political agendas to bring about social reforms.[1]

SELLING THE LAND

Developers at the turn of the century purchased parched ranch lands and sold them for five hundred dollars an acre to Midwestern farmers.[2] It took clever and resourceful men to convince a farmer from Illinois that the Valley could ever become more than second-rate ranching country. The developers ran advertising campaigns in major Midwestern newspapers describing the potential productivity of the fertile river lands, the cheap labor that was available on the other side of the Rio Grande, and the dependable supply of water.

These same developers chartered trains to transport potential buyers to the southern tip of Texas and set up model farms where Mexican and Mexican-American laborers tilled the virgin land and planted experimental crops. When the farmers got off the train, they were shown the results of the developers' capital investments and the Mexicans' sweat. They were carefully ushered back on board, wined and dined. Deals were made, broken, and remade; the land was sold to new owners in a few short years.

One developer recounted a common problem the developers faced at the time: How to distract the Midwestern farmers as the trains traveled through the rough, undeveloped ranch lands. A clever ploy involved the host of the trip calling for timely prayer meetings whenever the land outside was particularly unattractive. The window shades were drawn, prayers and hymns sung, and the shades reopened after the worst of the landscape had passed.

The developers touted a variety of crops, but all but a few were miserable failures.[3] Rice aroused considerable fanfare and interest. A mill was built in Brownsville to handle the expected production, but after only a few experiments it was discovered that the flooding of fields brought up the salts in the soil which quickly killed the crop. Cotton, however, was ideally suited to the climate, it was labor intensive, the market at the time was firm, and Valley farmers had already had some limited success growing it.

The Midwestern farmers were, of course, far from stupid. They were attracted by what seemed a dream that could not fail. Not only would a complete and intricate system of ditches and pumps regularly irrigate their fields year-round, providing water to the rich delta soil, there was a plentiful supply of laborers to work and harvest the crops. In an era before the mechanization of agriculture, inexpensive and dependable labor was a vital necessity. The farmers were not blind; within several hundred miles of the Rio Grande were all the Mexican laborers they would ever need.

The Midwestern farmers knew, or were quickly told by the developers, that the Mexican-American laborers were not only incredibly cheap but renowned for their hard work, their dependability, and their lack of viable economic options. The farmers knew, at least in general terms, of the conditions of Mexican peasants in the interior of northern Mexico. They could offer these men work at wages which would maximize their own profits. If particular Mexicans did not like the work, then they could easily be replaced by others.

THE LABOR FORCE

Mexican peasants were actively recruited from northern Mexico. They were offered high wages compared to what they earned in Mexico, and transportation was provided by Valley farmers to carry workers to and across the Rio Grande. The promises were real: farm laborers could earn higher wages north of the river, although working conditions were often exaggerated.

These recruits, along with poor Valley Mexican Americans, began the back-breaking work that eventually transformed the land into an agricultural vision. The laborers worked from sunup to sundown, hacking the hard, resilient mesquite to the ground and hauling it by oxen to large piles which were set afire. One visitor to the Valley at this time describes the glow of these fires and the rich aroma of mesquite and brush which filled the night air for days and days, month after month.[4]

With shovel, ox, mule, and cart, these same men dug the ditches, building the irrigation system which now crisscrosses the area. Almost invisible on land, this system is clearly revealed from the air. Large, wide canals shoot off the Rio Grande at right angles, branching to large ditches, smaller ditches, then even smaller ditches that are less than a few feet across. In the Lower Valley, steam-fed pumps originally raised the water to the level of the canals where gravity then took over and spread the waters to the dry lands. In the Mid-Valley area, where the lands were a few feet higher, steam pumps were used both to raise the water to the canals and to pump water through the irrigation system.

From the beginning, Mexicans and Mexican Americans (Anglo farmers rarely made a distinction between the two) were treated less as men, more as a nameless number of interchangeable bodies who were necessary to the success of the farms. Laborers worked from fourteen to fifteen hours a day, sunrise to sunset, six and one-half days a week.[5] For their labor they were commonly paid 50 cents a day, depending on the crop. With these wages they could barely purchase enough groceries to feed their families. Groceries often had to be purchased from a store owned by the farmer or grower. Sometimes the workers would be paid in credit, which they then used at the store. Not a few workers fell into debt.

One son of a Valley farmer described the situation on his father's land near Brownsville. His father recruited 150 men from San Fernando, about eighty miles south of Matamoros. These men, though hard working, could barely afford to buy the beans, flour, sugar, and other necessities at his father's store. He received $100 a month from his job as supervisor of the Mexican farm workers while they received 50 cents a day.

A former farm laborer described the situation:

Well, yes, people did suffer, because when the children came from school and the husbands would get home from work they would find nothing on the table to eat.[6]

This same worker outlined his life in the Valley:

I was born in 1903 in a ranch called San Vicente, which is located on [Highway] 511. My father was born where sugar cane was cultivated and processed into sugar. My mother was born in the Arenal which was located alongside of the river, about one-half mile from where San Vicente was. Later my parents moved to the Hacienda of Brule. There I was hired where sugar cane was cultivated and processed into sugar. Back then my father would earn a wage of 75 cents per day. At this time I was only twelve years old and worked as a water boy who would take water to the people in the fields. I was making 35 cents a day...when I was thirteen years old I worked picking sugar cane. I would get about 50 cents per day, but they would pay the older men 75 cents per day. When it came time to cut the sugar cane down, people would get hired by contract. I would work from sunrise to sunset. We used to work six and one-half days per week and the other one-half of the day we would get paid...Nobody ever complained...And if anybody did complain, I never found out about it. People only wanted to have some job so they could bring income into the household and that's what they had...During the War [World War I] there was a shortage of men to work. So at the age of fifteen I started working where the troops were stationed and since I already had working experience with animals, wagons, and other manual labor skills, I was very fortunate to be working there. My job was to carry dirt from place to place with a wagon. Because back then we didn't have the dumpers we have now and it took a little bit of skill to do the work. Since I was a brighter and more skillful worker than the rest, my employers learned to appreciate me more. My supervisor would appreciate me more because I knew how to work with the shovel very well, especially when they were making ditches for various purposes. I was earning a wage of $1.25 per day and to me it seemed like a lot of money, because the most I had ever earned was 35 cents per day when I was working as a water boy in the fields. When I was working for Mr. ——— I only got paid food to eat and the working experience.[7]

When asked, "How did people survive during this time?" this same worker responded, "People would do what I did. They would work at anything and everything they could find in order to survive.[8]

There are important disadvantages in any regional economy which relies solely upon agriculture: the lack of real job mobility, and the absence of opportunities for increased wages based upon experience, skills, or other positive job-related characteristics. Mexican laborers who became a part of the Valley's agricultural labor force in the early 1900s saw their quality of life, when compared to that in Mexico, improved. But their potential for continued individual advancement based on individual skills and ambition was severely curtailed by the nature of their employment. Only a minority successfully escaped the limitations of their employment as farm laborers.

Farm and grove workers were most often paid a daily wage. Regardless of how hard they sweated under the hot Valley sun, it was very difficult to accumulate capital. One could only hope to become a foreman or a supervisor of a crew. The dream of actually owning land remained, for most, only a dream.

Valley farm laborers had, in effect, three real options. They could earn their wages, then return to live on the south side of the river. This alternative most closely resembled the developers' and growers' conception of the ideal labor force. Or they could make their home in the Valley year round, as many chose to do, since political instability in their homeland and chances for higher wages in the Valley provided primary push factors. Or after finally saving a little money, the farmworkers could move north to better opportunities, higher wages, less discrimination. Although the exact numbers cannot be known, some Mexican workers and Valley Mexican Americans chose this last option.

There were exceptional individuals who were able to find good jobs, earn decent wages, gain new skills despite the economic system that had been established. The same Valley worker described above was able, at twenty-four, to leave the fields and find work as an assistant carpenter in Brownsville. He eventually bought a small city lot and built his own house. Combining some of the skills he had learned working at the army base during World War I with new ones he gained in Brownsville, he joined the ranks of the middle class. In 1954 he opened up his own small house-moving business. He is now retired and lives in the same house that he built in the 1930s.[9]

There were, too, some farmers and ranchers who treated their workers fairly and honestly. They helped them out when an illness, natural disaster, or family tragedy occurred. They also, on occasion, provided the money to further the education of a laborer's son or daughter who showed particular promise.

Overall, however, the system of economic relations that was constructed by the developers and the agricultural elite made it extremely difficult for incoming Mexicans and native Mexican Americans to prosper. As laborers erected the agricultural infrastructure in the Valley, as they dug the ditches, built the farm-to-market roads, cultivated the lands, and laid down the tracks, they received a poverty wage. Regardless of how hard and long one worked, the opportunities to lift oneself out of poverty were extremely limited.

As deftly as the new Anglo farmers developed their new farmlands and the new towns to support them, they in effect developed the conditions for long-term poverty. The agricultural elite could never control the flow of poor Mexican peasants from one side of the river to the other. Poor Mexican peasants in search of work soon outnumbered Mexican Americans as the Mexican Revolution caused many to flee north across the Rio Grande. Banditry and political instability continued to drive Mexican peasants north and into the Valley up to the 1920s.

The Valley's population grew in direct proportion to the number of Mexican workers who crossed the river in hopes of finding a better life. During the 1920s large numbers were required to plant, tend, and harvest Valley cotton and citrus crops. Cameron and Hidalgo Counties doubled their populations during the 1920s when the majority of irrigated lands came into full production. A high birth rate among Mexican and Mexican Americans also contributed to this population increase. By the 1980s the birth rate had fallen, but was still almost five children per Valley family, double the national average.

Blacks stayed away for a different reason.[10] The Valley became nationally known for its discrimination against blacks because of the Brownsville raids in 1906. Black troops had been stationed at Fort Brown and other frontier outposts for many years. They had served honorably and well from Fort Davis in

West Texas to the Gulf Coast. Relations between blacks at Fort Brown and the residents of Brownsville, however, had not been cordial. In 1906, a series of fights broke out between black soldiers and townspeople. Even today if one asks the descendants of these same townspeople what occurred, blame is quickly thrown on the black troops.

Accounts written by recent historians about these incidents give quite a different picture, one reflecting the racial discrimination against blacks both by Mexican Americans and Anglos.[11]

The entire black regiment that was stationed at Fort Brown was dishonorably discharged because of the refusal of all the soldiers to identify to their white superiors the black soldiers who were specifically involved. Almost seventy years later, President Carter reinstated honorable discharges to the few black soldiers still living, and they finally began receiving military benefits. Because of this incident, and others which preceded it, blacks number less than one percent of the total Valley population. Most of those blacks who do live in the Valley live in Harlingen.

POLITICS, VIOLENCE, AND RACISM

The city and county political machines continued to run smoothly. Judge James B. Wells not only ruled over all of Cameron County until the 1920s, but played a significant role in the politics of Hidalgo, Starr, and Willacy.[12] He also found time to influence politics at the state and national level as well. Others who followed him strove to manipulate the system of political patronage and favoritism as well as he had.

Such manipulations of the city and county systems involved direct control of the Mexican-American vote through payment of the individual's poll tax, the siphoning off of city and county funds for personal use, and the hiring of favored friends and relatives on the city and county payrolls. The graft and corruption were punctuated by acts of remarkable violence. Nowhere else is this more true than in Starr County. The struggle for political power in this county led, for example, to the murders of Judge Stanley Welch in 1906 and Gregorio Duffy in 1907.[13]

The farmers and growers also maintained political control through their private water corporations. These corporations were funded by general bonds paid for by the public, but were used to the best interests of the agricultural elite. The private water corporations served as part of the political patronage system and as a mechanism to control the growth of the development of the Valley. New towns and housing developments could not be established without the cooperation of the private water corporations to provide the necessary water lines. The Valley poor were the long-term victims of these water corporations because they ultimately had to choose, from the 1950s through the 1980s, between more expensive lands serviced by these corporations or far less costly areas where the water corporations refused to provide service.[14]

Overt violence in the region continued unabated. The Mexican Revolution of 1910 spawned increased violence and disruption along the border. General Pershing's expeditions into Mexico were in direct response to border raids by Pancho Villa and less-known bandits and social revolutionaries.

Peavy describes a battle in Matamoros that occurred in 1913 between loyal federal troops and the revolutionaries.[15] Perched on the railroad trestle that crosses the river, he had an excellent view of the defense of the city and the slaughter that took place. He recounts from his observation the sight of piles of bodies being burned in the streets of Matamoros—the piles burned for several days.

Bandits, both Mexican and American, continued to plague the river region making life extremely hazardous for the general population. The Texas Rangers were again called in and, as before, they enforced laws in a very discriminating manner.[16] They often chose not to distinguish between those who were outlaws and those who were simply Mexicans and Mexican Americans going about their daily business.

At about the same time, 1915, the infamous Plan of San Diego was revealed, which further stimulated racist fears and hatred for Mexicans and Mexican Americans.[17] A Mexican national named Basilio Ramos was arrested in McAllen. On him was discovered a precise blueprint for the takeover of American lands. The plan called for Mexicans and Mexican Americans to unite against their common Anglo oppressors and take control of the southwestern part of the United States. Blacks, Japanese Americans, Indians, and other racial and ethnic groups were to help. Hostages were to be taken, ransomed, and then shot. The Plan of San Diego may have been written by the Germans or the Mexicans to stir up the border during the Mexican Revolution or, perhaps, was even a local hoax. But the identity of its creators is less important than the local racist reaction to this ridiculous plan to overthrow the United States.

The Plan was used by the Anglo minority to justify and legitimize violence against Mexicans and Mexican-Americans in the Valley. Anders summarizes the situation in the Valley:

> Anglo gangs burned houses, forced Hispanic families to flee their farms and ranches, and confiscated their weapons, but widespread lynchings overshadowed all of these practices. Vigilante committees compiled "black lists" of suspected raiders or collaborators and marked them for death. . . . By the middle of September, the "San Antonio Daily Express" reported that "the finding of dead bodies of Mexicans. . . has reached the point where it creates little or no interest.[18]

The Texas Rangers and other Valley law enforcement agencies participated in the attacks. Within one six-week period nine Mexicans were killed while trying to escape from the San Benito jail.

Mexicans and Mexican Americans became so terrified that many crossed the Rio Grande to escape from the reign of Anglo terror. Valley farmers became concerned because they had no workers. It was then that a legislative subcommittee led by the Valley's State Representative J. T. Canales estimated that the Texas Rangers had summarily executed between 300 and 2000 suspects in the Valley without trial. The Rangers were severely discredited by this investigation, their numbers reduced to less than one hundred, and their major duties taken over by the newly created Texas Department of Public Safety.

The few Mexican-American GIs who returned to the Valley after serving in World War I were changed by their experiences. In defending their homeland from a foreign enemy, they became more aware of their rights as citizens of the United States. This awareness came at a time when the Anglo elites in the new Valley communities were consolidating their economic and political power, utilizing attitudes of race to subordinate Mexicans and Mexican Americans.

Gonzales documents one of the incidents which occurred:

> Two years ago in Falfurrias, Brooks County, the American Legion had a Fourth of July celebration and dance. For this purpose subscriptions were made from the merchants of town both Mexican and American. On the date of the celebration all the boys wearing the legion badges attended the barbecue. All went well. But in the evening when some of the Mexican [Mexican-American] boys wanted to dance, they were told that the dance was only for whites. This as might well be imagined was taken as an insult by the Mexican [Mexican-American] legionnaires. One of them who had received a decoration for bravery, snatched it from his coat lapel, threw it on the floor and trampled it saying, "If shedding blood for you Americans does not mean any more than this, I do not want to ever wear your colors, from now on I am ashamed of having served in your army.[19]

While this particular incident took place in Falfurrias, directly adjacent to Hidalgo County, it was, according to Gonzales, typical of what occurred in the Valley.

Racism was effectively used by those in power as a means of social control. Valley racism became institutionalized, a part of the formal and informal relationships that touched everyone on a daily basis. From the local police to the teachers in the public schools, racism pervaded the social system. Local community police hired by an appointed police chief, county sheriffs elected by a minority Anglo vote which controlled the ballot box, and the Department of Public Safety were all used to keeping Mexicans and Mexican Americans in their place. Many of these men were themselves Mexican Americans.[20]

There are a number of legal cases which suggest the nature of this institutionalized violence as it pertained to the relationship between farmer and laborer. One such case documents in detail how two farmers outside Lyford, in Willacy County, conspired to keep several Mexican Americans in peonage.[21] The men were originally arrested on charges of vagrancy, thrown in the local jail, then given the choice of working off their sentences in nearby fields. After paying off their fines by working for the local farmers for many weeks, the men tried to leave. They were apprehended by a deputy sheriff, returned to jail, and again fined by the local justice of the peace. Eventually the justice of the peace, the sheriff, and the deputy sheriff were all convicted of peonage.

This same racism that kept farm laborers in their place was easily translated to the new towns by the Midwestern farmers and growers. These new communities were established by the farmers as market centers for the new crops. In short order, the plats were laid out for Harlingen, Lyford, Raymondville, San Benito, La Feria, Mercedes, Weslaco, Donna, Alamo, San Juan, Pharr, McAllen, and Edinburg. The towns were situated directly on the new rail line that reached the Valley in 1904 and served as the region's first direct transportation link to the outside world.[22]

Mexicans and Mexican Americans in the new Valley towns, in some cases appoaching 85 to 90 percent or more of the total population, held little economic or political power. The Hispanic middle class was composed in part of those who began as merchants who served the "Mexican side" of town and gradually accumulated capital.[23] This middle class is remarkable both for its small size and its dissatisfaction with the dominant Anglo system. Some of these Mexican-American and Mexican men and women joined together in Harlingen in 1927 to form the first chapter of the League of United Latin-American Citizens (LULAC).[24]

The concerns of the Valley's Hispanic middle class were expressed very succinctly by LULAC members at a convention held in Corpus Christi in 1929. Among these concerns were:

> ...to eradicate from our body politic all intents and tendencies to establish discrimination among our fellow citizens on account of race, religion, or social position as being contrary to the true spirit of Democracy, our Constitution, and our privileges.... We shall denounce every act of peonage and mistreatment as well as the employment of minor children of scholastic age.[25]

Valley farm workers became less and less satisfied with their subsistence wages, the conditions of their work, and the racism which they encountered. When they sought to improve the nature of their work through efforts at unionization, the overt violence which has historically permeated this region was channeled in their direction.

Attempts at unionization in the late 1920s and 1930s met with repeated failures throughout the Southwest. Jamieson in particular describes in detail the failed strikes by Valley farm workers in 1937.[26] Strike breakers from Mexico could easily be trucked in and the threat of deportation of strikers who were not American citizens was employed. But over and above these constraints against unionization was the common use of local, county, and state law enforcement agencies to harass, intimidate, and crush the strikes.[27] This tradition of the ruthless use of the various branches of law enforcement to contain farm labor unions is clearly demonstrated as late as the 1960s by the actions of the Texas Rangers in the case of Allee vs. Medrano.[28]

THE BEGINNINGS OF CHANGE

The generation of Mexican-American GIs who returned home to the Valley after World War II, a generation who greatly outnumbered their fathers and grandfathers who had fought in World War I, would not tolerate the racism that they found awaiting them. Their exposure to how others in the United States lived and the rights they enjoyed was extensive. The Valley political and social system had to accommodate this new generation of Mexican Americans.[29]

Political bossism at the city and county levels did not fade away during these post-war years, although there was no one of Judge Wells's stature. The tyranny of bossism reigned most strongly in Starr County where another Hispanic family took control of the Guerra machine. In Cameron, Hidalgo, and Willacy, however, no single individuals were able to forge together as smooth an apparatus as in the days of Judge Wells. Several figures from the early 1940s to the present did make every effort to keep the status quo intact. Among these was Judge Oscar Dancy in Cameron County.[30]

Law enforcement, public education, and city and county government jobs continued to be the major sources of political favoritism and control. All positions, from sheriff to teacher's aide to county clerk came under the patronage umbrella. One established or curried favors with the higher-ups or did not get a job, regardless of qualifications. In a poverty economy, jobs themselves become spoils.

State and federal programs were filtered through this system of patronage. A poor Mexican American received extra money or food at Christmas time not from the U.S. government but from the largess of his particular patron. Such aid did not help the individual escape his economic circumstances, but it did help him and his family to get by.

The grosser examples of violence against individuals or groups that attempted to change the system are less in evidence from the 1940s to the 1960s. Troublemakers who sought to rock the boat were handled through the court system, if need be, or simply discredited in their communities. They were threatened with the loss of their job, however little that job might pay. Many of those who might have provided leadership among the poor and middle-income Mexican Americans left the Valley.

Immediately after World War II a number of Cajun shrimpers from Morgan City, Louisiana, began relocating their fleets and fishhouses to Port Isabel and Port Brownsville. As the shrimping industry grew in the Valley, it began, in contrast to Valley agriculture, to provide a few Valley men with decent wages.

A Valley Mexican-American or Mexican from across the Rio Grande could learn the ropes aboard one of the newly arrived Cajun trawlers and rise up from header, the entry-level position, to rigger, a journeyman, to captain. After ten years of shrimping, a man might, if he were ambitious and willing to work the long hours away from home, actually save enough money to buy his own boat. During the golden years of shrimping—the 1950s and 1960s—the most successful non-Anglos built up small fleets.[31]

In the late 1940s and early 1950s, some Texans and Midwesterners, especially those who had been stationed at the Air Force base in Harlingen during the war years, began returning to the Valley in the winter to take in the warm sun, walk the beaches, fish the bays. They wrote their friends, who were fighting snowstorms in Kansas, Illinois, and Iowa, about the advantages of living in the Valley. Tourism was not new to the area, but it is at this time that the potential for a major industry was first evident.

Agriculture remained king in the Valley. Cotton fields and citrus groves dominated the landscape. Many Mexicans who came as farm workers became American citizens, others did not but remained in the Valley. Mexicans still crossed the river when the farmers and growers needed additional labor. But the labor force, from the landowners' perspective, was far from ideal. While the strikes and unionization of the 1930s had subsided, the men and their families did not remain passive or submissive. During World War II the laborers had been sorely needed in the fields and they had, as a result, won slightly higher wages and improved workig conditions.[32]

But when the troops came back from the Korean War and national unemployment became a problem, the Immigration and Naturalization Service (INS) instituted "Operation Wetback" in which hundreds of thousands of Mexicans and Mexican Americans along the border were rounded up and sent back to Mexico. In the Valley it is estimated that in 1954 more than 70,000 men were summarily forced back across the Rio Grande.[33]

The Bracero Program, however, quickly solved the farmers' problem of who was going to harvest the cotton and oranges. Under pressure from the farm lobby, supported by Valley farmers, the Department of Labor (DOL) turned illegal wetbacks, recently driven south across the river, into legal *braceros* who were once again encouraged to work in the United States.

Agricultural mechanization gradually became cheaper than the price of Mexican and Mexican-American farm workers in the Valley. In the 1950s and 1960s the DOL began to insist upon a rising wage scale as well as decent housing and other working conditions which most American workers had long taken for granted. Valley cotton farmers began to replace their laborers with machines. Other crops, however, still required intensive field labor.

Attempts at strikes and unionization were met by farmers and growers with firm resolve. Local, county, and state law enforcement were used to break any threats of strikes. Intimidation, threats, and the legal system were now used most effectively, in contrast to the more overt violence of the 1920s and 1930s. While a strong movement towards unionization was taking place in California in the late 1950s, no such efforts were attempted with Valley farm workers until the mid-1960s.[34]

The recent population boom which has resulted in significant increases in the Valley's largest cities, Brownsville, Harlingen, and McAllen, is directly attributable to immigration from Mexico and from elsewhere in the state and U.S. Cameron County increased by about 70,000 in the 1970s, Hidalgo County by more than 100,000, and even tiny Starr by about 10,000.

During the 1970s and 1980s the Valley was continually used as a staging area by undocumented workers who were primarily from Mexico.[35] Such workers, the majority of which are young males, cross the river, reside in Valley communities and *colonias* from one day to up to several years, then move north to find more secure employment. Some, no one knows how many, settle in the Valley as permanent residents. Others return to their homes in the interior of Mexico or to Mexican border cities like Matamoros and Reynosa which have witnessed huge increases in population in part because of this migration.

There are not enough agricultural jobs for the Valley's labor force in the 1980s; the work has always been seasonal since the original infrastructure was constructed. Since the 1920s farm laborers have been forced to migrate north to find additional work in the fields to supplement their income. Few other labor intensive industries have appeared in the Valley to employ this labor force. A continuous flow of undocumented workers from south of the Rio Grande has translated into an increasing number of residents, both American and illegal alien seeking too few jobs.

In 1967, the United States formalized an agreement with the Mexican government called the Border Industrialization Program (BIP).[36] This program was to have a significant impact on the Valley and the entire Mexican-American borderlands area in the 1980s. American corporations would build or relocate plants (called *maquiladoras*) from nonborder regions of the United States to both the Mexican and American sides of the Rio Grande. Resources and materials would be assembled on the southern banks, then transported across the river with a minimum of tariff duties to American workers who would finalize the production process. The products would then be marketed in the United States. There are more than seventy-five maquiladoras in Matamoros alone in 1986, with an increased effort planned by the Mexican government.

CHICANISMO

National political movements in the last three decades have not passed this region by. Chicano ideology in the 1960s and 1970s, however, was filtered through the existing Valley political and social structure. Its impact was necessarily limited by the rigidity of the system already in place; potential for real change in the relationship between the Valley's rich and poor in most communities was minimal. There was a diversity of response in the Valley to Chicano ideas, a diversity that was reflected nationwide.

In Starr and Willacy Counties the political machines weathered these turbulent times virtually intact. However, in Cameron and Hidalgo Counties different communities reacted to Chicanismo to a great degree, based upon the vitality of their young, college-aged Mexican Americans. In Brownsville there were few protests, less immediate change. In some Hidalgo communities like Pharr, however, the Anglo-dominated political machines were thrown out, to be replaced by middle-class Mexican-American professionals and those who represented the disenfranchised Hispanics.

The success of Chicanos in Crystal City, one hundred miles north of Laredo, served in some ways as a model and hope for the Valley poor and the small Hispanic middle class. Chicanos were successful in registering first-time voters in Crystal City in 1963. In 1970 Crystal City Chicanos were able to vote out the Anglo political machine that had been established at City Hall and on the school board.[37] Chicanos in Crystal City then began instigating a set of reforms designed to benefit the poor Mexican-American majority in their city.

The backlash against the Chicanos in Crystal City was considerable. State officials were quite effective in shutting off state and federal funds. The city government bordered on bankruptcy. Its failures, regardless of the cause, were attributed to the Mexican-American takeover. Valley Chicanos noted with concern the reaction of Anglo Texans to self-government by Mexican-American majorities.

Even small and ineffectual protests by Valley Chicanos were met by harsh overreaction by the Anglo power structure fearful of Crystal Cities in the Valley. One tragic Valley example is the Pharr riot in the early 1970s.[38] A peaceful protest at the city hall in Pharr against police brutality quickly developed into a riot when the Pharr Fire Department turned high-pressure hoses on the protesters. But the "riot" which followed the protest was a police riot, during which an Anglo deputy sheriff shot and killed a young Mexican-American bystander. Young Chicanos were quickly rounded up, jailed, and two of the leaders charged with obstructing the police, a felony.[39]

Class composition in the Valley is, as has been demonstrated by Miller in the region's largest urban area, determined by ethnicity (see table 10). While only 2.6 percent of Miller's sample of Anglos earned less than $3,000, more than one-fourth of Mexican Americans earned a similar amount. At the other end of the income scale, 44.7 percent of all Brownsville Anglos earned $20,000 or more as compared to 13.7 percent of Brownsville

TABLE 10

Brownsville Household Income Distribution
and Per Capita Income by Ethnicity, 1978

INCOME LEVEL	% ANGLO-AMERICAN	% MEXICAN-AMERICAN
2,999 or less	2.6	11.7
3,000 - 4,999	0.0	14.9
5,000 - 6,999	7.9	13.7
7,000 - 8,999	6.6	12.1
9,000 - 11,999	9.2	13.3
12,000 - 14,999	7.9	11.3
15,000 - 19,999	21.1	9.3
20,000 - 29,999	28.9	8.5
30,000 or more	15.8	5.2
Total percentage	100.0	100.0
Total number	76	248

Source: Michael V. Miller, "Economic Growth and Change Along the U.S.-Mexican Border," Bureau of Business Research, Austin, Texas, 1982

Hispanics. In comparison to Texas and national figures, the Valley poor form a clear majority of the population, a class that is largely composed of Mexican Americans. The very small class of Valley rich is disproportionately Anglo, as is the small middle class.

Members of the Mexican-American middle class hold jobs in city, county, and state agencies, as teachers and as semi-skilled and skilled workers in the few manufacturing industries. Some of these Mexican Americans have achieved highly visible positions in Valley politics, media, the more prestigious legal firms, and other businesses.

It is sometimes argued that much "progress" has been made by Valley Mexican Americans because some Hispanics are members of the Valley's small middle and upper classes, hold elected positions, and perhaps maintain a high profile in their communities. It is, however, inaccurate to establish a legitimate trend based upon the unique experiences of a small number of very successful Mexican Americans. One indication of the difficulty that Mexican Americans in the Valley face in achieving upward mobility is how common it is for professional Mexican Americans to seek work outside the Valley. These well-trained Hispanics are forced to look elsewhere because they know that the positions that they qualify for locally will be given to others as a part of the patronage system.

As well, some middle- and upper-income Hispanics have joined the ranks of the Valley's traditional political elites. For these it often becomes in their own interest to sustain the status quo, thus perpetuating the poverty.

As demonstrated by the statistics that have been presented in chapter one, "progress" for Valley Hispanics as measured in upward class mobility has been extremely limited. This is certainly not to deny that some Mexican Americans have joined the ranks of the middle and upper classes. However, in comparison to other regions, "progress" in the Valley has been enjoyed by a very few. The myth of upward mobility serves to quiet dissent by promising a better future for those poor who will but try harder; at the same time the belief serves to blame the poor for their own poverty.

Those who believe most in Hispanic "progress" in the Valley are often those Hispanics who left the Valley to further their own economic futures and who now, having achieved upward mobility in cities far from the Valley, generalize their own personal success to those they left far behind.[40] These successful Mexican Americans romanticize their previous poverty, at the expense of reifying the Horatio Alger myth which pervades this region and much of American society.

These patterns of economic, political, and social development, which have of necessity been only schematically traced from the 1750s to the present, do, nevertheless, suggest some of the important historical roots of present-day poverty in the Valley. In the 1980s it is in part the burden of these historical relationships of wealth, power, race, and social class which help to maintain and create extreme poverty in these lands.

4. INDUSTRY, RESOURCES, AND THE LABOR FORCE: THE VALLEY AS AN INTERNAL COLONY

Vast stretches of farmland, grove, and pasture still dominate the landscape of the Lower Rio Grande Valley. Yet in the 1980s agriculture is no longer the pillar of the Valley's economy. Ranking third in dollar value after wholesale and retail trade and manufacturing (table 11),[1] Valley agriculture is still important because it employs more than 10 percent of the labor force. This translates into some 30,000 jobs (table 12).[2]

Farm workers plant, weed, grow, harvest, then pack a variety of farm products.[3] Truck crops are valued at approximately $130 million (table 13).[4] Valley onions are the biggest cash crop among all fresh vegetables, with cabbage, corn, cantaloupes, and a number of other vegetables grown in considerable amounts in comparison to the rest of Texas. Hidalgo County has the best soils for fresh vegetables and accounts for the majority of this production, although growers in Starr and Willacy Counties are increasing their production.

Cameron County contains soils more ideally suited for growing grains. This county also contributes the majority of the Val-

TABLE 11

Valley Industries by Dollar Contribution, 1981

SECTOR	DOLLAR CONTRIBUTIONS
Trade	$3,137,529,990
Manufacturing	928,674,990
Agriculture	578,266,000
Oil and Gas	541,600,000
Tourism	418,600,000

Source: Rio Grande Valley Chamber of Commerce, "Valley 2000," 1985

TABLE 12

Valley Industrial Sectors by Employment, 1967, 1980

SECTOR	1967 %	1980 %
Agriculture, For., Fish.	12.1	10.3
Mining (Gas & Oil)	1.3	1.2
Construction	5.2	5.1
Manufacturing	9.4	13.4
Transp. & Pub. Util.	4.6	3.6
Trade (Wholesale & Retail)	22.6	25.3
Finance	2.6	3.4
Service	20.4	12.9
Government	21.7	24.7
Total	100.0	100.0

Source: Heather Ball and J. Michael Patrick, "The Jobs of South Texas" (Austin, Texas: Texas Department of Agriculture, 1985).

TABLE 13

Value of Valley Vegetables, 1980

PRODUCT	VALUE
Onions	26,420,745
Cantaloupe	24,255,920
Cabbage	18,376,605
Bell Peppers	12,307,500
Honey Dew	11,260,800
Carrots	7,243,690
Lettuce	6,252,858
Broccoli	4,922,280
Watermelons	4,066,176
Cucumbers	3,787,719
Spinach	3,376,800
Tomatoes	3,114,025
Potatoes	2,012,400
Cauliflower	1,639,638
Sweet Corn	425,425
Total	129,462,581

Source: Rio Grande Valley Chamber of Commerce, "Valley 2000," 1985

ley's cotton and sorghum crops. Valley cotton was valued in 1984 at approximately $100 million and sorghum at about $55 million.[5]

The citrus industry has shown remarkably steady production over the last fifty years, with infrequent freezes the only real constraint to this viable Valley industry.[6] The value of oranges and grapefruits each has exceeded $100 million in previous years. However, citrus production is still recovering from the "Big Freeze," the worst cold spell in this century, which hit Valley groves during the Christmas holidays of 1983 and lasted more than a week. Over 90 percent of the fruit was destroyed and many of the trees were killed. Production in the citrus industry will suffer until the new trees reach maturity. It is estimated that levels of previous citrus production will not resume until 1992. When the new orchards do reach full production they will be more efficient and utilize only about half the acreage they previously occupied.

The Big Freeze underlines the continued importance of agriculture to the Valley. Thousands of farm laborers were put out of work by the vagaries of the weather. It is estimated that more than 7,000 jobs have been lost for the next several years, and that 3,000 to 4,000 jobs have been permanently lost because the new, smaller groves will require less manual labor.[7] Prior to the Big Freeze the Valley's unemployment rates were among the highest in the United States, but after the Freeze unemployment soared even higher. The McAllen-Edinburg-Pharr MSA, site of the majority of the citrus groves, registered the highest unemployment rate (19%) of any area in the United States in 1984. Cameron County was only a few rankings behind Hidalgo County.

Other important agricultural industries are sugar cane, which annually is valued at about $40 million, and corn, at approximately $25 million. Ornamentals such as flowers, shrubs, and small trees used for landscaping are a new industry which is gaining momentum in the Valley. In 1984 production from this greenhouse industry was valued at about $45 million.[9]

All that remains of the ranching dreams of the eighteenth-century Spanish are the grazing stock located in the northern portions of Hidalgo and much of Starr and Willacy Counties. While ranching operations take up large sections of land, production in 1984 was only valued at about $70 million.[10] Valley stockmen currently suffer from the nationwide trend of health conscious Americans consuming less and less beef each year. Some Valley stockmen say they are earning more from leasing their lands to deer and bird hunters than from their herds. Ranching in the Valley today brings about the same income as growing corn and raising plants in greenhouses. While Valley ranching is rich in tradition, its future is not bright.

Some eighty years after the Valley's brushland was converted into productive farmlands, the agricultural labor force remains not only poor but fearful of losing their jobs. As late as the 1960s about one-third of all Valley employment was related to farming and food processing. But by 1980 this figure had dropped to 10.3 percent. It is estimated that in fifteen years jobs in agriculture will compose 9.4 percent of all Valley jobs.[11] This estimate does not consider the loss of jobs from the Big Freeze.

A lack of part or full-time employment in the fields has meant that many Valley farm workers have been forced to work out of the Valley, to follow the harvests northward. Farmwork in the Valley, even in the best of times, has always been strictly seasonal, the summer and early fall months offering the least employment opportunities to the labor force. In the 1970s an estimated 100,000 migrant farm workers lived in the Valley, 10 percent of all migrant workers in the United States.

Valley farmers and growers have, in contrast, prospered over the years. The recent national trend which has seen small farmers forced out of agriculture, a trend reflected in other parts of Texas, is not evident here in the Valley. Valley farmers and growers, in general, paid off their land several decades before the high interest rates of the 1970s. The majority of Valley farms and groves are owned by some of the same families who originally developed the land at the turn of the century. Agricultural conglomerates and foreign-owned farms and groves remain, to date, a small segment of all land owners in the Valley. Mid-sized operations prevail, taking advantage of economies of scale, utilizing automation when possible, relying on the benefits in production from the generous use of defoliants and pesticides.[12] One major exception is the Valley citrus industry. Approximately one-half of this sector is owned by investors from outside the Valley.[13]

The most enterprising of Valley farmers and growers have reinvested their profits over the years in a vertical integration of the Valley's agricultural industry. They have managed to eliminate many of the middlemen, the processors, the haulers, the distributors, to contract directly with the large supermarket chains. Several of the largest corporations harvest, process, pack, and distribute farm products directly to the retailer. However, the majority of the Valley's agricultural products are not processed locally, nor is the majority of the processing done within the Valley more than grading and packaging. Other successful farmers and growers have invested their profits from their lands into diverse efforts, from car dealerships to shopping malls. As a group they remain, and have reason to remain, very optimistic about agriculture in the Valley.

Farmers and growers regularly threaten to increase the use of mechanization in the fields which would further reduce the need for workers. Among other reasons, this serves to keep wages for farm workers very low, a subject discussed in some detail in chapter five. A particularly interesting case in point is a locally owned corporation which has expanded its farming operations to Central America. This corporation is currently experimenting with growing a variety of fresh fruits and vegetables in Guatemala and Honduras which it would then export to this country. On NBC's Today Show John Alport reported that this grower was paying his Central American workers the equivalent of four dollars a day. A company spokesman stated that this wage was set by the Central American government and was considered a good wage by unemployed peasants. This foreign operation at the very least is an effective symbol of what might happen if Valley farm workers demand higher wages. It serves to keep farm workers afraid of losing their job, despite the low wages and dismal working conditions.

Valley farm workers and others in poverty have difficulty in purchasing the products that are grown, harvested, processed, and packed in the Valley. Food prices in the Valley are quite high when compared to other parts of Texas. Even though fresh vegetables, grain, beef, citrus, and fish are produced locally, this same food in Valley retail stores is quite expensive.[14]

In the fall of 1981 students in my Social Problems course monitored food prices in twenty different retail food outlets in Cameron County for four months. They collected and compared weekly food prices on a wide variety of items. Prices were approximately 20 percent higher than for similar items in other regions of Texas. The Valley poor pay more for their food than do affluent Texans elsewhere.

Shrimp prices were typical of products which are harvested in the Valley, but often cost more in Valley grocery stores than in San Antonio, Austin, or Dallas. It is cheaper to buy shrimp that was docked at Port Isabel or Port Brownsville in an Austin store than it is in nearby Brownsville, Harlingen, or McAllen.

TRADE

Valley agriculture, while still productive, is far less important in the 1980s than are retail and wholesale trade. This sector of the economy is six times as large as agriculture, three times greater than manufacturing. The retail and wholesale sector of the economy provides a quarter of all Valley jobs. However, these figures must be regarded very cautiously.

A significant segment of the retail sector is dependent on Mexico's roller coaster economy. Retail trade has always been closely tied to the Mexican consumer, especially in the Valley communities which border the Rio Grande. In downtown Brownsville, McAllen, Edinburg, and in their shopping malls, signs are often in Spanish; many of the sales clerks speak only Spanish, and are often undocumented workers.

When Mexican shoppers have money to spend, Brownsville and the McAllen-Edinburg area have boomed. A steady decline in the value of the peso, first beginning with a major devaluation in 1976, has seriously affected the Mexican consumer. Devaluation again in 1982, followed by controlled devaluation of the peso, has devastated retail sales in Valley border communities. Records of retail sales in 1983 as compared to previous years dramatically demonstrate the loss of revenues in many communities in Cameron and Hidalgo Counties.[15] Brownsville's booming downtown retail trade was severely hurt. Suddenly the traffic jams disappeared and sales clerks stood idly by in stores once jammed with Mexican shoppers. Estimates of the number of retail businesses that closed in Brownsville run as high as 200, including both small, family-owned stores and large chains.

A staggering inflation in Mexico boosted retail sales in Brownsville and other border communities in 1985 and 1986, but sales nowhere approximate the boom years. Downtown Brownsville has not recovered from the disastrous 1982 peso devaluation. Other Valley communities, less dependent on Mexican trade, are beginning to approximate prior levels of retail trade. Valley trade with Mexico has always been problematic: what was good for Valley merchants was not necessarily good for Mexican merchants or the Mexican economy.

Retail and wholesale trade, which includes the Valley's tourist industry, hires more than a quarter of all workers. The number of those employed in retail trade has increased substantially since 1980 (see table 14). From 1980 to 1984, despite the peso devaluations, the total number of jobs in the retail industry increased by about 4,000.[16]

However, while retail jobs have increased in number, wages remain low and stagnant. The average wage in the Valley in the retail industry is $3.35 per hour, minimum wage. Entry level sales clerks in downtown border communities earn much less than minimum wage, as low as $2.00 or less per hour. Sales clerks in towns not directly on the Rio Grande are most likely to start at $3.35 an hour. Assistant managers in convenience stores earn from $4 to $4.50 an hour. Opportunities for advancement are extremely limited and pay does not usually compensate for extra responsibilities and duties. Sales clerks will commonly work at a job for six months to several years and still receive minimum wage. Those who insist on higher wages are fired and a replacement is quickly found.

Retail trade reflects Valley poverty. A majority of stores and businesses, with the exception of those geared to the tourist trade, sells goods and services which the poor require. Although prices are often high in comparison to other regions, the quality of the product is likely to be substandard. Bottom-of-the-line goods are sold not only by locally owned stores, but national chain stores which in other regions of the United States cater to middle-income consumers. Lay-away and pay-back plans for purchases abound in the Valley. Those of limited means must often pay very high finance charges on goods that are already overpriced. Furniture stores, appliance stores, clothing stores, discount stores, voca-

TABLE 14

*Covered Employment by Valley Labor Force
for Cameron, Hidalgo, and Willacy Counties, 1980, 1984*

	1980	1984
Manufacturing	21,299	20,713
Durable Goods	7,023	6,379
Lumber & Wood Prod.	195	153
Furniture / Fixtures	—	—
Stone / Clay / Glass	880	1,186
Primary Metals	—	—
Fabricated Metals	440	616
Machinery	960	581
Electric Machinery	1,292	666
Transportation Equipment	—	—
Other Durable Goods	3,256	3,177
Nondurable Goods	14,276	14,334
Food & Kindred	4,896	4,954
Textiles	—	—
Apparel	6,585	7,050
Paper & Allied	—	—
Printing & Pub.	798	973
Chemicals & Allied	487	267
Petroleum & Related	—	—
Other Nondurable Goods	1,510	1,090
Nonmanufacturing	109,862	122,777
Mining	1,720	1,748
Construction	7,946	7,922
Trans., Comm., Util.	5,287	5,852
Wholesale Trade	10,580	10,483
Retail Trade	28,628	32,629
Finance, Insur., Real Est.	5,181	6,940
Services	15,837	22,166
Federal Gov.	2,766	2,507
State Gov.	4,774	5,113
Local Gov.	27,143	27,417
Total	131,161	143,490

Source: Texas Employment Commission

tional-technical schools, and car dealerships take advantage of the Valley consumer, demanding higher than average interest rates on goods of lower than average quality.

There is also a disproportionate number of retail stores which cater to the demands of Valley tourists. These stores sell everything from Mexican curios to expensive fur coats designed to appeal to the owners of the beachfront condominiums from

Dallas, Houston, and Monterrey. The Valley also has a thriving recreational vehicle parts and services business.

An often heard complaint of middle-income Valley residents is that they have no place to shop. While less true in the 1980s, such a complaint reflects the reality of the Valley economy. Retail trade is geared primarily for the poor who form the majority of the population and the tourist. The consumer needs of the Valley's middle class are met by a limited number of retail stores.

Wholesale trade in the Valley is far less important than retail trade. In 1984 total wholesale sales in the Brownsville-Harlingen-San Benito MSA and in the McAllen-Pharr-Edinburg MSA were $1,238,930,503.[17] Total retail sales in these same cities were $2,644,911,231, more than twice as much. Nondurable and durable goods compose about the same share of all Valley wholesale trade.

In the 1980s employment in Valley wholesale trade remained stagnant. In 1980 this sector employed 10,580, as compared to 10,483 in 1984. Entry level jobs begin at minimum wage, with very limited opportunities for advancement, as is the case in the retail sector. This sector was also significantly damaged by the 1982 peso devaluation.[18]

Port Mansfield, Port Isabel, and Port Brownsville were bright spots in the Valley's economy until the Texas oil bust and the *peso* devaluation. These ports, established respectively by the Willacy County Navigation District, the San Benito–Port Isabel Navigation District, and the Brownsville Navigation District, became vital parts of their local economies in the early 1980s. Tiny Port Mansfield bounced back from Hurricane Allen in 1983 and has been able to balance a growing recreational fishing industry with the demands of commercial shrimping and the off-shore oil industry.[19] Port Isabel harbors a large shrimp fleet which has supported the local economy since World War II.[20] The Texas oil bust has adversely impacted tourism in both of the communities.

Port Brownsville, the most significant of the three ports, has thrived in recent years as an importer of raw materials to Mexico.[21] In effect it has served as Monterrey's outlet to the sea, expanding as Monterrey has grown to be the second largest city in Mexico. Gross tonnage at Port Brownsville peaked in 1981 at about one million tons of cargo. However, as Mexico's economy has continued its tailspin, Port Brownsville has suffered. Several petro-chemical and ship building plants had thrived at the port, but the oil bust cut back production. These national and international trends are not peculiar to Port Brownsville; ports all along the Gulf of Mexico are enduring hard times.

Employment in industries at this port has decreased substantially since 1981. Marathon LeTourneau, a builder of offshore oil rigs, now employs 200 compared to almost 2,000. A Union Carbide plant which employed about 500 workers closed down. Both businesses were exceptional. A skilled welder can start at $6.00 an hour or more at Marathon LeTourneau, rather than at minimum wage, and workers at Union Carbide, while paid less than at comparable company plants in the United States, earned decent wages. Union Carbide also hired Valley residents in management positions and paid them well, by Valley standards, for their work. Port Brownsville is also home to the second largest shrimp fleet in Texas and a fishing industry which pays high wages to its best workers.

Members of the International Longshoremen's Union, Local 29, have also received good wages for their work at the port. The union, one of the only viable unions in the Valley, paid its workers during the peak of the port's activity up to $20.00 an hour with excellent benefits. The Union used Valley Mexican Americans. Such wages are unheard of in the Valley. Now, however, members of Local 29 work far fewer hours for half as much pay.

MANUFACTURING AND THE BORDER INDUSTRIALIZATION PROGRAM

Next to retail and wholesale trade, manufacturing is the most important sector of the Valley economy. Over the last three decades it has shown extreme fluctuations. In 1981 Valley manufacturing was valued at $928,674,990, almost double the value of Valley agriculture. But in the 1960s manufacturing was in serious trouble. Manufacturing jobs in Hidalgo County had declined by 21 percent, compared to the previous decade, with a 7 percent decline in Cameron County.[22] This trend changed again in the 1970s. Manufacturing jobs in Cameron County increased by 62 percent, with similar growth in Hidalgo County. More than 8,000 jobs were created in the Brownsville area during this period; similar growth transpired in the McAllen-Edinburg and Harlingen areas. In the early 1980s manufacturing jobs again took a nose dive. Valley jobs in durable goods declined by approximately 650, jobs in nondurable goods showing a net gain of only 58. In Cameron County about 2,200 jobs were lost in 1985, the majority in manufacturing.

This thirty-year roller coaster ride is best understood by examining the nature of the industry. Valley manufacturing is dominated by clothing and electronic assemblers. Workers are hired to cut and sew clothing which is then shipped north to major distribution centers. In the electronics industry workers help to assemble electronic goods, such as car radios, which are trucked to other factories outside the Valley for final assembly and/or distribution.

These manufacturing plants have been attracted to the Valley because of the Border Industrialization Program (BIP), initiated by the Mexican and American governments in the mid-1960s. The considerable turnaround in Valley manufacturing in the 1970s is directly attributable to BIP. The vast majority of workers in this sector today are employed by plants which relocated to the Valley, creating relatively large numbers of new jobs for the Valley's labor force.

In 1984 there were 7,050 men and women working in plants producing apparel, about one-half of all existing jobs in the nondurable goods sector of Valley manufacturing.[23] Only a slightly smaller number worked in plants producing electronic goods, accounting for a little less than half of all jobs in durable goods. Other kinds of manufacturing work include furniture, stone, primary metals, fabricated metals, machinery, electric machinery, chemicals, and petroleum and compose only a very small part of all Valley manufacturing jobs.

In McAllen, manufacturing employment accounted for 13.7 percent of all city employment, with those working in the apparel industry and electronics assembly plants accounting for 3,500 jobs. In the manufacturing sector only those employed in food processing plants had a similar impact on the local economy.[24]

Some of these new Valley plants are the sister operations of much larger plants on the Mexican side of the border. Products are assembled in Matamoros or Reynosa and shipped across the Rio Grande for final assembly and distribution by American plants and American workers. The other new plants in the Valley came as word spread that the Valley labor force was abundant, cheap, reliable, and non-unionized.

In the 1970s both twin plants and the other new plants offered jobs that the Valley labor force so desperately required. They were portrayed at the time by the Valley's business leaders as the solution to the Valley's long-time poverty. It was very easy then to ignore the obvious limitations of these new plants. They hired women and ignored the large number of unemployed men, offered very few chances for promotion or advancement, and were very sensitive to national economic trends. The companies brought their management with them, along with their supervisors and technicians, so that very few local residents were hired except as production workers. The majority of apparel and electronics jobs were given to women because women had held the jobs previously. Some of these plants immediately shut down in the first half of the 1980s, or in some cases relocated their operations, because of downturns in the economy. Through these actions the companies showed no long-term commitment to stay in the region.

These plants rarely paid above minimum wage and did not offer any training in skills that would prepare workers for higher paying positions.[25] Advancement within the plant job hierarchy was virtually nonexistent. Many of the workers were unable to afford the very products that they produced; finished goods were shipped north, then reshipped back to the Valley for sale. Women who sewed together jeans all day or night often could not afford to buy them in Valley stores.

In many ways jobs in these kinds of plants resemble farm work: wages are very low, there are no transferable or acquired job skills, no advancement, and the work is very unreliable. A major exception to this observation is that, unlike farm work which brings many into direct contact with pesticides and defoliants, these plants provide for relatively safe working conditions.[26]

The work of Stoddard and others has shed substantial light upon maquiladoras along the Mexican side of the border.[27] Maquiladoras have shown rapid growth since their inception. In 1966 there were 57 plants along the border employing 4,257. Ten years later there were 488 plants with 74,000 workers. In 1985 there were 720 plants with 240,000 employees. As the number of plants and workers has increased since 1966, so too has the value of their production. Since 1971 when the foreign exchange earnings of these plants was a little more than $100 million, earnings have increased by more than 1400 percent; in 1985 the value of maquiladora production was put at $1,450 million.[28]

A recent study has also argued that maquiladoras have a positive impact on the American side of the border.[29] Approximately 1,750 American companies employing more than one million workers do business with the maquiladoras on the Mexican side of the border. An additional 15,000 U.S. firms supply maquiladoras with materials; these firms employ 200,000 American workers. Along the U.S. side of the border there are 459 companies which are directly tied to the maquiladoras which provide 150,000 jobs. In Texas the maquiladoras generate 23,500 jobs.

Maquiladoras in Matamoros, Reynosa, and other Mexican border communities reflect similar trends. In 1967 there were only three maquiladoras in Matamoros. By 1975 the number had jumped to a high of 48. As of 1985 there were 37 of these plants employing approximately 21,000 Mexican workers. For this same year Reynosa boasts 18 maquiladoras, with three more in the process of relocation. Camargo, across from Rio Grande City, now has three small plants.

While Valley chambers of commerce continue to assert that maquiladoras have greatly benefited the Valley's economy, there has been no research to date which substantiates these contentions. Such research is vitally needed.[30] Maquiladoras have raised a certain amount of criticism, nationwide. A few critics have focused on the wages that Mexican workers receive, the composition of the labor force, and the socioeconomic impact on both the Mexican and the American side of the Rio Grande, among other issues.

Stoddard has correctly emphasized that the majority of American social scientists who have been critical of maquiladoras have failed to analyze these plants within the context of Mexican society.[31] This is certainly true in regard to wages. While workers in Matamoros commonly receive $1.30 per hour for their labor, a little more than one-third of minimum wage on the north side of the river, the Mexican wage is well within the range of general wages paid to Mexican workers in that border city.

Workers in Matamoros are unionized under the long-time leadership of Agapito González Cavazos. Cavazos, recently re-elected to his post as president of the Mexican Chapter of the Mexican Labor Federation (CTM), has controlled labor in Matamoros for three decades. Cavazos has created his own rogue union, which does whatever he wants it to.[32]

Stoddard notes that maquiladoras all along the border are significantly superior in wages, working conditions, and fringe benefits when compared to other kinds of Mexican plants and factories. He distinguishes between the different kinds of maquiladoras based upon ownership, suggesting that those that are owned solely by Mexicans offer the lowest wages and the poorest working conditions.[33]

Yet there are other issues that need to be addressed. Among these is a concern that these new plants in cities like Matamoros and Reynosa take jobs from American workers. Trico, for instance, a large producer of windshield wiper blades based in Buffalo, New York, recently relocated to the Brownsville-Matamoros area. It constructed two plants, a large plant in Matamoros that will, according to the company, employ about 1,000 Mexican workers, and a smaller facility in Brownsville where 400 will work.

Trico workers in Buffalo were unionized and paid between $10–14 or more per hour plus benefits. Mexican workers will receive about $1.30 per hour plus benefits, while workers in Brownsville will earn the minimum wage of $3.35. The move from Buffalo to the Mexican border makes excellent economic sense; Trico will save considerable costs on labor and not have to worry about labor disputes because the Mexican union in Matamoros has sweetheart contracts with all the maquiladoras. Trico has also placed itself in an excellent bargaining position with the union in Buffalo. Not only can it demand lower wages from the union, using its relocation as a direct threat that it will move all of its operations to the border if its demands are not met, but Trico may even succeed in busting the union.

The economic impact on Buffalo will be severe but Trico's move to Brownsville will have a minimal positive affect on Brownsville workers who will earn minimum wage. Trico, like other twin-plants, will bring its management, supervisors, and technicians along with them when they make the move or leave them in a smaller facility in Buffalo. It is far easier to see how Matamoros will benefit from this move than it is how either Brownsville or Buffalo will benefit.

Several Valley business leaders have urged the business community to develop small supply companies which can furnish parts to the Mexican maquiladoras. In this way the Valley could take greater advantage of the maquiladora industry. But such companies require venture capital which is in short supply in the Valley, a topic to be discussed below. Further, the larger Mexican maquiladoras are already tied to a supply network that is international in scope. The result is that while in some other regions along the border American businesses have directly benefited from the growth in the maquiladora industry, the Valley has shared in only a limited fashion.

Apologists for the maquiladoras argue, as do company spokesmen, that if maquiladoras do not relocate along the U.S.-Mexico border the plants will simply go "offshore." Many more American jobs will then be lost to workers in Hong Kong, Korea, Taiwan, and the Philippines. This particular issue is admittedly complex and beyond the scope of the present discussion. At the very least, however, the ability of these plants to quickly relocate to more favorable sites emphasizes how unsound it is to base any long-term solutions to Valley poverty upon the backs of maquiladoras. These plants have the capacity, as they have clearly demonstrated, to willingly accept the local tax breaks and infrastructure improvements provided by public bonds, then to pack up, almost overnight, and leave for greener pastures.

Of equal consideration in any discussion of maquiladoras are the general social and economic conditions which these plants help to create both on the Mexican and the American side of the

Rio Grande. Higher wages along the Mexican border have encouraged a rural-urban migration to Valley border cities which accounts in part for their large increases in population in the last two decades. Not only are wages higher in Mexican border towns but, relative to other regions in Mexico, there is less unemployment. Maquiladoras help to increase this Mexican rural-urban migration, with subsequent increases of undocumented workers crossing the Rio Grande.

Stoddard has painted a far rosier picture of the maquiladoras than is merited.[34] He demonstrates that there is little empirical evidence to suggest that the maquiladoras in and of themselves pull in Mexicans to border cities. But Stoddard's dilemma is that, having demonstrated the rapid growth of the maquiladoras, the growing commitment of the Mexican government to them, and the relatively high wages and safe working conditions, he then must claim there are only limited negative consequences for those who live on both sides of the river.

Matamoros, Reynosa, and other border cities have experienced incredible increases of population in the 1980s. Matamoros has grown by about 200,000 people in less than sixteen years, from 139,000 in 1970 to an estimated 325,000 in 1986. Reynosa has undergone similar growth, from about 137,000 in 1970 to more than 250,000.[35]

This new population is not just the result of a high birth rate among the indigenous population. A substantial portion is attributable to immigration from the surrounding northern Mexican states. Even the most superficial of trips through the city of Matamoros reveals large numbers of Mexicans living in newly constructed cardboard shacks and other substandard structures. Matamoros is developing a community of these cardboard houses which surrounds and is dependent upon the city dump.

There is an even greater strain on already limited city services in Matamoros, Reynosa, and other border communities in the 1980s. Electricity, potable water, sewers, all public services are in very short supply. This year Matamoros was forced to clear land for a new cemetery, its other two public cemeteries filled to capacity. Rain showers regularly result in major flooding because of an inadequate drainage system. Crime and health and education problems, all correlates of urban poverty, have increased in Matamoros and Reynosa as more and more people migrate to these cities.

The maquiladoras play an important, but not solitary, role in this migration flood. Mexicans are migrating to find employment, to find a higher quality of life. The maquiladoras are hiring workers, but only a fraction of those seeking work.

Whether or not Mexicans move to cities like Matamoros and Reynosa because they have specifically heard that jobs are available in maquiladoras is a spurious question; they simply know that life is better in the cities than in the countryside. Because of the deteriorating situation in the countryside, villages, and towns in Tamaulipas and other northern Mexican states, it makes good sense to look for better work along the border or in the United States. When Mexicans move to the cities many do not find work. Some of these, mostly men, but increasingly both men and women, seek work north of the Rio Grande.[36] Many, perhaps those less willing to take the risk of seeking work in a foreign culture where they will be treated as criminals, stay where they are. The situation in Mexican border cities adjacent to the Valley continues to deteriorate, despite Mexican government proclamations to the contrary.[37]

The constant influx of Mexican workers into the Valley, and the threats of Valley employers to use this work force, keep wages low for a majority of nonskilled and semi-skilled Valley workers.[38] Wages of workers in McAllen, Edinburg, and Mission demonstrate this trend. The 1984 median hourly wages of truck drivers is $4.70, guards $3.85, janitors $4.18, material handling laborers $4.40, switchboard operators $4.47, and computer operators $5.50.[39]

There are, finally, two additional issues that require scrutiny. The first is the impact of maquiladoras adjacent to the Valley upon the long-term health and safety of workers. There is evidence to suggest that twin plants in Matamoros and Reynosa have less regard for public health than the plants which Stoddard examined. For example, the Quimica Flour plant in Matamoros spilled an as yet undetermined amount of highly toxic hydrofluoric acid in 1980.[40] The long-term effects on Mexican workers who were treated has not been determined. Of equal concern, Matamoros and Brownsville residents were never notified of the spill, the extent of injuries, nor any other facts concerning the accident. In another case, two Matamoros maquiladoras have continued to dump waste in a landfill less than two miles from Lauro Villa Beach, that city's most popular summer resort. The Mexican Department of Urban Development and Ecology began supervising the illegal dumping site, but the two companies continue to use it.[41] These two examples and others strongly suggest that twin plants that are attracted to this region may be among the "dirtiest," those least concerned about maintaining a safe environment.

Finally, these plants are willing to condone practices by Mexican law enforcers that would not be tolerated in this country. Mexican state and local police have been used to break strikes in maquiladoras in Reynosa. A member of the American press who witnessed an act of violence by Reynosa police was held overnight in a Mexican jail and tortured by Mexican police.[42] Again, these actions suggest that this region may be attracting those plants which are qualitatively different from other twin plants along the border.

This is not to blame BIP for all of the Valley's economic or political woes, rather it is to stress that BIP at best is a mixed blessing for this region. Valley business leaders, however, continue to self-servingly argue that the greater the number of twin plants, the better.[43]

TOURISM

Tourism is not new to the Valley, but it is only within the last several decades that it has so profoundly influenced the Valley's economy; tourism ranks as the fifth most important industry in the Valley. Port Isabel and South Padre Island have, since the turn of the century, drawn sport fishermen and hunters from around the state and the nation.[44] Beginning with prohibition in the 1920s, Valley Mexican border communities became havens for those who chose to frequent the cantinas, casinos, and substantial red light districts.[45]

In the 1980s it is Midwestern senior citizens who are the most important component of the Valley's tourist industry. When the first big snowstorms strike Iowa, Missouri, Illinois and Wisconsin, thousands of the retired, called "Winter Texans" or "snowbirds" by the residents of the Valley, begin their long trek southward in their recreational vehicles and pick-ups with attached trailers. There are a number of other regions in the United States which offer attractive climates to those wishing to escape frigid temperatures and snow drifts, but none of these is as cheap as the Valley.

A majority of these Winter Texans are retired blue collar workers who are living on modest pensions. These couples (there are few singles) are quite content with relatively unsophisticated services. They seek out friends to play cards with, attend dutch suppers, square dances and any other excuse to socialize with old and new friends. This is not the race-track, hai lai, fancy crowd; it is the par three, shuffleboard bunch.

In 1985 the average Valley tourist spent $163.00 per week.[46] Of this amount, a third was spent on lodging, a third on food, 24 percent on automotive expenses, and 9 percent on other costs. While the average Winter Texan spends a total of 77 days in the Valley, he spends less than $13.97 per day, a very modest sum.

A good portion of the Winter Texans' expenses go toward rent in trailer courts. Two-thirds of all Winter Texans stay in their own recreational vehicles during their visits and pay rent to park where they can hook up to electric and water lines. The trailer courts compete for business by offering a variety of social events, recreation, and entertainment. Other activities most often include fishing, sightseeing, and visiting Mexico, which are all very inexpensive.

In addition to this kind of tourist, there are also those who visit the Valley for much shorter stays. Many of these tourists stay at hotels or motels on South Padre Island or in the surrounding area, or rent condominiums. Those who own or rent on the beach are upper middle-class tourists from Texas metropolitan areas such as Houston and Dallas and from Monterrey, Mexico.

South Padre Island has witnessed considerable growth since Hurricane Beulah in the late 1960s.[47] The number of condominiums grew rapidly until the first major devaluations of the Mexican peso in the early 1980s, followed by the Texas oil bust. At that time condominium development, which had peaked at over $100 million a year, came to a grinding halt. An estimated 1500 new units are now for sale and have not drawn interested buyers; the soft market has resulted in significant discounts in the selling price. Construction of retail stores has been considerable for the last three years, but this market has now become saturated.

Port Isabel has undergone considerable economic and political changes in the last decade as a result of the growth of tourism on South Padre Island. It has grown from a sleepy little fishing community to one dominated by developers and outside interests. The business center near the causeway which links Port Isabel with South Padre has become an area which caters to upper middle-income tourists and sport fishermen. Many low-income residents have been forced out because of soaring real estate prices; they have found homes in nearby inland communities.

Port Mansfield has seen similar development, although on a much smaller scale than South Padre Island. Real estate prices there have soared, as in Port Isabel, as Texans from outside the Valley buy lots and beach homes for investment and retirement.

Mexicans are a vital part of the Valley tourist industry, although they and other kinds of tourists take a backseat to the Winter Texans in terms of economic importance. Mexicans invested heavily in South Padre Island real estate prior to the peso devaluations.

College students on spring break also contribute to the tourist industry. In 1986 they were estimated to number more than 100,000 at South Padre Island.[48] Although their stay in the Valley is much shorter, these students are much bigger spenders than Winter Texans. The average college student spends about $300 during his brief visit to the Valley, enjoying the sun, drinking beer, and socializing with other students. The estimate of dollar impact of these tourists in 1986 was $30 million.

Developers plan to expand the island tourist industry, and one corporation has laid plans to turn the mouth of the Rio Grande into a 12,665 acre resort.[49] Billboards at the entrance to Boca Chica Beach announce the new development in glowing terms. DMJM of Houston is preparing plans to construct a new waterway system which will link the Brownsville Ship Channel to the river just above its mouth. Plans call for condominiums, malls, single-family dwellings, ten golf courses, and ferries to transport resort visitors from the American side of the Rio Grande to the Mexican side. It is estimated that the first stage of the project, Playa del Rio, will cost $20 to $30 million. A city of 150,000 is envisioned within the next twenty years. Whether this development project is ever completed remains questionable at this time; some local experts suggest that environmental impact studies and other impediments may prolong the construction of the project indefinitely.[50]

While tourism ranked fifth of all Valley industries, it is neither labor intensive nor does it pay, on the average, above minimum wage. For instance, in Hidalgo County in 1983 tourists spent $182 million. The industry, however, employed only 3,837 workers and paid them $34 million.[51] Assuming that each wage earner in this industry was paid equally, the average worker earned $8,861, only slightly above minimum wage. Of course, wages are not equally distributed; managers and supervisors earn substantially more than do maids, waitresses, kitchen help, and others. Too, these kinds of jobs, like jobs in most other Valley industries, provide for few opportunities for advancement, pay no benefits, and are seasonal.

Tourism brings in outside dollars which then help to stimulate the regional economy. Local property taxes, either directly through owning property or indirectly through paying rent, as well as local sales taxes, also contribute to the Valley's economic health. In 1983 tourists spent $77 million in Hidalgo County, with an additional $1 million generated by local sales taxes attributable to the tourist industry.

However, there are also several drawbacks to tourism in the Valley, factors which are rarely discussed by Valley businessmen and others who profit directly from the tourist industry. Winter Texans, for one, exert substantial pressure on the limited public services which the Valley can provide its full-time residents. Health care is one such example.[52] Midwestern tourists, most elderly, rely more heavily on health services, including ambulance and emergency room service, than does the average Valley citizen. Ambulance service in some areas of the Valley is problematic. Emergency rooms at the limited number of Valley hospitals are already hard-pressed to meet the needs of full-time residents. In a region characterized by an extremely low health status of the general population, hospitals vie for the lucrative tourist trade. Billboards and television commercials describe the various advantages of services the hospital can provide the elderly.

In certain specific cases tourists drive up the cost of living for full-time residents of the Valley. The Brownsville and McAllen-Edinburg housing market prior to the peso devaluation in 1982 is one example. An increasing number of Mexicans had invested in these real estate markets, buying the most expensive houses and, when these were no longer available, the more modest houses owned by the middle class. Prices for all levels of housing leaped upward as developers and builders who might have otherwise been encouraged to build low-income housing responded to the demand of Mexican buyers.[53]

The long-term instability of Valley tourism remains a very real problem to an economy with few reliable sectors. In 1979 the Ixtoc Two oil spill, the largest oil spill in the world, discouraged visitors from vacationing at South Padre Island.[54] The Island lost a complete season of business. Valley tourism is extremely sensitive to a variety of economic trends and fashions. South Padre Island is currently an "in" place for college students from the Midwest to spend spring break. But the Island, just as quickly, can become an "out" place, with subsequent loss of jobs and revenue.

The Winter Texans are as trendy as college students. Figures for Valley tourists since 1982 demonstrate the variability of the whims of those who choose to visit the Valley. In 1982 a total of 297,942 tourists visited the Valley, the majority being those who stayed for several months. The following year, more than 70,000 additional tourists visited the area. In 1984, 321,015 turned up, a drop of approximately 50,000 from the previous year.[55]

One of the more ominous aspects of Valley tourism is the recent involvement of Winter Texans in the politics of one Valley city. During 1985 these tourists were dissatisfied with what they perceived as inadequate services to their trailer courts. They were also disturbed by a proposed park planned directly across the street from one trailer court. They organized, attended city council meetings to voice their objections, and finally changed their legal place of residence in order to be able to vote in an upcoming election. Voting as a block, they managed to help elect an Anglo mayor and city council in a community that had been 88.5 percent Mexican-American.

Not surprisingly, full-time residents of this city took a dim view of the tourists' participation in what they considered to be their own affairs. They called into question the motives of Winter Texans who were unwilling to allow construction of a park designed for young children, one sorely needed by the community. When these tourists returned to the Midwest in the spring, the full-time residents were stuck with the political fracas that they had created, then abandoned. Winter Texans in this one community have, as a result of their participation in local politics, created an anti-Anglo backlash.

THE SHRIMPING INDUSTRY AND ECONOMIC OPPORTUNITY

Since World War II the shrimping industry has provided Valley men and their families with the best opportunity to escape poverty. There remains a crucial irony, however; working in the Valley's fishing industry relegates many to occupational discrimination. Valley shrimpers, like many commercial fishermen, have been ascribed a variety of negative characteristics which limit their social mobility and political participation in the community.[56]

Florida, Louisiana, and Alabama shrimpers discovered large reserves of brown shrimp in 1946 off the coastlines of South Texas. These shrimp migrated southward into Mexico's Bay of Campeche; the fishing grounds east of Veracruz were particularly productive. As markets for shrimp were developed, shrimpers from these states moved their operations to Texas to be closer to the best fishing. Cajun shrimpers were sometimes driven out of northern Texas coastal communities because local fishermen saw them as competitors—Louisiana and Texas shrimpers remain hostile to each other in the 1980s. Cajun shrimpers, however, found relatively little resistence to their industry in Port Isabel and Brownsville where the local labor force was anxious for the new jobs created by the shrimp trawlers and their on-shore facilities.

Today these two Valley fishing ports are among the most important in all of the United States. In 1984 Port Isabel and Brownsville, taken together, ranked sixth out of all fishing ports across the nation in terms of the value of the catch that was landed. The 23 million pounds of shrimp that were landed in 1984 were netted by a fleet of 400 trawlers employing crews and dockside personnel numbering around 1500.[57] The Valley shrimping industry has consistently produced harvests that are valued at $50 million or more since the late 1940s. The impact on the small community of Port Isabel and surrounding towns is substantial; the $50 million generates another $125 million that is distributed throughout the general Valley economy in the form of wages, rents, and retail sales.

The Gulf shrimpers who relocated their base of operations to the Valley required a labor force. In the beginning Valley residents worked on Gulf trawlers as headers, the lowest position on the boat. Headers, as the name implies, spend most of their time deheading shrimp. Such work is backbreaking—the header sits on a small stool on the rear deck of a trawler and, one by one, deheads the thousands and thousands of shrimp that the captain and rigman catch in their nets.

For this labor headers receive only room and board on the vessel and a small wage which is determined by the number of boxes, or hundred weight, of shrimp tails that they dehead. In 1988 the average header in these two ports earned about $6,000.[58] More important than the small wage, however, is the fact that the header is an apprentice. If he works hard and is willing to put up with the long hours at sea distant from family and friends, then in two years or less he can be promoted to rigman.

Rigmen are paid well, by Valley standards, for the work that they do. The median income for rigmen in 1988 was about $13,000, although the best earned as much as $24,000. The responsibilities and the skills required of rigmen on Gulf trawlers are considerable. They must prepare and fish the bulky nets, stand in for the captain when called upon, and also help to head the shrimp. It is not easy work; like all work on a shrimp boat it is backbreaking, repetitive, and sometimes dangerous; it is a rare fishing season that a shrimper is not lost at sea.

There are a number of Mexican Americans who began working on shrimp boats after World War II and, through hard work and ambition, worked their way up from header to rigman to captain. These men had a limited education (the average was junior high school) and few skills when they began working as shrimpers.[59] Some thirty years later more than a few had become captains or boat owners and their annual incomes had substantially increased. Captains of boats in 1988 earned on the average about $18,000 in these two ports, although the best earned up to $38,000.

A few of this same group of men were able to save their money and buy trawlers. Several now own small fleets of three to eight or more vessels. The income of these most successful Mexican Americans easily exceeds $100,000; by Valley standards these men are very rich.

While the Valley shrimp industry provides a small group of men and their families with good wages and economic security, many of these same commercial fishermen suffer discrimination in their communities because of the work they do. Landlords, store owners, and the police among others all maintain very negative attitudes toward these commercial fishermen. There are a number of very strong, but false, myths about this workforce; Gulf shrimpers are often stereotyped as irresponsible troublemakers who drink excessively. The actions of a few shrimpers are assumed to represent all those who fish for a living and the Valley mass media help support this stereotype. In fact, the majority of Valley shrimpers are married, own their own homes, work very hard for the wages they receive, consume alcohol at the same rates as the rest of the population, and are no more likely to break the laws than other residents.[60]

While shrimping has provided some Valley Mexican Americans with the opportunity for upward mobility, these same strong negative stereotypes limit their prestige within their communities. Also they are unable to participate actively in politics because of the daily demands of their work—during the six to eight month fishing season they are away from home two to three weeks at a time, return briefly to take on fuel and supplies, then once again sail for the open waters of the Gulf of Mexico. These shrimpers have been unable to form a strong union; their frequent attempts to strike against boat companies to gain better working conditions and higher wages have always met with failure.[61]

The outlook for the Valley's shrimping industry is not bright. An amendment to the Lacey Act in 1980 made it unlawful for Texas shrimpers to fish south of the Rio Grande.[62] Traditionally shrimpers from Port Isabel and Port Brownsville had netted 25 percent or more of their shrimp in Mexican waters. Fuel prices, insurance premiums, and other costs have also cut into their profits. The rise in imported shrimp has, in the 1980s, helped to keep the price of domestic shrimp low. While still a very viable industry, the golden years of commercial shrimping have passed.

Undocumented workers from Mexico compose a very significant segment of the labor force in the Valley's shrimping industry. A survey of Valley shrimpers in 1979 reported that more than half of the work force was composed of undocumented Mexican workers; the further north from the border, the fewer the number of Mexicans who work as shrimpers in Texas shrimp fleets.[63]

Mexican shrimpers fishing on Texas boats earn about 35 percent less than do American citizens although they perform the same duties as other crew members. Nevertheless, Mexican workers are drawn to work on Valley shrimp boats because they can earn much higher wages than on Mexican shrimp boats; headers on Mexican boats earn less than $2,000 per year as compared to approximately twice that on Valley boats.[64]

There has always been a demand for Mexican fishermen to work on Valley shrimp boats because of the strong negative stereotypes that prevail and the nature of the work that shrimpers must do; the indigenous labor force, in spite of very high unemployment and the very low wages that most jobs pay, has been unwilling to work as shrimpers on Valley trawlers. In 1987 major boat companies in Port Isabel and Port Brownsville worked out an agreement with the U.S. Department of Labor to allow a limited number of Mexican citizens to legally work on Valley trawlers.[65] Recent changes in the immigration laws and a renewed effort by the INS to arrest undocumented workers on shrimp boats in these two communities made it increasingly difficult for

Valley boat owners to hire the same numbers of Mexican workers as they had in previous years.

Before the program was initiated, announcements were placed in the Valley's major newspapers for three months which described the positions that were open. Wages were guaranteed; headers and riggers earned a minimum of $6,000 and $13,000, respectively, for six months of work. There were only ten replies to these public announcements, and only three American citizens actually showed up ready to work. One hundred and fifty Mexican men were then hired to crew Valley trawlers, a majority of whom had extensive previous experience working on Valley shrimp boats.

The Valley's shrimp industry clearly demonstrates the diversity of the impact of undocumented workers within this border economy. Unlike the majority of other Valley industries, Mexican workers have historically provided a vital labor force to the shrimping industry which is not competitive with the region's own labor force; without this labor force this industry could not survive.

Some previous studies of Mexican Americans in the Valley sought to develop personality or family characteristics which explained why poverty was so pervasive in the region.[66] The documented upward mobility of Mexican Americans and Mexicans in sectors where opportunities for advancement exist clearly demonstrates that there is no "deficiency" of character in Valley Hispanics which causes or contributes to their poverty. Valley Mexican-Americans have always worked very hard and long, whether in farm work, processing plants, cut and sew operations, or the shrimping industry. The stereotype of lazy, drunk Mexican Americans still is to be found not only in the Valley, but elsewhere in our nation. This stereotype serves to blame the victim.[67]

OIL AND GAS

Oil and gas production is also a significant part of the Valley's economy. In 1984 oil and gas production in the four counties totaled $676,447,271, ranking it among the top five

Valley industries. While the number of barrels of crude oil has remained constant since 1980, gas production has substantially increased, almost to double the value in 1984 than in 1980. The Valley is rich in oil and gas deposits and resources in the extensive bay system which have not yet been tapped. The oil bust has limited production and any need for drilling new wells. However, the Valley reaps little benefit from its rich oil and gas resources above that of wages paid to the work force of about 2,500. A minority of these workers, those with special skills, earn considerably above the average Valley income, but most earn minimum wage.

Most oil and gas is pumped to outside refineries. There are only two small oil refineries in the Valley and seven small gas plants, all of which had very modest production figures in 1984. Unfortunately, the Valley's oil and gas are resold to Valley consumers at relatively high prices.

In December of 1986 Texas consumers in Laredo paid 85 cents a gallon for unleaded gas, while in Corpus Christi they paid 80 cents, San Antonio 74 cents, and Dallas 85 cents.[68] In the Valley, however, prices were considerably higher: unleaded gas averaged 94 cents a gallon in McAllen, 92 cents in Brownsville, and 96 cents in Weslaco. Local dealers blame high gasoline prices on transportation costs while consumer advocates argue that the higher prices are an attempt to take advantage of winter tourists and their gas-guzzling recreational vehicles.

THE BANKING SYSTEM

Banks and the banking system are often overlooked but compose a crucial part of any regional economy. From 1972 to 1984 deposits in Valley banks and Savings and Loans increased on the average by more than 500 percent, while some deposits in some banks exceeded 1,000 percent![69] This phenomenal growth resulted in deposits which reached almost $6 billion by the end of 1986. These same banks, located in the poorest counties in the United States, were extremely reluctant to loan capital to Valley businesses to help stimulate the local economy.

Even the smallest communities, some of which are home to very large percentages of the poor, witnessed extraordinary growth in local bank deposits. Deposits in tiny Hidalgo, with a population of barely more than 2,000, have increased since 1972 by more than 1,000 percent to total almost $50 million in 1984. Deposits in Pharr, population 22,000, reached almost $100 million. Deposits in Brownsville and McAllen, Valley cities which are home to the largest number of poor, also grew by an incredible 1,000 percent over this same time period. New Valley banks were chartered and existing banks hired additional staff over the last decade. The labor force in the Valley's financial institutions actually increased from 5,181 in 1980 to 6,940 in 1984.[70] Over the same time period, jobs in other sectors of the Valley's economy were either holding steady or in decline.

The majority of the $6 billion deposits, according to interviews with Valley bankers, is from Mexican investors seeking to protect their savings against runaway inflation in Mexico. By the end of 1986 Mexican inflation was exceeding 100 percent, while inflation in this country was measured at less than 2 percent. These investments were originally spurred by the peso devaluations in the mid-1970s. Wealthy Mexicans find it very convenient to place their money in Valley banks that are, relatively speaking, close at hand.

Banks with such extremely large deposits might be expected to seek a return on their holdings by loaning it out to local businesses. In the banks' point of view, however, there is little impetus to invest in the Valley's poverty economy. Valley banks in the second quarter of 1985 loaned out only 61 cents for every dollar on deposit as compared to the national average of 80 cents on the dollar.[71] From 1980 to 1984, when Valley bank deposits were increasing by 150 percent, commercial and business loans increased by only 89 percent.

These figures, however, misrepresent the actual amount of loans Valley banks make to Valley businesses. If international loans, agricultural loans, commercial real estate loans, and loans to Valley corporations whose assets are valued at more than $25 million were considered, then Valley bank loans to Valley businesses would most probably be much less than the statistics suggest.[72]

Banks limit their loans to local businesses by imposing restrictive requirements to secure the loan. These include 150 percent or more collateral, high interest rates, and short repayment periods. Local bankers emphasize that new regulations of the Federal Deposit Insurance Corporation (FDIC) have severely curtailed their ability to reinvest their enormous deposits in the Valley's economy. Because of the regulations they say they are now forced to stiffen their loan requirements. Such limitations make it next to impossible for small businesses to obtain start-up loans or to expand their operations; those with 150 percent collateral would probably not require a loan in the first place.

There is no doubt that tougher regulations by the FDIC play an important part in limiting the number of loans Valley banks make to Valley businessmen. However, the majority of Valley banks, as suggested by the tremendous growth in deposits, are thriving at the very time the Valley's poverty economy is in serious decline. In contrast to the rest of Texas, only three Valley banks have folded since the oil bust, one of which was an uninsured Savings and Loan. Bank loans were also difficult to obtain prior to the FDIC's restrictions; Valley bankers have a short memory. Valley banks choose to send their capital out of the Valley. By selling money "upstream," Valley bankers were able to maximize interest rates that they receive, but to the detriment of the Valley's poverty economy.

Such lack of interest in the local economy is not unique to Valley banks, but a national trend. Valley banks, the majority of which are owned in the 1980s by large holding companies, have a limited stake in the Valley's economy; they are prospering even as the number of Valley poor increases. Only the minority of locally owned banks have consistently demonstrated interest in the region, especially those which have invested in farms, groves, and condominiums on South Padre Island.

What is unique here is the great disparity that exists between the large holdings of the Valley banks and the poverty of the local region. There is little leadership in the Valley's financial community, a role often taken by bank officers. With a few notable exceptions, Valley banks have spent more on promotional advertising than they have actively seeking viable solutions to the Valley's economy. In short, the Valley bears the brunt of bordering

Mexico, but receives no benefits from this proximity to another country.

THE PUBLIC SECTOR

One very important part of the Valley economy, often given little attention, is the governmental sector. This portion of the economy employs about 20 percent of the total Valley labor force. In 1984 those employed in federal jobs in the Valley numbered 2,507, while 5,113 worked in state jobs, and 27,417 worked in county and city jobs.[73]

Unlike many other areas of the Valley's economy, most jobs in the governmental sector pay well above the minimum wage (at least at the state and federal levels), provide for relative job security and advancement, and often offer additional benefits such as health insurance, sick leave, paid vacations, and retirement funds. Many of these jobs are filled by promotions from within the ranks so that Valley residents are given increased duties and responsibilities in return for higher wages and other direct financial benefits. Working conditions are almost always satisfactory, and the safety and health of the employee is not at risk.

The ranks of the governmental sector are disproportionately large when compared to other regions of Texas and the nation because a majority of Valley governmental workers are directly involved in agencies and programs which serve the poor. Johnson's War on Poverty had a significant impact on the Lower Rio Grande Valley of Texas in the 1960s, though not perhaps the intended one. The expansion of existing programs for the poor and the creation of new ones not only helped to ease the burden of those in need, but also provided thousands of Valley workers entry into the middle class.

Although cutbacks or hiring freezes in these poverty programs have severely affected the Valley poor, particularly during the Reagan Administration, the extreme poverty in the Valley still commands a relatively large number of federal and state poverty dollars. Federal, state, and local programs and agencies today employ significant numbers of staff in order to provide a variety of social services which include health, legal, and welfare aid, and programs targeted toward special populations such as children, the elderly, female heads of households, the disabled, the malnourished, and migrant farm workers and their families.

Since the 1960s these poverty programs have contributed to the growth of a small Mexican-American middle class in the Valley. Valley Mexican Americans with a high school or college education and political connections were not forced to seek work outside the Valley, as has historically been the case. These same government jobs, however, continue to form the basis of political patronage in the Valley.

There are also a large number of Valley workers who have indirectly benefited by programs designed for the poor. While not directly working for a government poverty agency, they nevertheless owe their job to federal and state dollars. The bilingual program in the 1970s pumped millions of dollars into Valley schools, as did programs especially geared for the children of migrant farm workers. These programs in turn hired additional teachers and support staff to carry out the directives of the program.

More recently, Texas House Bill 72 on educational reform in public schools has been an economic boon to local Valley economies. Since 1984 $212 million have reached Valley school systems, employing additional teachers and staff and requiring additional school construction. In the Brownsville Independent School District alone the annual budget increased from $62.1 million to $103.8 million since House Bill 72. Four hundred new teachers were hired in 1986, two hundred more in 1987. Local contractors in Brownsville estimate that one-half of all new construction in that city in 1986 is related to House Bill 72. A new $2.5 million elementary school and an $11.8 million high school were completed in 1988.

The food stamp program is another example of the importance of government dollars to the Valley's poverty economy. One-third of all Valley residents receive food coupons with which they can purchase necessary items in retail grocery stores. In 1986, $113 million was allocated to the Valley's poor who, in turn, purchased food items. Without this injection of federal dollars, the Valley's grocery and discount stores could not have prospered.

Federal health assistance increased substantially during the 1970s in the Valley. From 1969 to 1979 federal health dollars to the four Valley counties approached $825,000,000.[74] These funds not only benefited those who required health services, but created jobs and stimulated the economy.

The Valley's governmental sector depends in many different ways upon the continued existence of poverty in the Valley. Sudden cutbacks to federal, state, or local poverty programs undermine the Valley's economy, increasing poverty in the Valley. Ironically, any major decreases in Valley poverty would have a negative impact on the Valley economy, severely limiting employment in the governmental sector and adversely affecting the economy in many direct and indirect ways.

ALTERNATIVE ECONOMIES

Alternative economies have arisen as those seeking work struggle to provide the basic necessities for themselves and their families. While a majority of the work and markets in the Valley is legal, some is not, and some lies in the grey area between. In the Valley's poverty economy alternative jobs and markets remain a viable option to the limited opportunities in the traditional economic sectors.

One notable example is the drug and smuggling industry in Starr County. Anyone who has traveled the two-lane highway from Mission to Rio Grande City cannot help but notice the many new and large homes that line both sides of the road. Late model four-wheel drive vehicles sit in front of the large residences, satellite dishes abound. A quick trip down almost any side road uncovers any number of similar kinds of residences, some of which are still under construction. Such homes, some qualify as mansions, are particularly striking because they often stand less than a hundred yards from one or two room shacks in disrepair, outdoor privies in back.[75]

There is money in this town and there is not; there is a vital economy at work, as reflected in the homes and material possessions of the residents, and there is, too, a poverty common to the Valley. According to the statistics the poorest of the Valley counties, Starr County, has long been fueled by the smuggling of goods. As soon as the Rio Grande became an international border, there were products that one country needed that the other could provide in abundance and at a cheaper price.

A variety of goods from tobacco to firearms were smuggled across the river during the nineteenth century.[76] In this sparsely populated county there are many places where men can wade across the shallow Rio Grande waters carrying on their backs whatever is in fashion. Professional smuggling is one way out of poverty in Starr County, and today some families can trace their smuggling operations back to the 1850s. During the 1960s the product in fashion was marijuana; in the 1980s, it is cocaine. It is impossible to measure how much income is derived from drug traffic in Starr County, but its impact on the local economy is considerable.

Illegal drug trade in Cameron and Hidalgo Counties has increased significantly since 1985. According to local and federal law enforcers, drug traffickers have shifted some of their operations to these counties from other parts of the United States. Recent drug busts involving unusually large amounts of cocaine and marijuana in these two counties, as well as a rash of drug-related murders, emphasize this point.[77]

However, drug smuggling in these two counties is not yet an integral part of the culture as it is in Starr County. In Starr County drug smuggling, and the smuggling of other goods over the last one hundred years, has become a part of the economic and social system which is vital to the well-being of many of its residents. This county is by no means unique; other counties throughout the United States, including several in California, also reflect this same trend. What makes Starr County somewhat unusual is the historical dependence upon an alternative economy. The volume of smuggling throughout the rest of the Valley counties is greater than in Starr, but because of Starr's small population the impact of this illegal trade is both more obvious in this county and more integral to the economic welfare of its citizens.

People as well as drugs are also daily smuggled from Mexico into the Valley. Thousands of illegal aliens are transported across the Rio Grande into the Valley every year; the number has increased as Mexico's economy declined. Drugs are much more lucrative, but "coyotes" who smuggle undocumented workers into this region do quite well. Electronic goods, firearms, and stolen vehicles also pass across the river illegally into Mexico. Although there is the risk of getting caught and being incarcerated, the payoffs for this illegal work are attractive, especially if one has only limited hopes or opportunities for finding decent work.

The poverty economy encourages many, especially the poor, to trade goods and services among themselves. Many low-income residents construct their own homes. If one is good at a particular skill, mixing concrete for instance, then he will exchange labor with others who might have experience in framing or roofing. Goods and services are bartered, from home-grown garden products and small livestock to a brake job, circumventing the high costs of the mainstream Valley economy.

Flea markets are extremely popular. The small stalls, booths, and tables serve as markets for goods which low-income people cannot purchase through the conventional economy. In addition to produce, second-hand items from appliances to clothing are offered for sale at cut-rate prices.

Valley poor, in particular those who live near the Rio Grande, often shop in Mexican towns for goods and services which they cannot otherwise afford. Food staples are purchased, often at considerable savings, along with other necessities such as prescription drugs and medical services. While the Valley's affluent frequent the restaurants, bars, and boutiques which cater to their wealth on the south side of the river, the Valley's poor roam the *mercados* and large department stores in search of good buys.

AN INTERNAL ECONOMIC COLONY

The rich Valley farmlands continue to be among the most productive in the nation. The irrigated fields produce a variety of citrus, vegetables, and grains twelve months out of the year. Large herds of cattle graze the northernmost areas of the four counties. Shrimp and diverse species of fish abound in the Gulf waters. Oil and gas lie just beneath the surface of the wetlands and the bays; there are oil fields that have been mapped but remain untapped. The vaults of Valley banks are stuffed with the dollars of Mexican investors. The population of the Valley is rapidly increasing, while along the Mexican side of the Rio Grande the population is booming because of migration. The labor force, perhaps the Valley's richest resource, is hard working, patient, and determined.

The Lower Rio Grande of Texas is very rich in resources even as its people are among the poorest in the United States. In part this is because the regional economy is premised upon poverty. It is poverty which shapes and drives the Valley's economy. Agriculture, manufacturing, tourism, each new industrial sector has been grafted on the existing economic arrangements between rich and poor and helped to strengthen those superior-subordinate relationships. The twin plants that come to the Valley in the 1980s do so to take advantage of a labor force that will work for minimum wage. Tourists come for the cheap prices created by cheap labor. With the exception of shrimping, few industries have developed which provide the opportunity for upward mobility to the poor. The government sector has thrived on federal, state, and local poverty programs, but is entrenched in patronage politics.

In many ways the Valley resembles an internal economic colony.[78] The majority of the Valley's resources are exported out of the Valley to the interior of this country. The poor of the Valley are left with high prices for the products that they themselves produce, low wages, high unemployment, and the myriad consequences of poverty for which they themselves are often blamed. The Valley is not poor because of its lack of resources, it is poor because of the ways these resources are controlled and distributed.

5. "LIKE ALWAYS, EDDIE, LIKE ALWAYS": POLITICS, JOBS, AND LIVES

> People would always be waiting for jobs to open up and some kind of assistance. So the government gave some assistance to the people, by giving them food by a man named Eddie who was in charge of this program. I was the kind of person who never liked to get assistance from the government. I always looked for ways to work and even with Eddie being my neighbor, not once did I ask him for assistance. Till one day his heart spoke up and asked me how we were going to pass Christmas. My reply was, "Like always, Eddie, like always!" He then gave me a voucher for some food, but never again did I get assistance.[1]

Nothing is of greater importance in the Valley than having a regular job. In a region where unemployment has been the highest in the nation for many years, jobs in and of themselves become invaluable commodities over which individuals struggle in behalf of family members and friends. Government positions in the Valley comprise 20 percent of the labor force; budget times at public agencies become annual wars as positions are eliminated, created, or maintained. Victors celebrate and the losers do not forget.

Favors in a poverty economy also become matters of crucial importance. Favors ease the financial burden of those who work full time, but still are in or close to poverty, as well as of those who are unemployed. Favors, regardless of size, are always returned. The control of jobs and favors and, through them, the control of people is a vital component of all local political machines.

There has never been representative government in the Valley.[2] From the time this region became part of the United States, the political system has only reflected the veneer of democracy. Politics in the Valley has been a private realm in which those in power divide what spoils there are, while those in poverty clamor outside the gates. Ruling elites manipulate the system to their own benefit, perpetuating control through electoral politics,[3] the overt force of the police, Department of Public Safety, and the Texas Rangers,[4] and occasionally the judicial system. In a land where people still remember when their lives were not safe from bandits, Texas Rangers, and other warring factions, the threats of the powerful are still meaningful.

South Texas political bossism is no longer as evident as it once was. In Cameron and Hidalgo Counties, the political machines are no longer an Anglo phenomena; Mexican Americans have been elected to office in ever-increasing numbers.[5] Yet the impact of the existing political structure on the poor in the 1980s should not be underemphasized. The poor are intimidated, threatened, blamed for their own poverty. The majority remain passive in a system that would quickly punish them for acting in their own interests. A few, the exceptional, somehow manage to succeed against all odds.[6]

ELECTIONS

The poor are actively discouraged from voting. In the 1980s, as in past decades, only a small number of the eligible voters are registered and vote regularly. Turnouts in local elections commonly range from 15 to 20 percent or less of the electorate.[7] School boards, water districts, city and county commissioners are all elected by a very small minority of the total possible voters. Of those who do vote, a disproportionate number are of the middle and upper class. In some Valley towns neighborhood "politiqueras" are paid by local politicians in proportion to the number of votes they can deliver; this tradition of "voting" poor Mexican Americans dates back to the 1850s in cities like Brownsville. These women tell their neighbors which candidates to vote for, then provide transportation to and from the polls.

The poor are regularly misled by campaign promises, charges against the opposing candidate, and a variety of other political ploys that mask real political interests. Campaigns are a series of verbal attacks upon the opposition, calling into question the credibility, dignity, and honor of all those who are disloyal enough to support another candidate. Even if the poor in the various Valley cities were able to distinguish between candidates through the political advertising fog, there have been few candidates who in fact represent or even understand their needs. In the 1970s and 1980s, there have been many Mexican-American candidates who have run and won positions in the name of the poor, then gone on to represent their own or upper-class interests.

Attitudes of fatalism among many of the Valley poor are largely justified. From their own real experiences in the past, there is little hope of change. They know their politicians usually lie; they accept the temporary favors of beer and fajitas at *pachangas*. They shake the hand of the newest political candidate because most know that the beer, the fajitas, and the handshake are about all they are going to get if the candidate is elected.

The poor are also rightfully scared of losing what little they have. If they vote for a candidate who is not elected, if they actively campaign for the man or woman of their choice who does not win, then the long arm of the machine can take away their job, their privileges gleaned from favors, and their standing in the community. The election or reelection of city commissioners usually corresponds with firings or demotions of men and women in city agencies and private businesses. Pressure is placed upon public school principals to fire certain teachers and hire others, just as it is in the offices of the police, firemen, city manager, and other city departments. The same is true for businesses which derive any part of their revenue from city or county budgets.

The poor, in the end, have more to lose by voting than they do by not voting. If they vote and their candidate loses, they may suffer recrimination; if they vote and their candidate wins, all they have gained is an official who may dispense small favors to them. It is not surprising, given these conditions, that so few regularly cast their ballot.

JOBS

In the spring of 1972, two workers for a county health agency were called to a colonia north of Harlingen to inspect the

sewage and drainage facilities. Noting that the roads were un-
paved, one of the workers suggested that the colonia residents as
a group complain to the appropriate county agencies. The worker
told the residents that if they went as individuals to complain,
they would be ignored; but if they went as a group of ten or
twelve, then the county government could not ignore them.

The two workers returned three hours later to their agency,
were called into the supervisor's office, and fired. The supervisor
told them that they were being fired for "political propagandizing."
When the workers protested that such was not the case, the
supervisor told them that he knew that they had meant no harm,
but if he did not fire them then he would be fired. The workers
accepted their fate, knowing that if they complained further, they
would get into more trouble.

Almost all city, county, and some state and federal agencies in the Valley are a part of local systems of political spoils.
While job descriptions normally restrict the hiring of applicants
who do not qualify, these are waived by agency employers. Unqualified and/or incompetent workers are routinely hired; they
then maintain and often run agencies and programs to the immediate loss of those served. Public monies are mismanaged, not
necessarily with the intent to defraud, although the Valley has
had more than its share of corruption, but from incompetence
or a lack of proper supervision. Not only are the roads, sewers,
schools, health care systems, and parks in bad condition because
of the misapplication of public funds, the ways in which the
existing funds are used often do little to ameliorate the situation.
There is limited public debate; the rhetoric of elected officials and
confusing media coverage cloud the issues. Public issues become
muddled in the mire of personalities, and the serious questions
about the ability of a particular level of government to provide
services are never asked.

The system of political spoils extends to the private sector
as well. The poor are often manipulated and controlled whether
they work for a public agency or for private business. Again the
threat of loss of job and/or favors is paramount. Middle-class
professionals who are self-employed and small businessmen are
more secure in their jobs. However, the ability to profit from a

liquor store, gift shop, or gas station in a particular Valley community is often dependent upon not displeasing those in power.

MASS MEDIA

There is a real absence of information by which the public could make decisions that would affect political policy.[8] The electronic and print media do not provide the information necessary to reform the political systems in Valley towns and cities. There are three commercial television broadcasters: KGBT in Harlingen, KRGV in Weslaco, and KVEO in Brownsville, a recent addition. The local news that is broadcast is remarkably one-sided; little if any mention is made of chronic problems or attempts by those outside machine politics to solve them. Personal-interest stories highlight the impoverishment of a particular family during the Christmas season in order to raise funds for the family or a charitable organization, but there is no broader analysis of the Valley's political, economic, or social problems. KVEO's news team was disbanded in 1986, management citing poor ratings. The series "Taxi" and "Wheel of Fortune" replaced the six and ten o'clock news on this station.

The Diocese of Brownsville purchased the Valley's short-lived Public Broadcasting television station when it went bankrupt. The potential of Channel 60 (KMBH) is great—conceivably it could begin to provide the Valley with a wide range of educational and informational services, as well as entertainment, not currently available. In particular, alternative sources of national and local news would be of considerable value.

However, television stations are very expensive. KMBH's current budget, approaching one million dollars per year, must depend heavily upon monies from the Diocese as well as local support from the public. It remains to be seen whether or not the station can support itself and the extent to which it will be able to fill the void created by the censorship in the Valley's commercial media.

Since the early 1980s the quality of the news reported in the three Valley newspapers has risen substantially. All three papers now hire reporters who do investigative reporting.[9] However, since the papers pay so little, few competent reporters stay more than a year before they are hired away by other state newspapers. Another real problem is that newspaper circulation is extremely low.[10] The *Brownsville Herald*, the only daily newspaper in Brownsville, has a circulation in both its English and Spanish editions of approximately 9,000 in a community of 100,000. Other Valley cities face a similar problem; total Valley newspaper circulation is only about 75,000. Reading a newspaper requires an eighth grade reading level. It also requires an interest in and a habit of reading. In Brownsville about a quarter of the population has less than an elementary education, and many of those who have graduated from junior high school do not have the necessary reading skills. Newspaper reading is not a part of the socialization process of a majority of Valley citizens.

Information about the events in Matamoros and Reynosa is almost totally absent, although these cities now count a total population exceeding half a million. Only recently has one Valley paper begun to cover some of the major events in Matamoros with regularity.

The Valley public is not regularly informed about even the most important local news. For example, several years ago when tapes of brutality by the night shift of the McAllen police force were shown on all the national news programs, the presentation by Valley stations was extremely cautious and restrained. There is no question that if the tapes had not been shown first on national television, they would never have been shown in the Valley by local broadcasters. There is, in effect, active censorship; broadcasters are very selective in what they choose to air and the particular slant they give to a story.

The control of information in the Valley is part of the political control. On numerous occasions I have discovered information about events in the Valley only from reading the *Corpus Christi Caller*, the *Texas Observer*, *Texas Monthly*, or academic journals. It is next to impossible to find out how state congressmen and senators voted during legislative sessions or to follow their voting records in any coherent fashion. In the absence of reliable information, there is an abundance of half-truths and half-lies.

News coverage in the Valley is controlled by a combination of watchful advertisers, who pressure broadcasters to avoid "controversial" news, and the extreme political conservatism of the newspapers themselves. None of the television stations is owned by corporations located in the Valley or that have an active interest in the Valley. The three major newspapers are part of a national chain, Freedom Newspapers, widely known for its conservative editorials and positions on domestic and foreign affairs. Editorials are rarely written by local publishers or editors but emanate instead from the national corporate office.

CONTROL OF OUTSIDE FUNDING

A large amount of money from outside the Valley has been targeted in recent years for specific Valley problems. Education and health dollars from federal and state sources have been substantial. The existing political structure, however, serves as an important gatekeeper in the distribution of these monies. A majority of these monies serve to fatten the influence of those charged with their supervision, and sizable portions of these public monies have been misapplied.

In 1981 I read with interest a Request for Proposal (RFP) in the local newspaper. The RFP concerned monies made available from a federal agency to study local problems in the shrimping industry and to develop solutions. At the time, I had just completed such a study for the Department of Commerce through the Sea Grant Program at Texas A&M University.

I visited with the elected official who was to award the contract to the bidder who both provided the lowest bid and demonstrated the most professional competence. Explaining that the study had just been done, I suggested that the contract be withdrawn from bidding. The official saw no reason for a withdrawal. I then contacted the federal agency involved and expressed my reservations. The spokesman of that agency was very reluctant to hear my complaints, so I sent several letters to him and his agency questioning the proper use of their monies in the Valley.

Hearing from colleagues that the local official was planning to award the contract to a friend of his, I decided to bid on the contract myself to demonstrate to the federal agency that the contract was not awarded fairly. Consulting firms in Dallas and Houston also expressed concern about the sincerity of the local RFP which they had seen advertised. We decided it was in our own best interests to document closely the actions of the local official.

On the appointed date the official awarded the contract to his friend's consulting firm. This firm had no experience in the shrimping industry and no experience in compiling social science surveys. Their bid was $99,000. Of the seven other bids submitted, mine was the lowest at $38,000, the average around $60,000. Our calls and letters to the federal agency funding the project were not well received. We were given the message that the agency would rather not get tangled in the political problems of a local government, regardless of the merit of our concerns. However, after some weeks, we were told that the matter had been turned over to the Department of Justice.

Three months later the award for the contract was withdrawn by the federal government, which cited irregularities in the procedures to select a contractor. No criminal charges were brought. The local official held a press conference, duly reported in the local media, in which he portrayed the federal government's decision as another in a long line which demonstrated its insensitivity to the needs of the Valley poor.

There is no reason to believe that this incident was in the least exceptional. The federal agency's response was typical, the agency had enough problems without getting embroiled in local politics. Typically, the grant money would have gone to friends of the official, who would have lined their own pockets and have done substandard work. The local firm was too incompetent to have performed the task, but it would have wielded influence in the community by hiring personnel and purchasing equipment and supplies. Not only would the money have been wasted, but it would have lent support to the existing system of political spoils.

Much of the monies that come from outside the Valley must be filtered through a political screen composed of elected officials and the men and women they have hired to work in local agencies and programs. In the end, the monies and the work of outside agencies are far less effective than they might be.

ATTEMPTS TO REFORM

It is tempting to question why more Mexican-American leaders have not emerged from the poor or the middle class, or even the rich, who would, through their own personal experiences with the Valley's political system, then serve to catalyze the formation of a strong opposition. Such a concern neglects the imposing nature of the Valley political system. Historically, individuals have had little legal recourse, although this situation is changing in the present decade. What can one do against a system that can swiftly and crudely make life miserable for not only the individual, but for those who are closest to him?

When Jorge, a staff member of a high school, was asked to chair a task force on the drop-out rate in a Valley school district, he did so gladly because he was concerned about the problem. He interviewed teachers, collected available statistics, organized meetings of reluctant administrators and counselors, and studied solutions with committee members. Upon presenting a final report which criticized various aspects of how drop-outs were handled by the school district, he was systematically ignored by his superiors. Growing frustrated, Jorge talked to a newspaper reporter who eventually wrote a story about the results of the task force. Jorge was not rehired even though his previous evaluations had been extremely good. Word was also passed around to other employers in the community that Jorge was a "trouble-maker."

An individual defined as a "deviant" by the political structure often pays a heavy psychological price.[11] He thinks that if the resistance he is confronting is so strong, then he must be at least partially wrong. He questions his own sense of values, his ability to make a valid judgment of the issue at hand. He backs away from the conflict, rethinks the situation. Sometimes such an individual becomes self-destructive, sometimes he leaves the Valley, or sometimes he is simply coopted, eventually becoming a cynical advocate for the system which he had formerly criticized.[12]

Organizations are more difficult to isolate, discredit, and coopt.[13] The same methods are employed as with individuals, but the legal system is more likely to be called into play. What is unique about the Valley is that so few political organizations or groups matured—a sign of the overwhelming strength of the political structure. Over the years, groups which demonstrated any signs of oppositional behavior were quickly broken through discreditation, overt violence, and/or the legal system. One major exception is the farm workers' unions, yet even these organizations, whose successes can be measured in very real terms, have weathered the struggle against the Valley elite only by their ability to accommodate and develop in relatively unique ways.

When Eugene Nelson organized a strike at La Casita Farms just outside Rio Grande City in 1966, the real impact of his efforts was minimal. The strike was little more than a small protest at the gates of the largest agribusiness interests in Starr County.[14] Only a handful of farm workers joined the California activist who had worked under César Chávez. Reaction against the strike on the part of the growers was predictable. Much as they had done in reaction to the attempts at unionization in the 1930s, the growers relied on the use of law enforcement and the legal system as well as strike-breakers from the Valley and from Mexico.

However, thousands of supporters greeted a march by fifty-some farm workers from Rio Grande City to Austin on July 4, 1966, to protest wages and working conditions. Some observers thought the marchers became the most important symbol of Valley farm workers' resistance. Many Hispanics now feel that the sight of poor farm workers marching to the steps of the Texas State Legislature had a lasting influence on a generation of Mexican Americans who became involved in Texas politics for the first time. John Connally, then Governor of Texas, tried in vain to blunt the impact of the march by meeting with farm workers in New Braunfels, a small community outside San Antonio. He may have had some inkling of how the state and national media would react to the sight of poor Mexican Americans asking for decent wages, but he could not have known at the time how important the march was to become as a symbol for not just farm workers from the Valley, but for all Texas Hispanics.

The Texas Council of Churches and the Catholic Church in the Valley, reflecting the mood of the Civil Rights Movement sweeping the nation, gave support and tacit approval to several organizers of Chávez's United Farm Workers who followed in the footsteps of Eugene Nelson.[15] A small number of Valley farm workers went on strike the following summer. Growers reacted as they always had, but one incident in particular reflected real political differences between the 1930s and the 1960s. Two farm workers were badly beaten by Texas Rangers on June 1, 1967. In the landmark case of *Medrano* v. *Allee* that went all the way to the Supreme Court, a number of state labor laws were repealed and the Texas Rangers were enjoined from participation in any future labor disputes. In the 1960s, for the first time, the farm workers used the legal system, however tedious, to retaliate against the farmers and growers and to protect their own legal rights.

The particular facts of this case justify examination in some detail. What is at once evident is not only the cruelty of the Texas Rangers against local farm laborers, but the concerted attempts of the Rangers, County Sheriff, and other law enforcement officers to break the strike.

Citing from the uncontested facts of the case as they appeared before the Supreme Court:

> Later that month, when the president of the local union and others were in the courthouse under arrest, they shouted "viva la huelga" in support of the strike. A deputy sheriff struck the union official and held a gun at his forehead, ordering him not to repeat those words in the courthouse because it was a "respectful place." As the strike continued through the year and the Texas Rangers were called into the local area, there were more serious incidents of violence. In May 1967, some union pickets gathered in Mission, Texas, to protest the carrying of produce from the Valley on the Missouri-Pacific Railroad. They were initially charged with trespass on private property; this was changed to unlawful assembly, and finally was superseded by complaints of secondary picketing. The Reverend Edgar Krueger and Magdaleno Dimas were taken into custody by the Rangers. As

a train passed, the Rangers held these two prisoners' bodies so that their faces were only inches from the train. A few weeks later the Rangers sought to arrest Dimas for allegedly brandishing a gun in a threatening manner, and found him by "tailing" Chandler and Moreno, also union members. Chandler was arrested with no explanation as was Moreno, who was also assaulted by Captain Allee at the time. These two men were later charged with assisting Dimas to evade arrest, although by Allee's own testimony they were never told Dimas was sought by the Rangers. Indeed, because the officers had no arrest warrant or formal complaint against Dimas, they could not then arrest him, so they put in a call to a justice of the peace who arrived on the scene and filled out a warrant on forms he carried with him. The Rangers then broke into a house and arrested Dimas and Rodriguez, another union member, in a violent and brutal fashion. Dimas was hospitalized four days with a brain concussion, and x-rays revealed that he had been struck so hard on the back that his spine was curved out of shape. Rodriguez had cuts and bruises on his ear, elbow, upper arm, back, and jaw; one of his fingers was broken and the nail torn off. . . . During this entire period the Starr County Sheriff's office regularly distributed an aggressive anti-union newspaper. A deputy, driving an official car, would pick up the papers each week and bring them back to the Sheriff's office; they would then be distributed by various deputies. The District Court included copies of the paper in an appendix to its opinion; a typical headline was "Only Mexican Subversive Group Could Sympathize with Valley Farm Workers." The views of the Texas Rangers were similarly explicit. On a number of occasions they offered farm jobs to the union leaders, at the union demand wage, in return for an end to the strike. The Rangers told one union member that they had been called into the area to break the strike and would not leave until they had done so.[16]

Spirits among some farm workers and organizers in the Valley were buoyed in 1968 when Antonio Orendain began serious attempts to organize a union. There was hope then that Orendain could quickly form a union on the strength of his political skills and the financial and moral support of the United Farm Workers Union in California.

A number of other local grass-roots organizations had been or were being formed at this same time. Colonias del Valle developed out of the efforts of the Texas Council of Churches and the Catholic Church; its stated objectives were to improve living conditions in the Valley's colonias. At the time, the majority of colonias lacked any dependable source of safe water, many colonia residents hauling their drinking water from the irrigation ditches and storing it in oil drums. The existing water districts refused to supply water lines to the colonias, citing the expense as prohibitive. Colonias del Valle was instrumental in forming the Military Highway Water District, the first not-for-profit water corporation in the Valley specifically created to meet the needs of the poor.

About this same time students at Pan American University in Edinburg and in some Hidalgo County high schools organized a chapter of the Mexican-American Youth Organization (MAYO). MAYO was concerned with a number of local issues, including civil rights. A chapter of the Political Association of Spanish-Speaking Organizations (PASO) was also started at this time. PASO was composed of predominantly middle-class Mexican Americans dissatisfied with the political status quo. A chapter of the Brown Berets also appeared.[17] This group portrayed itself as the vanguard of the new order, offered its services as a security force, but in general enjoyed little credibility among other political organizations. In California, the Brown Berets grew in number, while in the Valley they were looked upon by most Mexican Americans as extremists.

In the early 1970s, as the effort continued to organize Valley farm workers, La Raza Unida Party ran slates of candidates. The political backlash to the Pharr riots in 1971 lent support to their efforts. In San Juan, Mexican Americans ran for and gained control of the City Council and the Mayor's office; their model was Crystal City.

In 1972 La Raza Unida garnered considerable support in the Valley. In Hidalgo County, where it was strongest, the party received 29 percent of the vote cast. In Starr, voters gave it 18 percent of the total vote and in Cameron, 15 percent. Two years later, in 1974, the party received a smaller share of the total vote but in Hidalgo County, for instance, it still mustered 23 percent of all voters.[18]

At the same time, the UFW helped sponsor "Ya Mero," a Spanish-language newspaper which ran editorials on local elections and printed stories that were of interest to Mexican Americans. The paper attempted to lend journalistic support and credibility to the new Mexican-American political groups.

Attempts at unionizing Valley farm workers, however, met with one failure followed by another. Farm workers remained fearful, intimidated by the growers; sixty years of history could not be erased by the promises of a few California organizers. Growers were very successful in their use of Valley and Mexican scabs to break strikes. Also, Orendain was not another César Chávez. Arguments soon surfaced between Orendain's organization and the UFW in California. In 1975, Orendain split from the UFW to form the Texas Farm Workers (TFW) union. A few years later, disagreements within the TFW led to yet another split and the formation of the International Union of Agricultural and Industrial Workers (IUAIW).

None of the three farm workers' unions has signed a single contract in the last twenty years with a Valley grower. Yet the accomplishments of the unions, chief among them the UFW, have been considerable. Through their efforts, along with several other sympathetic organizations such as the ACLU, farm workers could receive workers' compensation in 1984, a legal right granted to other American workers in 1922. Farm workers today also can receive unemployment insurance, a right that the majority of American workers have enjoyed since 1935. As a result of the farm workers' unions' lobbying efforts, the short-handled hoe has been outlawed by the Texas State Legislature, working and safety conditions have been improved in the fields, and some of the most abusive of the labor practices utilized by labor contractors and growers have become less common. Living conditions of farm workers and other working poor in the colonias have been bettered because of efforts similar to those of the Military Highway Water District. Even most critics of the labor union movement in the Valley would agree that the unions have brought about considerable improvements.

On the other hand, farm workers in the Valley are still faced with major problems. The number of agricultural jobs has remained static over the last decade at the same time that the Valley population of farm workers increased. A deteriorating economy in Mexico has meant there are much greater numbers of undocumented workers crossing the river looking for agricultural work. At the national level farm labor jobs continue to decline, in large part because of automation.

The Big Freeze in 1983 was a tragedy for farm workers, who were put out of work by the thousands. The citrus industry is not expected to recover full-scale production until the 1990s, and then fewer farm workers will be needed because the new groves will be more labor-efficient. The Big Freeze dealt an additional blow to the UFW in the Valley. A major consumer boycott had been planned to put pressure on citrus growers to raise wages. The boycott has been indefinitely postponed.

Farm workers still do not receive a living wage for the work they do. They currently are guaranteed only the state's minimum wage of $1.35 per hour, although there is a lobbying effort to raise their wage to federal minimum standards. Farm workers are still fighting against the Bracero Program, now referred to as the Guest Worker Program. If farm workers from Mexico are allowed temporarily into this country, then American farm workers know that their own wages will remain substandard. The right to collective bargaining is still not legally theirs; it appears that it will be a long time, if ever, before the Texas Legislature grants such a right.

The UFW has survived and continues to put political pressure on local and state politicians to meet the needs of farm workers. The majority of other Hispanic organizations begun in the 1970s has not fared so well. The Brown Berets have long since disappeared in the Valley; MAYO has been dissolved; PASO is no more. Colonias del Valle, along with several other grassroots groups, has gone through a variety of changes and, in its present form, has arguably become a part of the traditional political system.

Several of the young Chicano leaders and members of the antiestablishment organizations in the 1970s have become respected members of their communities and hold elected and appointed positions at the city, county, and state levels. They are in part responsible for some of the positive changes that have occurred in the Valley in the last decade. In particular, the Valley's judicial system is no longer plagued by racist attitudes toward poor Mexican Americans. Most city councils now have Mexican Americans on them; in not a few cities they hold a majority vote. Similarly, a younger generation of Mexican Americans now holds sway on local school boards. At the county level, there is proportional representation by race.

The majority of activity against the status quo in the Valley in the 1970s took place in Hidalgo County where La Raza Unida won almost one-third of the vote. To some degree, the greatest signs of reform have also taken place there as well. In Cameron County there was much less political unrest as reflected in the formation of Mexican-American political groups. The civil rights movement and the political dissatisfaction with the existing system had less impact on Starr and passed by Willacy County.

The successes of Valley farm workers in the last two decades would not have been possible without Texas Rural Legal Aid (TRLA). The Association of Texas Trial Lawyers sent a lawyer from Austin in 1970 to set up legal services for the poor. He was not well received by the legal community in Hidalgo County and was investigated by several lawyers sent from the county bar. But in a matter of six months, TRLA was actively pursuing almost a thousand cases. TRLA spend several years knocking down strict voter registration laws which discouraged the poor from voting. Although the poll tax was outlawed in 1964, registration laws required all voters to re-register annually and made it difficult to register new voters, particularly the poor.

An organization with limited funds and staff, TRLA was swamped by the immediate needs of the large number of poor—needs ranging from divorces to wage claims. TRLA began focusing on the problems of farm workers in 1975, and increasingly became involved in defending the rights of farm workers against the long-time abuses of growers and labor contractors, some of whom were Mexican American. Offices were set up across Texas to serve migratory farm workers. While TRLA lost its share of cases, it managed to change the essential relationship between growers and those they employed. Those growers who exploited farm workers through unfair wages, poor working conditions, or harsh treatment for the first time became legally liable for their excesses. The courts repeatedly ruled in favor of farm workers when their civil rights were abused, as in *Medrano v. Allee*.

Two related cases reflect the progress that has been made in legal rights for the poor. In 1976, an Hidalgo County farmer named Miller shot and wounded several striking Mexican-American farm workers who stepped on his melons. The case received national headlines, but was virtually ignored by Valley media. An Hidalgo County jury composed of an Anglo majority found Miller innocent of any wrong-doing.

Ten years later, Miller's son was tried on four separate indictments for aggravated assault for shooting at Mexican undocumented workers trespassing on his father's farm. One of the Mexicans, José Reyes Santillan, drowned while attempting to escape the shots. A jury in the courtroom of Judge Arturo E. Guerra, Jr., found Chesley Labron Miller guilty and the judge sentenced him to four years in prison.

Not only were both Millers indicted for their respective charges, something that would not have happened prior to the 1970s, but the later trial of Miller's son was overseen by a Mexican-American judge. A number of Mexican Americans were on the jury and a Mexican-American attorney represented the legal interests of Mr. Miller.

However, as recently as 1983, mass charges of police brutality against poor Mexican Americans have been recorded. Of particular note is the McAllen Police Department's C Shift, the night shift, which for a period of about a year systematically terrorized area poor people. The McAllen Police Department recorded suspects on an overhead camera as they were booked at the city jail in order to prevent charges of police brutality. However, a series of these video tapes, which aired on all three national network news programs, showed Anglo and Mexican-American policemen ruthlessly attacking and beating handcuffed prisoners without cause. A series of criminal and civil proceedings against those involved were initiated. Several policemen have been convicted in criminal and civil suits.

TRLA helped secure changes in the selection of grand juries and trial juries. Formerly, Mexican Americans were routinely eliminated because of education and language requirements. An increasing number of Mexican Americans graduating from Texas law schools has meant a growing number of Mexican-American lawyers who are more sympathetic to the needs of the Valley poor. A review of the membership of the Cameron and Hidalgo County Bar Associations reveals that Mexican-American lawyers were virtually nonexistent prior to the 1970s. There are notable exceptions; for instance, Reynaldo G. Garza, Sr., the first Hispanic to be appointed to a federal judicial district. But in a region in which 80 percent of the population is Mexican American, more than 80 percent of all Valley lawyers were Anglos before 1970.

There is still a considerable discrepancy between those lawyers, regardless of ethnicity, who will represent the poor in court and those who will represent the rich. Lawyers, regardless of race, take cases which can generate the most income. When the poor get divorced, want to sue each other, have wage claims, or are taken advantage of by merchants, the private attorney can expect little in return for his services.

In the 1980s TRLA finds itself, like other Valley social service agencies, understaffed and overworked. The Reagan administration has cut back funding and would like to see TRLA and other state legal services for the poor put out of action. While TRLA has grown substantially in the Valley—it now has a multimillion dollar annual budget—its future is far from certain. There still remains a tremendous need for legal services for the poor as evidenced by the demands on TRLA's present staff. For every 15,000 people in the Valley, there is but one TRLA lawyer.

More than a handful of former TRLA lawyers have left to set up their own practices in the Valley. This modest influx of TRLA lawyers into the Valley's legal community has helped to change the attitude of many lawyers toward low-income clients. It has also provided TRLA with a credibility that it did not at first receive among local lawyers.

VALLEY INTERFAITH

By far one of the most important changes in the political arena has been the creation of Valley Interfaith, a grass-roots organization of low- and middle-income residents. Valley Interfaith is the result of the organizing efforts of Ernesto Cortez, who is associated with the late Saul Alinsky's Industrial Areas Foundation (IAF).[19] There are seven other chapters in Texas, each organized in a similar fashion.

The Diocese of Brownsville, under the direction of Bishop John Fitzpatrick, requested that the IAF send community organizers to the Valley in the early 1980s. Valley Interfaith, the end result of that effort by professional community organizers, is a set of Valley community groups centered around Catholic parishes. There are a few non-Catholic churches which belong, but they are the exception rather than the rule. The strength of the organization is derived from the common thread of religion, the underlying leadership of the Bishop, although he maintain a low profile, and an attempt to develop leaders from within.

Members of Valley Interfaith, which claims a membership of 5,000, have in common a set of religious beliefs which motivate and legitimate their actions against the political system in place. The traditional methods of intimidation by social isolation, threats, and peer pressure all have far less impact upon a large group than upon an individual. Valley Interfaith is financed both by individual parishes and the Diocese; thus it can offer a permanent umbrella to its members. It is less easily intimidated by the threat of lawsuits or actual lawsuits brought against it because of its financial resources and membership which can furnish legal talent when necessary.

This organization is attempting to develop its own leadership. It sends its best and brightest off to national IAF seminars and workshops which teach political strategies for confronting the existing political system. Leaders then return to put into practice what they have learned.

Not surprisingly, the opposition to Valley Interfaith has been very loud and strong. The most serious charge against Valley Interfaith, repeated in the media, has been that the organization is nothing but a front for communists and radicals; in short, that the Bishop has allowed his parishes to be taken over by Ernie Cortez and his henchmen, all outsiders.

Attempts to discredit Valley Interfaith have largely failed for the reasons mentioned above. The group has an intimidating membership, credibility, financial stability, and is developing a leadership. Its biggest problem is a lack of any long-term political agenda. Some of its new leaders have already been coopted into the existing system; they have taken their new leadership skills and sought individual recognition. But a more important impediment is that Valley Interfaith has failed to develop a comprehensive plan which would strike at the heart of local problems.

Still, Valley Interfaith has accomplished in a very short time what neither the farm workers nor any other Valley group has yet been able to achieve—a viable opposition political movement. The parishes, albeit at very different levels of participation dependent on the support of their priests, have become politicized. While farm workers were never able to garner wide support in the Valley, Valley Interfaith has been able to organize around religion to the point that the poor and some middle-income residents have taken up the reformist banner in the name of biblical teachings.

Valley Interfaith's biggest success to date was in lobbying Governor Mark White's administration for special funding for Valley problems, including the development of the colonias, indigent health care, and financial support to those put out of work because of the "Big Freeze." The group has also been effective in using its clout to persuade the Environmental Protection Agency to reconsider its decision to permit burning of toxic wastes in the Gulf of Mexico off of Brownsville.[20]

Community issues of concern to the poor have not yet been directly addressed, although they are being closely studied by different Valley Interfaith task forces. The ability of Valley Interfaith to win not only political battles at state and federal levels, but at community and neighborhood levels will be the key to the long-term viability of the organization.

If organizations like Valley Interfaith are to succeed they must also politically re-educate their people—a very difficult task. The poor in the Valley have been forced to accept their situation.

If they are easily intimidated, it is because they have suffered punishment so many times before. If the poor are easily silenced, it is because the threats against them have been very real and their legal recourse minimal. If the poor are politically apathetic, it is because apathy is one realistic way to accommodate to a political system in which a very few have all the power.

Valley Interfaith is attempting to resocialize its members by calling upon shared religious values and teachings. Such values dictate a different response than the one used to sustain the status quo. Even attempts to persuade by calling upon a higher motivation than earthly concerns is doomed to failure, however, if immediate results are not produced. The poor must soon see what their membership in Valley Interfaith has brought them.

The Valley's Mexican-American middle class is not without representation in Valley Interfaith. To a degree the participation of the middle class demonstrates an even larger leap of faith than that of the poor. Those who are middle income have much more to lose. It is surprising, then, to note how well represented are the middle class in Valley Interfaith. Teachers, doctors, social workers, and some attorneys have been very visible in the organization and have assumed positions of leadership.

BOSSISM AND RACISM IN THE 1980S

Since the 1970s a number of Mexican Americans have sought elected office in Valley cities and towns and won, replacing Anglos who served as mayors, on the city council, and school board. The power base of Valley communities has broadened to some degree in order to take in these Mexican Americans from the new middle class. Today many Mexican Americans are elected to positions of local power and, to the best of their ability, consistently represent the interests of the ruling community elites.[21] In political rhetoric only do they demonstrate a concern for the poor. This is of course not new to the Valley: the political machine in Starr County has long been run by a handful of wealthy Mexican-American families, and their attitudes toward the poor differ little in substance from those of affluent Anglos in Cameron and Hidalgo Counties.

Bossism in the Valley in the 1980s is not dead, it just has become more bi-racial. Contemporary Mexican-American politicians in the Valley (excluding several notable exceptions who have strongly and consistently advocated for the poor) protect the same class interests as did their Anglo predecessors. They may certainly be more sensitive to the cultural needs of their constituents, but it is difficult to discern how in fact material needs are better met than before. This point is not made to diffuse the importance of Mexican Americans gaining positions of leadership in the Valley, only to emphasize that the interests of class generally transcend racial affiliation.

Racism in the Valley has not disappeared. In the past it served as a convenient ideology by which the economic and social structures were given legitimacy. Now it is more likely to be employed as a strategic political tool. However, since in a number of communities in the mid-Valley 90 percent or more of the residents are Mexican American, race in these towns is far less important than is class.

There is a tendency for those unfamiliar with the Valley to overgeneralize about the region, to suggest that relationships of race and class are identical in each community. There is, however, some diversity, in part dependent on the characteristics of individual community elites. Leaders in one Valley community may have been more farsighted than those in another. Yet this diversity does not negate the general patterns of political behavior within all Valley communities.

Local community leaders long have competed among themselves for state and federal monies and programs as well as other public services. A long-term result of such a strategy has been the duplication of services in a region in which public resources are severely limited. For example, for two decades Harlingen, McAllen, Edinburg, and Brownsville have struggled among themselves for superiority in commercial air service. When one city secured a commercial airline, the others always viewed it as their real loss. There has never been a unified attempt to centralize airport services to best accommodate regional needs of residents and tourists. Harlingen is geographically the logical choice to locate major airline services; passengers from McAllen, Edinburg, and Brownsville would have to travel no more than forty minutes to reach the airport.

Lack of regional perspective also blinds community politicians to the mutual benefits that could be obtained if Valley towns worked together toward common objectives. For instance, only recently has a coordinated advertising campaign been launched to attract tourists in the Valley. While other Gulf Coast communities marshaled regional efforts to lure the Navy to locate its vessels in their respective "homeports," the Valley's feeble attempt fizzled for lack of planning and coordination. Other areas along the Gulf coast began to coordinate their plans more than two years before Valley leaders began similar efforts.

Political parochialism has thus fostered a resistance to economic change in a majority of Valley communities. Local elites, as a rule, are fearful of any kind of change that may offset their control and have historically made decisions that retarded economic growth. Immediately after World War II, San Benito, then a town of about 12,000, had an opportunity to get an airport which could have served its needs, and those of Harlingen and Brownsville. The local power structure was afraid of what such change might bring to their community, and Harlingen, then about the same size as San Benito, got the airport. Today, because of this and other aggressive decisions made by Harlingen leaders, its population is three times the size of San Benito, and it is one of the most vigorous Valley towns. In a similar manner, McAllen, although it is certainly not without problems, has fostered an economic climate that has attracted some outside industry.

Most who live in Texas know that people in the Valley are very poor, but they still do not know how poor. Most Texans still believe that Valley poverty is no different from poverty elsewhere in Texas. A casual visitor to the Valley may be initially impressed with the ways in which the Anglo minority seems to exist in relative harmony with the Mexican-American majority. The Valley today, however, is far from tranquil. The long months of sunshine, the warm breezes, the pleasant faces on street corners, all mask real and deep class divisions and racial antagonisms kept fresh by a political structure which controls jobs, favors, financial resources, and lives. Public education and health care are two areas in which this political system is clearly revealed.

6. THE MISEDUCATION OF THE POOR

The Valley poor in the 1980s are constantly told that they must get an education if they are to escape poverty. Nevertheless, the Valley has a very high drop-out rate and a work force which is one of the least educated in the United States. Since the poor do not seem willing to improve their chances by staying in school, many in the Valley, including the poor themselves, blame lack of education for poverty.[1]

National figures indeed show that those not finishing high school earned a median income of $9,221 in 1983, while those with a college degree earned $34,709.[2] If the Valley poor would only get an education, one might conclude that they could find good paying jobs and escape poverty. The solution, however, is not so simple.

At the same time that Valley elites urge the poor to get an education, they operate the public school system as part of their political patronage. Public education is highly politicized in the Valley, and its primary importance, as far as the elites are concerned, is not the education of the young but the resources that provide jobs, salaries, and contracts for services. One result is that the quality of education in the Valley is quite low. Students are exposed to limited educational opportunities by teachers who often lack basic skills. Administrators are poorly trained. The elites know quite well the inadequacies of the educational system they have created. For many years they have sent their children to private schools in the Valley or to the public schools on the "good" side of the tracks.

While education is an important factor in achieving financial success, a wide body of literature demonstrates that opportunity along with the socioeconomic status of one's family are of greater importance.[3] Graduates of Valley schools face a dismal job market; there is a very real possibility that they may remain unemployed for long periods of time or find jobs that only pay minimum wage. Those in fact who do manage to become well educated must often search for jobs outside the region, especially if their families are poor and they lack the social and political connections that would allow them entry into the extensive patronage system.

However, schooling is very important because it teaches beliefs and values about ourselves and the larger society.[4] Public education in the Valley encourages complacency, conformity, and passivity, and discourages active participation in political life. Students learn early not to question those in authority, not to complain, not to participate for fear of failure or criticism.

In recent years Valley school districts have received substantial increases in funding from the state. This funding has not translated, however, into better schooling for the poor.

A VALLEY SCHOOL SYSTEM

The Brownsville Independent School District (BISD) demonstrates in detail how public education works in the Valley. BISD differs from other local school districts only in size; the enrollment of about 34,000 makes it the twelfth largest school district in Texas. Full-time faculty and staff number approximately 4,100 and the annual budget exceeds $100 million.

Public education was initiated in Cameron County in 1875, at a time when the population of the entire county was only about 12,000.[5] Wealthy Mexican Americans and Anglos sent their children to private schools in Monterrey, Saltillo, or north to Texas boarding schools. The small Valley middle class which could not afford to send their children away to school helped to support local private schools throughout the Valley. Families were assessed tuition and sometimes the balance of the school costs was paid by the wealthier members of the community. The children of the poor, both on the ranches and in the towns, did not go to school and were not encouraged to attend. The more affluent felt that education would make them dissatisfied with their position in life.

The quality of these private schools varied greatly, dependent upon the resources of the community. Rural areas commonly had the worst schools; straw-thatched roofs and dirt floors were commonplace, teachers only a little more educated than their students.[6] On the other hand, two or three schools maintained relatively high standards of education. Incarnate Word was established in Brownsville in 1853 by French nuns for the daughters of affluent Mexican Americans, Anglos, and Mexicans. In 1865, St. Joseph's Academy in Brownsville was founded by the Oblates for the sons of the rich, and some years later Villa Maria was founded for their daughters.

Valley public schools were a disaster from the start. Many of the poor did not attend and those who did received an inferior education. While historical data on BISD enrollments are incomplete, available figures strongly support these observations. In 1886 only 480 out of a possible 1,818 school-aged children attended public school in Brownsville.[7] Of those who did attend, a sizable minority showed no improvement in tests given at the end of the scholastic year in reading, writing, and mathematics. Materials, including slates and textbooks, were in very short supply. Many parents kept their children at home because of the poor conditions of the buildings which were described as "being unsuited for school purposes being small, dark, and damp."[8] The public schools were in session less time than the private schools; as many as seven to eight months in a year were devoted to vacations between classes.

By the turn of the century, BISD enrolled only a third of the total school-aged population. And of these, many did not regularly attend; in fact, one-quarter of the students who could attend actually did so. Less than 2 percent of the school-aged population in Brownsville attended public high school in 1898.

RACISM IN PUBLIC EDUCATION

Data from the high school annual of BISD, "The Palmetto," suggest the nature of the system.[9] From its beginning, BISD was administered by Anglos and taught by Anglos to an Anglo student majority, even though approximately 90 percent of the population was Mexican American. In 1918, there was not one Mexican-

American administrator, faculty member, or student in the high school senior class. Only about 22 percent of the students in the sixth grade were Mexican American.

The first non-Anglo to teach in the twentieth century in BISD was a female Spanish teacher in 1924. The following year a Hispanic female joined her in the Spanish department. Several years later, a female Hispanic taught as an assistant in the physical education department. No other Mexican Americans taught in BISD until the 1940s.

This pattern continued through World War II. In 1942, there were no Mexican-American administrators and only one Mexican-American faculty member, but the number of Mexican-American students had increased in the senior class to almost 50 percent. By 1969, ratios of Mexican Americans to Anglo administrators and senior students began to approximate that of the general Brownsville population, but still only about 50 percent of the teachers were Mexican Americans.

Most Valley communities that were large enough maintained separate elementary schools for whites and middle-class Mexican Americans in the "good" neighborhoods.[10] Until the 1950s and the national demand for integrated and equal education without regard to race, Valley communities which could support separate junior high schools did so. By high school many students had been effectively eliminated from the education system. In smaller towns like Mercedes, for example, there was only one junior high school and, prior to the 1950s, few Mexican Americans attended. Thus it was that in Valley high schools in areas where the Mexican-American population outnumbered Anglos four to one, Anglo students formed a majority of the student bodies.

Up to the late 1960s the speaking of Spanish was forbidden in school and on the playground. The message conveyed to Mexican-American students was that the language and culture learned at home was inferior to English and Anglo-American ways. Teachers, administrators, and counselors, although there were certainly exceptions, did not encourage Mexican Americans to continue their education. Through the 1950s, as a rule they were not even encouraged to finish junior high school.

Such discrimination against the majority of students, when combined with the real economic pressures most students felt to support their families, resulted in extremely high drop-out rates.

The norm was that only the brightest and most motivated Mexican Americans graduated from high school. Of these, even fewer attended college. Anglos, on the other hand, almost always graduated from high school, regardless of individual skills or talents, and many went on to college.

Valley public schools from the beginning were administered less to produce educated students than they were to control financial assets and jobs. For example, from the earliest days of public education, teaching certificates throughout Cameron County were bought and sold openly by politicians in return for political favors.[11] Teaching jobs were too valuable a commodity to be awarded on merit alone. In Brownsville, as in other Valley towns, the public school system became nothing more than a system of political spoils.

Anglos, with the help of a few Hispanics, dominated this system of spoils as they did city and county governments. In Brownsville, a community in which more than 90 percent of the population was Mexican Ameican, wealthy Anglos governed the school board without opposition year after year. The racial composition of the BISD School Board reveals this practice. From 1915, the date at which records first become available, to 1940 no Spanish surnames appear on the seven member school board. From the latter years of World War II to the mid-1960s, Anglos generally maintained a five-to-two majority in a community in which they were less than a 10 percent minority. The Board only began to be more representative of the population in the mid-1960s when Mexican Americans finally formed a majority.

Brownsville Mexican Americans seldomly were hired as teachers prior to World War II, nor did they serve as administrators. One retired Mexican-American teacher remembered that "lack of education" was always given as the reason so few Mexican Americans worked for the school system, except as janitors and cooks. When she was at last hired at an elementary school in the early 1950s, she felt that it was only because she was more qualified—she had her Master's Degree—than the Anglo candidates. She was the first Mexican-American teacher at that school, and she remembers that she was not welcomed by her Anglo colleagues.

THE QUALITY OF EDUCATION

During the early years, the quality of education was also problematic because of the shortage of qualified teachers. In Cameron County in 1914 there were only eighteen who held state certificates out of a total of sixty-nine teachers. Thirty-two of the remainder held county certificates which were literally purchased from county officials. At about the same time, BISD employed a total of twenty-eight teachers, only two of which held state certificates.[12]

BISD has throughout its history hired BISD graduates. Typically, BISD teachers have graduated from the school system, attended Texas Southmost College, Pan American University-Brownsville, Pan American University-Edinburg, or nearby Texas A&I. This practice results in an educational in-breeding, perpetuating a low level of skills.

More recently, qualified teachers from outside the Valley have been hired; but they seldom stay with the system for longer than three years. These teachers find it difficult to work in a system in which there are few professional standards. While they complain of overcrowded classrooms, lack of materials, and too much paperwork, all common criticisms of public schools around the nation, what disturbs them the most are the ways in which their schools perpetuate the problems.

Standardized test results emphasize that many BISD teachers are poorly qualified. In the spring of 1986, BISD teachers and administrators took the Texas Examination of Current Administrators and Teachers (TECAT). The TECAT was uniformly criticized around the state as "too easy"; 96.7 percent of all state teachers and administrators passed the test on basic reading and writing skills. However, 175 certified teachers in the BISD failed this same examination—approximately 9 percent of all instructors and administrators when it was first given. Another group of 190 teachers did not take the test, in effect quitting, rather than risking failure. One teacher in BISD who held a certificate, when asked by a local reporter about the TECAT, remarked, "The education was applied to us by God,...and I don't believe that no mortal has the right to take it away from us."[13]

Approximately two-thirds of all Valley school districts fall below the TECAT state average (see table 15). Santa Maria Independent School District ranked lowest in the Valley, 20 percent unable to pass the test. At the other extreme, all teachers and administrators in tiny San Perlita passed the test. Teachers and administrators in BISD ranked twenty-sixth out of thirty-one Valley school systems. BISD spent $70,000 in the summer of 1986 to prepare personnel to pass the second TECAT offering.

Standardized tests of college juniors and seniors majoring in education suggest the nature of the problem in the Valley. Edu-

TABLE 15

Valley School Districts by TECAT Scores, 1985

SCHOOL DISTRICT	% PASSED	RANK IN VALLEY
Brownsville	91.4	26
Donna	93.3	24
Edcouch-Elsa	89.3	29
Edinburg	95.4	17
Harlingen	96.7	11
Hidalgo	91.3	27
La Feria	97.4	8
La Joya	93.4	22
La Villa	93.5	21
Los Fresnos	96.1	14
Lyford	97.6	6
McAllen	97.1	9
Mercedes	96.1	13
Mission	96.0	16
Pharr-San Juan-Alamo	94.6	20
Port Isabel	96.2	14
Progresso	100.0	1
Raymondville	96.3	12
Rio Grande City	87.2	30
Rio Hondo	97.0	10
Roma	93.2	25
San Benito	93.4	22
San Isidro	97.5	7
San Perlita	100.0	1
Santa Maria	80.0	31
Santa Rosa	95.0	19
Sherryland	97.9	5
South Texas	100.0	1
Valley View	90.5	28
Weslaco	95.3	18
Texas State Average	96.7	—

Source: Texas Education Association

cation majors are now required to pass the Examination for the Certification of Educators in Texas (ExCET) before receiving their teacher's certification. The passing rate in Texas in 1986 was 80 percent, while at Pan American University-Edinburg it was 65 percent and at Pan American University-Brownsville it was 54 percent.[14] In previous years students who received their certification at the local college and university would then teach Valley students, in effect passing on their inferior education to a new generation of students.

Brownsville public school teachers have always received low salaries relative to teachers elsewhere in the state, and such salaries have not attracted the best teaching professionals. Entry-level salaries at BISD ranked in the bottom one-third of Texas teacher salaries prior to recent changes. A Brownsville teacher just out of college with certificate in hand could expect, as recently as 1985, to receive about $13,000 per year. On the other hand, administrative salaries at BISD from the early 1970s to the present rank in the top one-third. In 1987 the superintendent of BISD earned $80,016, the deputy superintendent received $63,178, and the deputy superintendent of curriculum received $52,400. These individuals also obtained as much as $5,760 for travel expenses. BISD's three assistant superintendents and twenty program directors earned between $32,938 and $52,500.

Recent attempts by the Texas legislature to raise salaries have meant that starting salaries for newly certified teachers beginning at BISD in 1986 were approximately $19,000, with those with the most experience and advanced degrees able to earn about $32,000.

Previously financial considerations forced many of the best BISD teachers to find jobs in other professions or teaching jobs in other parts of the state. There is still considerable pressure to get an administrative job with a much higher salary and an air-conditioned office. (Until 1985, BISD had few air-conditioned classrooms despite the climate.)

The dissatisfaction of many BISD teachers with their wages and with the conditions of their work—poor facilities, a lack of classroom materials, and a high student-to-teacher ratio—did not result in a strong push toward unionization or militancy. Teachers were afraid to complain for fear that they would lose their jobs.

A teachers' association developed at BISD, as did other similar organizations throughout the Valley, but these groups functioned more as social gatherings and an arm of the administration than as effective tools to gain benefits. In the late 1970s a chapter of the American Federation of Teachers was finally formed in BISD, but its small membership has not been able to win any real concessions.

The quality of Valley teaching is also reflected in the results of the Texas Educational Assessment of Minimum Skills (TEAMS) test. Mastery of the TEAMS test, like TECAT, was mandated by House Bill 72 to be a requirement for graduation from all Texas high schools, although the test was judged by many critics as being far too easy.[15]

Nevertheless, Valley students as a whole did quite poorly on the test. Only 71 percent of all BISD eleventh graders who took the test in 1985 passed it (see table 16). BISD ranked twentieth out of all Valley schools, the majority of scores falling well below the state average. Not surprisingly, given TECAT results, San Perlita Independent School District had students who performed among the best of all Valley eleventh graders. At the other end of the rankings was Hidalgo Independent School District, where only 50 percent of the students passed both parts of the test. These scores for Valley students fell into the bottom third percentile of all state students taking the test. Students at Hidalgo Independent School District, for example, scored in the twentieth, fifteenth, and twentieth percentiles when compared statewide for math, reading, and writing, respectively. Students at nine Valley schools scored among the lowest 5 percent of any students in the state. These same schools comprise one-third of all Texas schools that were subsequently monitored by the TEA because of poor performance on the TEAMS test.

A closer examination of the TEAMS results for juniors at BISD is alarming. Such students had particular trouble in the language arts. Although 79 percent of those who took the test "mastered" it by achieving passing scores, only 39 percent passed the section on punctuation, 41 percent on sentence structure, 44 percent on proofreading, 56 percent on drawing conclusions and distinguishing fact from opinion, and 62 percent on determining the main idea from a story.

TABLE 16

Valley School Districts by
11th Grade TEAMS Scores, 1985

School District	% PASSING MATH	% PASSING LANG.	% PASSING BOTH	RANK IN VALLEY BY % PASSING BOTH TESTS
Brownsville	82	79	71	20
Donna	72	78	64	22
Edcouch-Elsa	87	84	79	10
Edinburg	80	82	73	18
Harlingen	84	84	78	13
Hidalgo	62	60	50	26
La Feria	89	83	81	7
La Joya	70	72	62	23
La Villa	—	—	—	—
Los Fresnos	85	89	79	10
Lyford	90	87	82	6
McAllen	88	89	83	5
Mercedes	79	83	69	21
Mission	88	86	80	8
Pharr-San Juan-Alamo	79	81	72	19
Port Isabel	86	83	79	10
Progresso	88	83	80	8
Raymondville	85	87	78	13
Rio Grande City	71	70	62	23
Rio Hondo	91	91	85	3
Roma	65	67	56	25
San Benito	84	86	78	13
San Isidro	88	96	88	2
San Perlita	100	100	100	1
Santa Maria	—	—	—	—
Santa Rosa	80	89	75	17
Sherryland	79	85	77	16
South Texas	—	—	—	—
Valley View	—	—	—	—
Weslaco	94	87	85	3

Source: Texas Education Association

At BISD, 82 percent of the students were defined as having "mastered" the math part of the TEAMS test, but the actual results are disheartening. Only 41 percent passed the section on formulas, 43 percent on geometric properties, 45 percent the sections on fractions and measurement units, and 48 percent on multiple operations. The proportion of students passing the sections on geometric formulas, equivalencies, equations, proportions, and percents were only a little higher. In both components of the examination (language arts and mathematics) students showed they were unprepared when compared to other Valley and Texas students.

EXPLANATIONS OF POOR
EDUCATIONAL PERFORMANCE

It was in vogue in the mid-1960s and early 1970s for BISD administrators to explain away low scores on standardized tests as the result of cultural bias against Hispanics. There was some truth in this explanation at the time, but low scores continued without exception into the 1980s, long after standardized tests had been made less culturally biased.[16] BISD students were frequently used by national testing services in attempts to make tests less biased against Mexican Americans.

During the 1970s, the sons and daughters of migrant farm workers were held as bringing down test score averages, thus suggesting that BISD was in fact doing a better job than it appeared. Considerable amounts of federal and state funds were forthcoming and special programs were set up to meet the needs of the children of migrant farm workers.

Administrators have long blamed the lack of financial resources for low test scores. The school district certainly has in the past been restricted by its tax base compared to other systems of its size around the state. In 1985, BISD's taxable property values were $1.79 billion, down $.29 billion from the previous year. However, local tax dollars comprise only a fraction of BISD's 1985 budget: $83.8 million comes from the state, $14.8 million from the federal government, and only $14 million from local sources. Recent attempts by the Texas legislature to provide school districts with state funds based upon the financial resources of the school district have meant considerable increases in state dollars to BISD. No longer can BISD administrators blame the poor performance on inadequate funding.

BISD is not the only school system in the Valley which has failed to translate its financial resources into quality educational opportunities. The Point Isabel Independent School District (PIISD), for instance, has for decades been the richest district in the Valley. Its tax base not only includes the high-rise condominiums on South Padre Island, but half of the tax-rich Port of Brownsville. Its taxable property base is now valued at almost $1 billion, third highest in the Valley, while enrollment in the community of less than 6,000 is approximately 7 percent of the size of BISD's enrollment. Nevertheless, its students continue year after year to score among the lowest of any school district in the Valley. PIISD boasts a large football stadium, a new, well-paid football coach, new football and band uniforms, a new high school, a new junior high, and the best in educational materials and technologies. But, along with BISD and other Valley school districts, its students are receiving inferior educations.[17]

Since 1980 BISD administrators have attempted to divert attention from their own mismanagement by complaining loudly about the impact of illegal aliens upon the school district.[18] Federal monies have been generated from these complaints, but the real scope of the problem is minimal. By BISD's own count, children of illegal aliens account for less than 4 percent of the total enrollment and are most heavily concentrated in the elementary schools. Nevertheless, BISD officials repeatedly blame these students for many of the problems throughout the system.

State and federal funds have in recent years provided millions of dollars for BISD bilingual programs. It is now clear that the problem is less with students than it is with the quality of the programs that serve them. Other school systems around the state have developed bilingual programs which are effective; such programs are managed by qualified administrators and staffed by competent teachers.[19] The bilingual programs in the BISD and in many other Valley school systems are initiated by administrators with unclear objectives and taught by unqualified teachers. The result is often students who are functionally illiterate in two languages. BISD to date has no means of evaluating its program, let alone taking positive action to improve it.[20]

The school board has been perhaps the weakest link in the school system. Less than 20 percent of the public regularly votes for the BISD school board and board members have not been reluctant to fill their own political agendas before meeting the needs of public education. School board members have traditionally been local businessmen with limited, if any, experience in education. As a rule, board members send their own children to private schools in Brownsville.

PUBLIC APATHY

The citizens of Brownsville have taken as little interest in the education of their children as they have in other matters of public policy.[21] They have mistaken the exploits of their children on the athletic field or in other high profile programs for academic excellence. Their passivity is in part a reflection of their own lack of education—a parent with a fourth-grade education finds it very difficult to question the college-educated teacher who is supposed to be teaching his son. When my wife and I visited with teachers and administrators at the semi-annual parents' night at one BISD high school with an enrollment of approximately 1500, we were two of twelve parents in attendance.

This passivity on the part of parents has been encouraged by administrators and board members. It is part of the traditional relationship between the minority of Anglos in power and the majority of Mexican Americans in poverty. Parents are constantly misled, both about the quality of education their children receive and the real problems in their school system.

The discussion thus far has focused on the quality of public education, but one must not forget the other important functions that schooling provides. The beliefs and values of school trustees, administrators, and teachers are transmitted daily to students. The policies of each school, the ways in which students are treated by the system, the morale that pervades every school, all emanate from the school hierarchy.[22]

Students who complete their education at BISD are not only educationally disadvantaged, they are also often demoralized. They have been taught that intelligence is the ability to memorize and score well on multiple choice tests. They have rarely had a chance to develop their writing skills. They have been steered away from many academic courses which would have prepared them for college.[23] While they are unusually polite and well-mannered, they are all too willing to simply sit in class and never participate; they are intellectually passive. Their educational experiences have successfully encouraged this passivity, an adaptive stance that will serve the system that created it well, even as it serves the students ill.

A majority of students who go through BISD do not have a terrible time. The halls of BISD's high schools are not unpleasant places to walk, students do not appear glum or reticent. Their days are filled by teachers who entertain them, often pleasantly. Students are passed along from one year to the next until they drop by the wayside because as juniors or seniors they still cannot read. The few who are not passed turn seventeen and are still in ninth grade. Principals and assistant principals, with several notable exceptions, tend to the daily routines.

Students at BISD and other Valley schools are constantly bombarded with a litany that emphasizes the importance of obtaining an education, but rarely are they given the personal guidance or the tools to achieve it. Students do learn first-hand about powerlessness; they have little sense that they or anyone else can change their schools because those who make such an attempt are quickly suppressed and ridiculed. What some students learn in school is to present an image of passivity as a protective shield against the intrusions of an institution. Some become masters at pretending that they do not care about what goes on around them, a good defense when one can do little to control one's life.[24]

The drop-out rate is another indication that all is not well. Both TEA and BISD estimate that the chance of entering the school system at the kindergarten level and exiting as a senior with a high school diploma is 50 percent.[25] BISD has argued that much of this loss is due to students who transfer to other school districts.[26] I have not found that to be an accurate description of the situation. Students are bored and discouraged, and would rather earn $3.35 an hour than sit through another day of classes.

Students who develop any problems, educational or otherwise, are ignored by the school system. It is only within the last several years that drug problems have been tentatively addressed. Students with emotional problems, some of them quite serious, are thrown into various generic programs which do not meet their particular needs. Athletes are given special attention and favors, and continue to graduate among the least skilled of all students. The program for gifted and talented students serves only the one percent who score the highest on standardized tests, leaving other bright students to face the boredom of the average classroom.

The real question becomes why so many students in the Valley stay in school, given these conditions. In part it is because of the social functions that school offers. One can see and be seen, meet with friends, develop relationships with a girlfriend or boyfriend that may become serious, eventually leading to marriage. Particular extracurricular programs such as football and band undoubtedly serve to keep some students attending school.[27]

Valley students also stay in school because of their families. Many low-income families encourage their children to stay in school,[28] and when BISD students do drop out, it is not without some guilt. Poor mothers and fathers want their children to enjoy a higher quality of life, and they realize quite well that education is the key. Yet more than half eventually leave, preferring to take their chances rather than endure a system that promises them much but provides them little.

There are some administrators and faculty who do care. The McAllen public school system, under the direction of an innovative Mexican-American administrator concerned with his students, has attempted with some success to turn his schools around. Test scores have improved along with student and faculty morale. This district has also received its share of criticism from a skeptical community. In communities in which standards of educational proficiency have never been established attempts at reform are viewed by those in power as subversive.[29]

THE IMPACT OF HOUSE BILL 72

H. Ross Perot's special committee recommended a number of immediate changes to improve education in Texas in the 1980s; the intent of House Bill 72 was to bring rapid reform to an educational system in serious trouble. Changes included providing for the minimal competence of Texas teachers by giving them the TECAT, administrating the TEAMS tests as a requirement for grade advancement and graduation, substantial raises in teacher salaries, lower student-to-teacher ratios, and a number of other measures.

House Bill 72 has already transformed BISD and other Valley school districts in various ways. Teachers now earn a reasonable wage for their work; by Valley standards an extraordinary wage. Hundreds of former Valley teachers have returned to the profession, and many in other kinds of work have gone back to college to become certified.

House Bill 72 is making life a little harder for incompetent administrators and teachers in BISD and other Valley school districts. Even the slightest attempt to apply standards of minimal proficiency and competency has suggested that one out of eleven teachers is incompetent. TEAMS testing of students at different levels has raised some issues which are not going to disappear. Not only do BISD students do poorer on these tests than students around the state, a condition that has come to be accepted by BISD, but BISD students do less well than other Valley students. House Bill 72 has brought a modicum of accountability to BISD. The new laws have required that BISD reduce its very high student-to-teacher ratios, hire certified teachers, and begin to evaluate itself using statewide procedures. Towards this end, BISD hired its first professional in-house researcher in 1985 to begin measuring the results of TEAMS, the dropout rate, the efficiency of various programs, and other important data.[30]

But House Bill 72 only serves to emphasize the seriousness of the problems that BISD faces, along with other Valley school systems. BISD is a microcosm of the larger community; the political and economic decisions made in the name of education in BISD reflect the same kinds of political and economic forces at work in other areas of life in Brownsville.

The BISD school board, along with the administration, also can easily avoid House Bill 72. For example, in 1986 the board voted not to promote students unless they are reading at their grade level, as mandated by House Bill 72.[31] Sixth-grade students not reading at sixth-grade level would not, therefore, be promoted to the seventh grade regardless of the class grades they received during the year. But then in the spring of 1986, the board was presented with a dilemma: if they stuck to the new standards encouraged by House Bill 72, more than five thousand elementary students would not be promoted to the next grade level, thus not making room for incoming students. With little public dissent, the board voted to change the standard it had recently passed, promoted the unqualified students, and promised to give them "special attention" the following year. In short, despite House Bill 72, nothing changed—the district simply accommodated the demands from Austin, then provided for business as usual.

To make matters worse, Valley public school teachers recently expressed their annoyance with the compulsory TECAT by voting-out the very legislators who had tried to improve public education. A minority of public school teachers formed an organization called "The Force" and campaigned hard against those Valley state representatives who voted in favor of House Bill 72. The result is that in 1986 Valley schools have lost their most important political representatives in Austin.

Under growing pressure from a minority of the BISD board, dissatisfied parents, and a Valley Interfaith task force on education, the BISD board commissioned a consulting firm from outside the Valley to study problems in the administrative structure of the system. Unlike previous studies, this study was done by a qualified firm with many years of experience. The firm analyzed the current administrative hierarchy, and recommended 175 broad and sweeping changes, among which were a total revamping of the hierarchy, and the monitoring and evaluation of both administrators and programs.

To date, none of these recommendations have been acted upon. The BISD board has argued that the changes require additional funds which are in short supply. Recent board elections have effectively eliminated any opposition as voters in Brownsville once again displayed their apathy at election time. In this election BISD administrators were particularly effective in running and electing candidates sympathetic to their concerns.

TEAMS scores improved in 1987, however BISD still fell in the bottom one-third of all Texas public schools. Nevertheless, the improvement in scores was hailed by the administration as a major victory and announced in the media with some fanfare. What little public pressure that had been placed upon the system to improve immediately dissipated.[32]

HIGHER EDUCATION

Opportunities for higher education in the Valley have historically been more available to the Anglo minority than to the

Mexican-American majority. In the past the few Mexican Americans who graduated from local high schools lacked financial resources and/or were inadequately prepared for college-level courses. For many years Valley Anglos ran the college boards, administered the programs, and taught the courses to predominately Anglo students. Unlike the public school districts, the quality of education offered was relatively high because direct political intervention was less severe in higher education and because the student body, predominantly Anglo, were relatively well educated—graduates of Valley private schools or products of college track programs in the public high schools. A few college and university departments were competitive with other state schools, while Valley teacher education and other programs have been substandard for a very long time. Within the last two decades college and university enrollments rapidly expanded as Mexican-American students finally gained access to Valley higher education. However, larger student bodies have not resulted in significant increases in Mexican-American college graduates as a number of serious problems remain.

The Valley is served by one state university, Pan American University in Edinburg (PAUE), with a branch in Brownsville (PAUB); one community college, Texas Southmost College (TSC) in Brownsville; and two state vocational-technical schools, Texas State Technical Institute (TSTI) in Harlingen with a branch in McAllen, and a vocational-technical division of TSC. Student enrollment at Pan American was approximately 10,000 in 1986, while 1,500 attended the Brownsville branch. A similar number attend TSTI, and about 5,000 are enrolled in the academic and vocational-technical schools at TSC.

An increasing number of Valley Mexican Americans are attending college. Census figures show that the number of Mexican Americans with some college or who are college students has roughly doubled since the 1970s. College-educated Mexican Americans, however, constitute only 14 percent of all Valley Mexican-American adults while Valley Anglos with some college education or a college degree comprise 43 percent of all Valley Anglos.

A dual system of higher education has long been in place. In the 1980s the Mexican Americans who graduate from high school with the motivation and the economic resources to attend college usually lack the academic preparation to do well. The majority of Anglos, by definition affluent, attend colleges and universities outside the Valley where any secondary school deficiencies in basic skills are supplemented by remedial course work. These students are much more likely to obtain a college degree.

The history of Texas Southmost College is illustrative of this trend.[33] Records from the earliest yearbooks available (the school was founded in 1925) give a clear indication of who controlled the institution and who was served by it. For forty-five years a community college in a city with a population 90 percent Mexican-American was run by an all-Anglo board and all-Anglo administrators for an almost completely Anglo student body instructed by an all-Anglo faculty. The first Mexican-American teacher was not hired until the mid-1950s. By 1960 there were four Mexican-American faculty, composing 18 percent of all teachers at the institution, and as late as 1970, Mexican Americans composed only 12 percent of all faculty. It was not until the hiring of the first Mexican-American president in the early 1970s that there was a conscious and consistent effort to hire Mexican-American teachers at TSC. By 1985, 36 percent of the faculty were Hispanic.

What is perhaps even more surprising is the racial composition of the student body at TSC. Records are not available prior to 1940, but in that year only 15 percent of the student body was Mexican-American. Over the next forty-five years the ratio of Mexican Americans to Anglos reversed itself. By 1985 Mexican Americans accounted for more than 93 percent of all students attending the school, Anglos the minority.

For many years an Anglo board ran TSC, which, until the 1970s, was a very modest institution with a very limited budget and few jobs. In 1960 there were only twenty-two faculty working at the college. Even in the 1980s, TSC remains secondary to BISD in terms of financial resources. TSC's budget in 1986 was about $16 million, compared to more than $100 million for BISD. Because of its small size, TSC historically remained relatively free of the political intervention prevalent in BISD. The quality of education it provided was set not by political hacks but by educators. For this reason, the quality of education at this community college was, over the years, relatively high. Teachers were not always hired just on merit, but those who were hired usually did have to possess the minimum degrees that were required, although there were notable exceptions. In general, teachers were left alone to do their jobs, relatively unencumbered by the political favoritism and other problems that face teachers at BISD. In consequence, those who attended the institution could receive a reasonable education.

TSC retained relatively stringent academic standards by administering an entrance exam and a set of core requirements in the freshman year. Those who passed the entrance examination faced tough courses to stay in school. There were no developmental or remedial programs. Until the 1970s this policy in practice meant that Mexican Americans were systematically eliminated.

A small number of Mexican Americans who attended TSC graduated from it, then went on to other institutions to complete their education. Several of these former TSC graduates are now well-known leaders and professionals in the community, but they are the exception rather than the rule. The college made no attempt to provide those Mexican Americans who did gain entrance with any special guidance or expertise. Moreover, there was only a limited degree of cultural sensitivity to Mexican Americans in this Anglo institution, and certainly such an atmosphere was not conducive to retaining these students.

The first Mexican-American president of TSC, Dr. N. Oliveira, radically changed the institution. He threw out the entrance examination and opened the door to all students who had high school educations. Students financed their educations by qualifying for federal Pell Grants which paid for tuition and books. In 1986 approximately 60 percent of all students at TSC received some kind of federal assistance. At the same time there was a considerable effort to hire Mexican-American faculty, limited only by the scarcity of Mexican Americans who possessed the appropriate academic qualifications.

While the number of entering freshmen soared from a few hundred in the early 1970s to over three thousand just ten years later, the number of graduates in the 1980s remains about the same. More than one-half of first-semester freshmen flunk out or withdraw before the start of their second semester. By the sophomore year, classes are reduced to about one-third their original size. Even the majority of those who manage to reach their sophomore year do not graduate in June. Only from 25 to 30 percent—no more than 300 students—actually walk across the stage at graduation to receive a diploma. Of these, an even smaller number continue an education at an upper-division college or university.

An often-heard explanation of this trend was that many TSC students transferred to other state colleges and universities. But a recent institutional polling of students who withdrew from TSC found that the biggest reason for leaving was financial. Students responded that they could not attend college full time and also manage the full-time or part-time jobs that were necessary for them to continue their educations. Only about 5 percent stated that they were transferring to other schools.

Border community colleges in Texas, Arizona, New Mexico, and California have a much higher percentage of Anglos than they have Mexican Americans.[34] While the high percentage of Mexican Americans at TSC should result in increasing numbers of graduates, this has not been the case. The average student at TSC in 1986 attends school in the mornings or evenings and works at a part-time or full-time job. The campus is almost completely empty of students from noon until seven o'clock at night. While it is commonly held that everyone who wants to get a college education can afford to do so through grants, loans, and scholarships, in reality the poor of the Valley find it extremely difficult. Federal Pell grants provide tuition and books to a majority of students at TSC, PAUB and PAUE, but students often feel compelled to drop out of college and take a minimum-wage job to support themselves or their families.

Sophomores who graduated in 1986 from TSC are indicative of the problem. Only 314 graduated from a sophomore class of approximately 1,000, suggesting that academic preparation still remains a crucial impediment to those seeking a college degree. The majority of sophomores were either forced out because of grades, or will not graduate in the normal two-year period because they cannot attend full time.

A closer look at the group of sophomores who did graduate reveals a common pattern: only 3 percent did so in two years or less. If a student enrolls full time for four semesters, each semester taking a minimum of fifteen credits, then he should graduate within the prescribed two years. If he attends summers or takes more than fifteen hours per semester, he can graduate in less than two years. Most students who graduated in 1986 first attended TSC four years or more before they actually graduated. Almost half first began taking courses six years before they graduated.

These data and interviews with students at TSC portray a typical student who attends the college for one or two semesters, drops out to work, to start a family, or for other reasons, then later may return for a few courses, perhaps at night. Over the course of four to seven years or more, a minority of these students may accumulate enough course credits to earn a degree, a quite different pattern than that followed by the average middle-class student.

Standardized test scores emphasize the poor preparation of entering TSC students. ACT scores over the last decade have consistently ranked these students in the second percentile (i.e., 98 percent of the nation's youth scored better on the ACT than they). A standardized reading test, no longer in use in 1986, consistently measured their reading abilities at between seventh and eighth grade levels. Interviews with the institution's reading instructors indicate that in 1986 little has changed. Math skills, as measured by a test developed by TSC's mathematics department, reflect similar deficiencies.

In 1983, TSC received a federal grant to develop remedial courses for the large number of students who entered the college with inadequate preparation in English and mathematics. From the evaluations of the program to date, considerable improvement has been made in reading and math skills among students taking the remedial courses. These students then are theoretically channeled back into regular college courses.

The actual impact of remedial courses upon Valley college students remains to be seen. It is quite possible that remediation will do nothing but discourage many students with inadequate preparation from continuing in college. There is resistance on the part of the students. Too, it is clear that the solution to this problem in the long run lies not with college remediation programs, but with the public schools that are creating the problem.

PAUE and PAUB have had to confront the same problems that have faced TSC. These two institutions are governed by regents who are appointed by the governor and have been much less burdened by the Valley patronage system. The result has been somewhat higher academic standards. However, as with TSC, a majority of the incoming Mexican-American students fail to graduate because they lack adequate skills and/or financial resources.

The tenure system at TSC, PAUE, and PAUB has done much to preserve the quality of education. Faculty in general have been protected by the most obvious attempts to hinder their performance in the classroom, their interest in campuswide issues, or, to a lesser degree, political participation in the community. Unlike school teachers in Valley public schools, college-level teachers have been able to maintain a certain degree of professional integrity.

Students who are the first in their families to attend college often are the first also to have graduated from high school; their parents are not able to judge the quality of education their children receive. Parents demand little of the colleges, assuming that their sons and daughters are being given the best education possible. As a result, educational changes and reforms come not from demands of the community or the students, but from within the institutions themselves. However, as with all educational bureaucracies, Valley colleges are very slow to change, cautious to the extreme.[35]

The two Valley vocational-technical schools, TSTA in Harlingen, with a new branch campus in the McAllen area, and the vocational-technical school at TSC, have a total enrollment of approximately 4,000. Both institutions have serious problems. For many years students have been offered courses with poor instruction which provide them no marketable job skills. After one year or more in the secretarial program at TSTI, many young women find themselves behind the counters at Wal-Mart or Gibson's. Both educational institutions have also been very faddish, obtaining state or federal monies for instructional programs that were inappropriate to the skill levels of their students and the job market.[36]

Reading levels at TSTI in 1976 were on the average between fifth and seventh grade for all incoming students. Such skill levels make learning how to be a dental assistant or a diesel mechanic difficult, regardless of the other skills a student may have. Little has been done to help students, although in teaching a single semester reading course at TSTI, I found that the average student did improve his skills over a period of four months, most often from a sixth-grade to an eighth-grade level.

The vocational-technical schools have been a part of the political spoils. The teachers lack a system of tenure and suffer from low salaries; turnover is very high, and there is little, if any, faculty participation in important institutional decision-making. Morale over the years has been low. The administration of these programs has not been of good quality, nor has the institutional leadership. The vocational schools have been treated, unfortunately, as the stepchildren in the educational system.

There are several different private vocational-technical schools in operation in the Valley which vary considerably in the quality of education that they offer students. Among the least effective are two branches of the North American School of Education, recently closed by the TEA for failure to keep adequate records of federal funds secured for students. These private vocational-technical schools charge relatively high tuitions, between $2,500 and $3,000 per year, which students pay through federal grants and loans. It is estimated that the North American School of Education received more than $3,000,000 from federal loans and grants to students during its brief tenure in the Valley. These monies will have to be repaid by Valley students who are particularly vulnerable to these kinds of enterprises.

The available data demonstrate that the Valley's public education system has served to perpetuate and lend strength to the political and economic systems which foster discrimination and inequality. In a majority of Valley communities those in power have used, and continue to use, educational institutions to better their own interests. Valley public schools continue to produce a population of drop-outs and the worst educated graduates in the United States. One of the Valley's richest resources is its young, and they are systematically neglected.

7. NO MONEY, NO DOCTOR

For generations, poor Valley residents have worked at jobs and been forced to live in conditions which are detrimental to their health. When sick, they have been denied access to professional health care because they lacked the money to pay for the services. Valley hospitals and private physicians have rarely provided the care that the majority of the population required, although they have made some effort to convince the public that their "charity work" was sufficient. Poor Mexican Americans thus came to rely on alternative sources of treatment such as *parteras* (midwives) and *curanderos* (folk healers). These alternatives were not only considerably cheaper, but usually more sensitive to their patients' cultural background.

As a result of this dual system of health care, the health status of Valley Mexican Americans is among the lowest in the United States. Like education, the health status of the majority of the population was less important to those who ran the Valley than was the political and economic control of the jobs, services, programs, and fiscal resources of the health care system. Racism also played an important part in the allocation of health services to the poor. But unlike education, there have been recent signs of real changes in the 1980s; in the last decade the health status of the poorest Americans has improved.

HEALTH STATUS

Health status data must be eyed critically, interpreted both within the cultural context of the Valley as well as in terms of the very real health needs of those in poverty. Several researchers have noted the poor quality of Valley health data and cautioned against drawing conclusions based upon statistics alone.[1] One major problem with such data is that a large number of health problems go unreported. The Valley poor often cannot afford professional medical care, so their health concerns, though perhaps quite serious, do not enter the statistics gathered by local, state and federal health agencies.[2]

The Valley poor regularly use alternative sources of medical care which may include doctors, dentists, midwives, pharmacists, and mental health professionals practicing in Mexico. Similarly, the maladies of those who seek help from folk healers or midwives may go unreported. Some health researchers as well as local health professionals minimized some of the most alarming indicators of health status by suggesting that alternative forms of health care adequately compensated for the lack of access to professional medical services.[3]

Death rates of the Valley's population are an example of potentially misleading statistics. Taken at face value, the recorded death rates of 6.6, 5.7, 6.0 and 7.0 per 1,000 population for Cameron, Hidalgo, Starr, and Willacy Counties, respectively, compare favorably with the rate of the state of Texas, 7.6.[4] However, it must be remembered that the Valley population is skewed heavily toward the young. Median age in Cameron, Hidalgo, Starr, and Willacy is 25.0, 24.1, 22.8, and 24.7, respectively, compared to a state median of 28.2 and a national median of 30.0. The proportionately very large numbers of young are much less likely to suffer fatal illnesses or other major causes of death; therefore, death rates among the general Valley population, which compare favorably to the rest of Texas, are misleading. Diseases related to older age cohorts, for instance, those including heart disease, heart attacks, and cancer, are relatively lower in the Valley than in Texas.

A more telling statistic is the death rates from infectious and parasitic diseases, double the rates in the rest of the state of Texas.[5] The death rates from dysentery and amebiasis are twice that of Texas whites and four times the rate of Texas blacks. Death rates of Valley residents from ill-defined causes were three times that of whites in the rest of Texas.

Infant mortality rates in the 1980s and in prior years also argue against the extremely poor health status of the Valley population and, like death rates, must be viewed with some caution. The four counties which compose the Valley have relatively low infant mortality rates when compared to other counties in Texas and the United States. Various researchers have, however, argued that this is because of the inflated number of live births and the deflated number of deaths before the infant reached one year of age.[6] A large but unknown number of Mexican women give birth to their children in the Valley, in part because they would prefer to rely on the Valley's relatively superior health care and because they seek U.S. citizenship for their newborns. These same women may then return to Mexico with their infants whose health then goes unreported in the Valley statistics. This problem with infant mortality rates is one that is shared all along the U.S.-Mexico border region. An additional related problem is that Valley *parteras,* midwives, have historically not recorded complications in birth out of fear of civil or criminal action against them; women who give birth with the help of parteras have similarly not reported to officials infants who died during delivery.[7]

The Ten State Nutrition Survey, 1968–1970 and the 1970 Field Foundation medical survey of Hidalgo County farm workers both described the nutritional deficiencies in the general Valley population and the special populations of welfare clients and farm laborers which compose large segments of the Valley's population.[8] Incidences of heart, lung, scalp, and musculoskeletal disabilities were consistently high in these studies. According to one physician:

> High blood pressure, diabetes, urinary tract infections, anemia, tuberculosis, gall bladder and intestinal disorders, and eye and skin diseases were frequent findings among the adults. Almost without exception, intestinal disorders, eye and skin disease were frequent findings among the adults. Most of the children had chronic skin infections. Chronically infected draining ears with resulting partial deafness occurred in an amazing number of the smaller children. We saw rickets, a disorder thought to be nearly abolished in this country, and every form of vitamin deficiency known to us that could be identified by clinical examination.[9]

Medical facilities, trained personnel, and programs to provide health care have always been in short supply in the Valley.[10] As late as 1976, Cameron County had only 80 percent of the patient-care physicians of the rest of the counties in Texas, 25 percent of the dentists, 70 percent of the pharmacists, and 50 percent of the physical therapists. As recently as 1970, Brownsville had only one hospital with 162 beds for a population of 50,000. Mental health facilities, alcohol/drug abuse, and psychiatric services all have been available only on a very limited scale. In 1976 there was only one board-certified psychiatrist in Brownsville, and there were no psychologists. There were, however, several individuals who claimed to be psychologists, but were not licensed by the state.

The number of unwanted pregnancies is alarming, as is the average age at which young females, the majority unmarried, give birth.[11] The incidence of congenital birth defects is quite high, however relatively few potential parents seek genetic counseling.[12]

AIDS education is still grossly inadequate in the Valley in 1988. The number of actual cases remains undetermined because those who suffer from the disease are likely to be sent outside of the Valley for treatment. The number of cases reported in Mexican cities which border the Valley is not known. A number of Valley and Mexican health educators have expressed a concern for the importance of AIDS education in public schools as the disease spreads to the heterosexual community in other parts of the country.

Health statistics, regardless of how suggestive, mask the real disparities in health status between rich and poor. When disease rates in Cameron County are broken down by income level, the differences are staggering.[13] Rates for gonorrhea among low-income groups were nine times higher than for the nonpoor, for syphilis more than four times, for amebiasis six times, and for tuberculosis and hepatitis three and four times, respectively. Differences in reported disability status of poor and nonpoor adults in Brownsville were likewise significant.[14] Poor adult males were twice as likely to suffer from some kind of disability as those who were affluent, and poor females were three times more likely than affluent females to suffer some disability.

The conditions under which the poor must work helps in part to explain this great disparity in health status. Farm workers are typical of those poor in the Valley who for years have worked long hours in intolerable conditions. The effects of long-term exposure to pesticides and defoliants remains a major concern among farm workers. In contrast to earlier times, farm workers and other Valley poor now have some access to the legal system, and they are more likely to bring litigation because of employer practices or injuries suffered on the job.

The conditions under which the poor must live also contribute to their low health status. The estimated 70,000 who live in colonias, among the poorest of the Valley's poor, often do not have adequate sewage, sanitation, drainage, nor a safe supply of drinking water.[15] Overcrowding is more common here than in other Valley residences. There are no parks, sidewalks, paved roads, or lighted streets. Standing water after even a light rainfall is common. Serious flooding occurs after heavy rains, which then erodes outdoor privies and septic tanks. Crimes of violence often go unreported.

Living conditions for the poor in the Valley's urban areas, discussed in detail in chapter one, also contribute to low health status. Although many of the residences of the poor initially are impressive, a closer inspection would reveal many problems including several structural defects, inadequate outdoor plumbing, no heating system, and overcrowding. Federal grants in the 1970s have improved some barrio homes; these monies are now in short supply.

ACCESS TO HEALTH CARE

The major impediment to the health of the poor is lack of access to professional health care systems. The Valley medical establishment, with a few notable exceptions, has provided consistent medical care only for those who could afford it. Private physicians and hospital staff, who were themselves Anglo, served the rich, who were also largely Anglo. Up until the mid-1970s few new physicians or medical facilities were drawn to the Valley even though its population was rapidly expanding. The rich continued to seek specialized medical care outside of the Valley when the need arose, something that the poor could not do.

Valley doctors are not only physically, but intellectually isolated from mainstream medicine. Once having graduated from medical school, they found themselves at tremendous distance from Texas medical centers. They faced health conditions among the poor that were monumental when compared to the urban experiences of their colleagues in other regions. One common response was to ignore the medical problems of the poor and to concentrate on those patients who could afford their services.

Not only was it difficult for poor Mexican Americans to gain access to adequate medical care, but when they did manage to receive care they often found it culturally insensitive. Mexican-American doctors and support staff or Anglos who spoke fluent Spanish were rare. A visit to a physician or a stay in a Valley hospital could result in an economic disaster—bills that it would take years to pay—as well as an insulting experience at the hands of those with little knowledge of Mexican-American culture. As late as 1977 at least one Valley hospital still, as a matter of hospital policy, refused to release patients who had not paid their bills in full. In practice this meant that the hospital staff physically restrained patients from leaving their rooms, a policy which Texas Rural Legal Aid lawyers eventually discouraged.

An alternative system of medical care flourished in the Valley and directly across the border because it was cheaper and more aware of Mexican-American sensibilities. The very existence of such an alternative system of care is a strong reflection of the real health needs of the majority of those who lived in the Valley.[16]

Parteras, for example, were chosen over private physicians because few of the poor could afford to give birth to their children with the aid of doctors or in a hospital; even today it is estimated that approximately 50 percent of all Valley births are by parteras.[17] A bill in 1988 for prenatal care and birth, without complications, may add up to $2,000 at Valley Baptist Medical Center. This one bill of $2,000 constituted about 25 percent of the average annual income of Valley families; it is far beyond the means of most Valley workers who receive the minimum wage and no health benefits. It has always made good economic sense for most Mexican Americans to use *parteras*.

Parteras, unlike physicians and hospitals, have been sympathetic to the needs of Mexican-American women. Not only is there a common language and culture, but a common set of class values. When added to the shared bond of female treating female, giving birth with the aid of a partera has made for an altogether different kind of birthing experience than that allowed by Valley hospitals.

But cultural bonds between parteras and their patients should not be overemphasized. The majority of Mexican Americans would prefer to have their babies under the best professional medical supervision possible, regardless of the insensitivity of doctor and staff. A majority would prefer prenatal care by a trained physician as well as birth delivery and subsequent care. Many poor Mexican-American women know quite well that parteras cannot handle the complications that might arise during birth, complications that occur in approximately one out of every ten deliveries. These same women realize that there are some parteras who cannot provide adequate care even in a normal birth.

Parteras in the Valley had, until five years ago, remained unregulated, and the licensing procedure by various Valley cities is still grossly inadequate. Even licensed Valley parteras differ drastically in their competence, and those who place their trust in the hands of these women do so at the very real risk of their own and their newborns' lives.[18]

In spite of the very low health status of the Valley's poor, much of the medical community and the elites who control the Valley have firmly resisted major changes in the availability and delivery of health care services.

THE POLITICS OF HEALTH CARE

The politics of health care in the Valley account in large part for the poor health status of those in poverty. Private physicians run the health care system in their own best interests. Any state or federal system of health care has been viewed as "outside" competition which takes money out of the doctors' pockets. Private physicians have excluded competing systems of professional medical care and individuals who may champion them through the manipulation of hospital boards and the city, county, state, and federal governments. The health care of the general population has rarely been the primary consideration in these decisions.

Health care in the Valley has been a particularly lucrative business. For years doctors have been able to charge whatever rates they chose for often inferior services because the poor were both uneducated as to common medical practices and had few medical choices. It is only since the mid-1970s that public health facilities have become available to the majority of the poor. The Valley's legal community has become quicker to represent the poor who suffer at the hands of some Valley physicians. One result is that the number of suits against Valley doctors has risen steadily since the 1970s.

It was quite easy for professional medical standards, in isolation, to become lax. Doctors have always protected the mistakes of their own. In a region where the poor would not complain and the rich could, if necessary, seek specialists outside the Valley, abuses often remained hidden. The poor to this day are still much less likely to complain of improper medical services or treatment.[19]

Valley doctors since the 1900s have been very active in their communities. Their names often appear on lists of school boards and city councils.[20] Physicians have been leaders of their communities, perhaps to a greater extent than elsewhere. Those few with business acumen either invested in or began nonmedical businesses, from citrus groves to construction.[21]

Valley doctors grew or remained insulated from the medical needs of the majority of the community, out of touch with the average Valley citizen. They sent their children to private Valley schools, then to colleges ouside the region.[22] Some of their sons returned to the Valley to follow in their fathers' footsteps as physicians and dentists. They socialized with each other and others of the upper class, maintaining standards of status even as their medical standards declined. There were almost no Mexican Americans among them.[23]

At the same time that the majority of doctors in the Valley were among the most respected in their towns, they were as a collectivity exerting their political clout to keep federal, state, or county health care systems from developing in the Valley. Regardless of the real needs of the Valley poor for inexpensive health care, doctors within their county medical associations and as individuals lobbied long and hard to make sure that no health care facility that they could not have ultimate control over was built in the Valley.

Several grassroots organizations, including the farm workers with the help of the Catholic Church, finally were able to start a clinic for the poor in Harlingen in the early 1970s. Eventually this federally funded clinic, Su Clinica Familiar, developed satellite branches in Brownsville and in Raymondville, in Willacy County; a similar facility was initiated in Hidalgo County at the same time. Clinic doctors, a majority with the Public Health Service, were initially treated as lepers by the Valley's medical community. Not a few Valley doctors referred to the treatment of impoverished farm workers by government clinics as but another example of communism.[24] The satellite clinic in Brownsville was not built without a tremendous political struggle and was forced to construct facilities outside of the Brownsville city limits, making it difficult for many to reach.[25]

Many doctors in Brownsville have refused to accept poor patients on Medicare and/or Medicaid, claiming that collecting fees from the federal government was too time-consuming and costly. At the same time, these doctors have done everything they can to keep low-income patients from receiving health care from other professional sources.[26] The medical community in Brownsville has been typical of other medical communities throughout the Valley.

A different kind of conflict erupted in McAllen in the early 1980s between two different groups of physicians. McAllen now boasts two new hospitals, right across the street from each other, and each at this time is doing its best to drive the other out of business. It is questionable whether the needs of McAllen's poor will be served in the long run by this duplication of medical services.

No regional Valley hospital was ever promoted or allowed to develop; private, for-profit hospitals predominate. One reason given for the absence of a state or county hospital is the area's lack of financial resources, the inability of the region to provide for the construction and long-term operating budget of such a facility. But as evidenced by the resistance to the federally sponsored clinics begun in the Valley in the 1970s, the greater truth is that there are none because the Valley medical community strongly resisted public health care in any form for many, many years.

A relatively large number of health programs, in addition to those mentioned, came to the Valley in the 1970s and 1980s. From 1969 to 1979, Cameron, Hidalgo, Starr and Willacy Counties received, respectively, $301,969,000, $423,000,000, $60,176,000, and $37,046,000 in federal health care funds for selected programs.[27] A number of existing programs were funded and a number of new programs were initiated which targeted specific poverty populations. These include Medicaid, Aid for Families with Dependent Children, migrant health programs, community health centers, family planning, and a number of programs within the United States Department of Agriculture such as the National School Lunch Program, Food Stamps Bonus Coupon Program, and Women's and Children's Nutrition Supplementation Program. Programs with the Alcohol, Drug, and Mental Health Administration also were initiated or strengthened.

This significant influx of health care dollars and programs gave many of the Valley poor access to professional health care for the first time. Most Valley health care experts now agree that these monies have made a considerable difference in the health status of poor residents.

Zavaleta demonstrates that birth rates, mortality rates from infectious and parasitic diseases, medical problems in women relating to obesity, high blood pressure, and cancer have all been positively influenced by federal and state-funded programs.[28] Birth centers now provide some low-income women with an alternative to parteras. At the Brownsville City Clinic, for example, women who run a high risk of problem births can receive care during pregnancy and childbirth services at the same cost as that charged by parteras.

Su Clinica Familiar is another example of the success of outside health dollars. Su Clinica Familiar served approximately 30,000 patients in 1986, 400 a day in its various satellite clinics. An additional 60,000 patients are in its active files. Patients, a majority of whom are or were farm workers, pay on a sliding scale and receive, in return, first-rate care.

The evidence that is available suggests that in the last decade the health status of the Valley's poor has improved substantially, in large part because the poor now can get services comparable to those available to the rich. That such is the case underscores the fact that the Valley poor do not prefer alternative health care systems; there is little reluctance to use medical services when they are affordable.

The quality of funded health services in the Valley, however, remains uneven. A recent investigation by State Senator Hector Uribe of the regional branch of the Texas State Mental Health and Mental Retardation facility in Harlingen revealed that some buildings were substandard and that understaffing was common. The Valley has not received its share of state funds in the past because health was not considered an important priority by Valley legislators.

Moreover, the outlook for continued improved health status among the poor is bleak. Under the Reagan Administration there has been a continual effort to cut back on programs which directly impact the health status of the Valley's poverty population. Fewer health dollars in this region mean fewer health services from fewer programs. Public health officials in the Valley are concerned that recent and planned cuts will seriously damage the general health and well-being of the poor.

Added to this concern is the fact that several Valley hospitals have recently been purchased by national hospital chains. Locally owned hospitals provided unsatisfactory health care to the poor, the hospital chains may provide even worse care for the medically indigent. These corporations operate hospitals as efficient businesses in which care is provided only to those who can pay.

While these same chains spend much effort and money in public relations attempts to convince the public that they are serving the poor, this is not the case. In the Valley several hospitals recently acquired by national chains have stopped providing any care except for fees. While by law they cannot turn away those who come to them with medical conditions requiring emergency care, they circumvent the law by intimidating and harassing indigent patients. When one comes to the emergency room requiring immediate attention, he or she is asked by hospital staff if they have medical insurance or the money to pay for the health services.

If the potential patient does not have insurance, or some other means of immediate payment, then staff from the business office begin a series of personal confrontations designed to drive the service seeker from the hospital. Poor people are more easily intimidated than those who are more affluent and/or better educated, and in the end many, regardless of their medical needs, leave the emergency room without treatment.

Such circumstances as these are not unique to the Valley, but a charade played out in many other areas of the United States in the 1980s. Communities across the nation are increasingly faced with bulging health care costs that cannot be met by the poor, nor absorbed by hospitals. In Texas the Health Facilities Commission, the state agency which regulated the construction and development of hospitals and was able, in part, to limit competition between not-for-profit hospitals and hospitals owned or proposed by large corporations, was abolished by the lobbying efforts of the Texas Medical Association.

The Texas Legislature in 1985 passed the Indigent Health Care Bill, four separate pieces of legislation, which was designed to help those who could not afford professional medical care.[29] In the Valley this legislation was greeted by health advocates and consumers with much anticipation. But there is a strong indication that the bill will remain underfunded or will be eliminated because of the state's current crisis brought about by falling oil prices.

The reaction of county government to the Indigent Health Care Bill has been consistent and typical of its response to the health needs of the poor. Valley counties must make contributions to health care expenses in partnership with the state of Texas. Valley counties have been extremely reluctant to take on these costs, citing already overextended annual budgets. To provide monies for the health care of the poor would lessen the power of the county spoils systems because other budgetary items would suffer. Among these are funds to build and maintain county roads, funds which have long been a vital part of the spoils system.

Mexico is often blamed as the primary cause of poor health in the Valley. Sharing a border with Mexico does contribute to some of the special kinds of concerns which plague the Valley, such as communicable diseases, industrial and agricultural pollution, and contamination of shared natural resources.[30] The entire U.S.-Mexico border has serious health problems which are just beginning to be addressed.[31]

However, to lay the principal blame for poor health on Mexico is a convenient strategy often used by Valley elites. Proximity to the border aggravates health problems in the Valley, but certainly is not their major cause. The health status of the majority of the poor who live in the Valley is determined in the 1980s by the allocation of medical resources. It is this politics of health care which has, at least temporarily, improved the health status of those most in need.

8. IGNORING THE OBVIOUS

It is tempting to vilify the wealthy and the middle class in the Valley, all those who either direct the system or who, at the very least, participate in it and enjoy the rewards, thus perpetuating the status quo.[1] The real people who fill these classes are not demons; they do not necessarily consciously discriminate against the poor; most are no more or less mean-spirited than you or I. The affluent of the Valley simply have developed ways to profit from the poverty which surrounds them and, at the same time, ignore it.

MENTAL BARRIERS

Both the Valley middle class and the Valley rich have constructed a variety of barriers against the extreme poverty. These class barriers allow these privileged members to sustain a system of economic and social inequality and still live their lives relatively guilt-free, safe in the belief that the poor are neither their fault nor their responsibility.

Many of these barriers are mental. The affluent simply do not see the depth of poverty, even when it is directly before them. They question the credibility of research about poverty or quality of life in the Valley. Unfortunately, some earlier studies were misleading or detailed racial stereotypes which were offensive to Hispanics. Researchers are often considered "outsiders," whose findings are not accurate. When a recent study described Brownsville as the city with the lowest quality of life in Texas, followed closely by other Valley cities, letters published in the *Brownsville Herald* questioned the scholarship of the authors and their knowledge of the area.[2]

State and national journalists are similarly ignored as being ignorant of the "real" situation or as being politically or racially biased. Articles which have appeared in the last five years in the *Wall Street Journal, Newsweek,* and *Time* have described various aspects of poverty in the Valley but were dismissed as sensational journalism.[3] Articles in statewide publications such as *Texas Monthly* receive a similar response. A recent documentary by Bill Moyers was described by a Valley paper as reflecting the views of the "Eastern liberal establishment." A recent article in *Newsweek* which compared the poverty in Valley colonias to poverty in Appalachia was virtually ignored by the Valley's electronic and print media.[4]

The affluent are very defensive about poverty in the Valley. It is a sore point with many of them. They feel that there is poverty just as bad in Austin, San Antonio, or Dallas, and that local Valley poverty is an "impolite" topic of discussion. Those Valley residents who criticize Valley poverty are given the cold shoulder or challenged at a personal level to come up with solutions.

Those who are willing to discuss the Valley's immense poverty fall back on stereotypes and myths about the local poor. These myths are traditional in Texas: the poor have more children to collect more welfare; the poor do not want to work even if given a job; the poor leave school because they are not motivated to succeed; the poor have always been that way so any programs to change them are doomed by their very nature to failure; and the poor will always be poor in the Valley because of Mexico.[5] These and other stereotypes about the Valley poor have little basis in fact despite their prevalence among all classes in the Valley, including the poor.

How can a person of reasonable intelligence and sensibilities fail to see the poverty around him? It is a matter of becoming desensitized to the commonplace, to the visible poverty which one cannot avoid. In the Valley this is easier to do, and to justify, than in many other areas of the United States.

The Valley poor are not invisible, but their poverty is less dire than Mexican poverty.[6] Many of the affluent act on this premise, buttressed by their daily experiences. A trip to Reynosa or Matamoros for dinner cannot hide the living conditions of the

Mexican urban poor. Toothless women in rags beg on the streets, their small children strapped to their backs. If one leaves the main streets, then the Mexican hovels are immediately visible even from a passing car. From this perspective the Valley might not be heaven, but it is so much better than Mexico that any economic or political changes to the Valley system need be only minor. Since the Valley is isolated from mainstream America to the north, a comparison of Valley poor to Mexican poor, rather than to the poor in Dallas, Houston, Corpus Christi, or San Antonio, is natural.[7]

Personal contact between rich and poor is very limited. Affluent Valley women, for example, must deal regularly only with maids, gardeners, repairmen, retail clerks, service workers, and a very few other low-income people. It is maids that affluent females are most likely to talk with in a relatively relaxed setting within their own homes; maids become the upper- and middle-class woman's peephole into poverty.[8] The beliefs, opinions, and circumstances of maids are often generalized by wealthier women to represent all low-income people. However, maids are no more reliable sources of information about low-income groups than other working poor, and may be strongly biased in their remarks to their employers. They may fear that accurate descriptions of their daily lives would shock the women for whom they work. They may be reluctant to counter the stereotypes and beliefs of their employers for fear that they would lose their jobs.

Language is one important barrier in the Valley to social interaction.[9] Many Anglos whose families have lived in Valley cities directly adjacent to the border for more than one generation are fluent in Spanish. But the further from the Rio Grande, the less likely it is that Anglos speak Spanish. Competence in English is one characteristic of class among Valley Mexican Americans; low-income Mexican American are more fluent and, therefore, more comfortable conversing in Spanish. An affluent Valley Anglo is likely to have problems communicating with a poor Mexican American, especially in mid- and upper-Valley towns. Interaction between rich and poor in the Valley is thus hindered to a great degree.

This communication difficulty is particularly true among new Anglo professionals in the Valley. Their first predictable reaction is one of surprise. They often voice frustration in trying to communicate with people they meet in stores, at meetings, and in other public and private situations. The most well-meaning of these often take Spanish lessons or classes, but few master the language.

Those of the middle or upper classes who work with the poor do not necessarily help to break down existing stereotypes about the poor.[10] Familiarity with the needs of the poor does not mean that one is in sympathy or can empathize with those needs. The opposite may, in fact, be true. Social workers, teachers, businessmen, secretaries, mailmen, doctors, lawyers, law enforcers—in short, all who have daily contact with the poor—may regularly have experiences which strengthen existing class and racial stereotypes.[11]

Teachers and social workers may grow frustrated by resources or political constraints, and they may thus become apathetic or outwardly hostile to the poor. Middle-income professionals, especially Anglos not from the Valley, often find it difficult to work with the poor on a daily basis. Burn-out among teachers and social workers is common—one becomes overwhelmed by the sheer magnitude of unnecessary suffering. Hostility to the poor can become a reaction to those who one realizes cannot be helped.

A cohort of five social workers, for example, was hired to protect children in Cameron County against physical and psychological abuse. It soon became clear that the child abuse problem among the poor was much greater than had been suspected and that the resources of the agency were inadequate. The social workers became concerned that they would get "stuck" with a case in which a child died and they would be held legally and morally responsible. The social workers then developed strategies to dodge such responsibilities, including the referral of cases to other agencies, dumping cases on a naive social worker who did not realize the tragic potential, or simply refusing to take cases and, by their refusal, pressuring the supervisor to reassign cases to someone else.

Middle and upper-income groups develop among themselves explanations for the behavior of those poor with whom they interact daily. These explanations seek both to describe the poor and to analyze at a superficial level why the poor cannot or will not conform to the expectations of the affluent. These explanations are usually variations of "blaming the victim," blaming the poor for not being able to adequately cope with poverty or escape it.

Public school teachers must justify in their own minds the reluctance of their students to show enthusiasm for topics which do not interest them. Teachers are sometimes very surprised, especially at the high school level, when their students drop out. Rather than seek an explanation based on social fact, they may rely instead on mythical stereotypes about the educational aspirations of low-income Mexican Americans. Similarly, at TSC, English teachers are continually amazed that their students take little interest in British literature.

Paradoxically, those who are the best-educated are often the least knowledgeable about the Valley poor. Physicians have demonstrated a consistent lack of sensitivity to low-income people.[12] Like social workers, doctors get very frustrated with the recurring medical problems they encounter, some of which may be the result of either improper personal hygiene, a reluctance to monitor one's illness or take the prescribed medication, or a belief in folkways and mores which are unacceptable to the doctor. Again, stereotypes about the poor are likely to provide handy explanations for why patients "refuse" to get better. Those who directly work with the poor, then, do not necessarily become any wiser for their experience.

PHYSICAL BARRIERS

Physical barriers also limit the contact between rich and poor. The Valley is segregated by class; neighborhoods reflect these differences not only in the size and maintenance of residences, but in the availability and condition of streets, sewers, power lines, water lines, and other necessities. In earlier times one's race determined where one lived in a Valley community. Poor Mexican Americans lived on one side of the tracks, except in the cities along the Rio Grande, while richer Anglos lived on the other; only the boldest of middle-income Mexican-American families dared to live on the Anglo side of town.

Residential integration of Anglos and Mexican Americans is now a fact of life in most Valley towns. What distinguishes Valley neighborhoods is the stark contrast in appearances between those which house the minority of affluent Anglos and Mexican Americans and those which shelter the vast majority of the poor.

The richer classes in the Valley have physically isolated themselves from those in poverty.[13] High fences, a profusion of burglar bars, and other security measures separate the rich from the poor. Treasure Hills in Harlingen is in the southern part of the city, squeezed behind Valley Baptist Medical Center on one side, and the Arroyo Colorado on the other. Its broad, paved streets sweep past expensive new homes, lawns fed by underground sprinkler systems, and high wooden privacy fences. It is possible to catch glimpses of patios and swimming pools surrounded by tables with colorful umbrellas. Some of the most expensive Treasure Hills homes line *resacas,* small lakes which run throughout the development. In Brownsville, the Los Ebanos subdivision is a similar enclave, located immediately behind St. Joseph's Academy, the school of choice for the upper-middle and upper classes. Like Treasure Hills, there is only one street into the development and one out.

Many of the Valley's most wealthy maintain condominiums or single-family residences on South Padre Island.[14] South Padre Island affords the most affluent a chance to get away from the routines of their communities and to socialize with those of their own class from other parts of the Valley. South Padre Island is also a favorite spot of the Mexican rich, especially those from Monterrey. Both affluent Valley Anglos and Mexicans maintain a fairly strict segregation. Poor Mexican Americans cook the food of the rich Anglos and Mexicans, clean the rooms of their vacation homes, maintain the exteriors of the condominiums, and dispose of their garbage.

The residences of the Valley wealthy are no grander than in other parts of the state; they are certainly much less imposing than the homes of the wealthy in Dallas or Houston. Nevertheless, compared to the tiny wood-framed houses of the majority of Valley residents, the homes of the rich in McAllen, Edinburg,

Harlingen, Brownsville, and Rancho Vieho seem like castles. In a similar manner, the material possessions of the rich—the boats, condominiums, cars, clothes, and other accoutrements—stand out starkly in the Valley. The Valley's upper class does not necessarily lead a more opulent lifestyle than those in other regions; rather it is the contrast between the affluence and the poverty which surrounds them that is so striking.

The wealthier classes in the Valley have socially and physically distanced themselves from the poverty at the same time that they have justified it in their own minds. The end result is that the wealthy have become desensitized to the poverty around them. This lack of sensitivity can be measured by the low participation and membership in local voluntary groups which ostensibly serve the poor. While very few Valley civic associations have targeted the poor as worthy of their efforts, among those that do provide help, it tends to be more symbolic than real. Indeed, such organizations generally spend little time or money providing services, but expend much work in organizing and publicizing their efforts.

These voluntary associations are composed of members who find it is much easier to ignore the problem than to face it, or, alternatively, to select a problem so small that it is imminently solvable. For instance, voluntary associations as well as public institutions and private businesses often single out particular families in need at Christmas, raise money to buy them food, then forget about them until the next Christmas.

Those affluent active in voluntary groups attempting to address poverty are overworked and are likely to give up in frustration after a time. These few well-meaning people soon grow intimidated and depressed by the enormity of the problem. Private Valley foundations are overtaxed by the number of individuals and groups seeking funds for very reasonable projects. Again and again, one finds the names of the same people in different voluntary service groups and religious associations. For those who do take up the banner, the hours are long, and few peers are likely to congratulate them when they have done a good job. In the Valley there is almost no history of what may be defined as the philanthropic tradition, the sense of obligation by those of wealth to repay with their own time, work, and money the communities in which they were raised. There are a few exceptions, but those who give of their time or money to the community are held in no greater esteem by peers than those who do not.

The United Way annually raises funds for agencies which provide a variety of services to the poor. Each year many sincere people spend their energies raising monies to help the less fortunate. But these funds barely scratch the surface of what is required. One result is that agency directors must fight each other annually for their small share. And, as the funds have become tighter in recent years, the battles have intensified.[15]

THE MIDDLE-CLASS DILEMMA

The middle class of the Valley is in a genuine predicament with regard to the poor. They can on occasion empathize with the problems of the poor, especially if they themselves have escaped poverty. On the other hand, the political system can punish those who err from supporting the status quo; hence those who work for real social change run the risk of losing the favor of those in power.

Elsewhere in the United States the middle class composes a majority of the population and holds some political clout. In the Valley they are a minority with little authority or influence. Further, the middle class in other regions of the country has a number of ways to buffer themselves from the demands of the rich—the threat of poverty remains, to some degree, an abstraction to many in the American middle class. In the Valley, however, one can lose one's job for the offense of supporting the wrong political candidate or being judged a "trouble-maker." In this poverty economy there are few jobs waiting for those who are fired or pushed out. The only remaining option is to move to another region.

Valley Mexican Americans who have worked their way into the middle class must be cautious because they realize how much they have to lose. If one starts in poverty, suffers its indignities only to rise above it all, then there is a very human tendency to want to preserve those gains at any cost. This class realizes that it is best to conform to the demands of those who make the rules and run the system.

The cooptation of the middle class, both Anglo and Mexican American, is quite prevalent. This cooptation is facilitated in part because the middle class finds it much more easy to identify with the lifestyle and amenities of the rich than those in extreme poverty and with little education. In contrast to other regions, class lines between the middle and upper classes in the Valley are more obscured. In practice, one finds those of wealth more open to social and political contacts with those directly below them. Similarly, distinctions within the middle class between those of greater and lesser affluence and social status are less rarely made. One is a "professional" if a social worker, policeman, welder, teacher, lawyer, or any of a number of occupations; in effect, all that is required is that one is not poor.

Middle-income families, then, are likely to mingle with both the wealthy and those who in other areas would be labeled lower middle class. One may still be snubbed by those of a higher class, but the social contact at work, at parties, in homes, in restaurants, etc., is much more likely to occur than outside the Valley. This state of affairs causes many middle-income professionals to speak of how "laid-back" and "unstuffy" the Valley is; class pretensions and restrictions are less intense as long as one is not a member of the lower class.

Thus it becomes easier for people of moderate means to ignore the poverty around them, poverty of which they do not approve, but which they may support by their participation in the system and by their indifference. The attitude of the Anglo and Mexican-American middle class toward poverty in the Valley is complex, a mixture of a denial and loathing of the conditions of poverty, fear they may fall into it, and not a little jealousy for those of wealth.

The upper and middle classes who help to maintain the Valley social system are not much different from other Texans. They have become accustomed to extreme poverty, learned to live among and surrounded by those who are in extreme need; poverty simply becomes another fact of life. One thinks of ways to ignore poverty, justify it, perhaps even legitimize it because it is, after all, part of the human condition. There is a banality in this accommodation, an acceptance of extreme poverty as mundane. As life goes on unabated from one day to the next, one year to the next, the Valley's affluent rather effortlessly perpetuate a system of gross economic, political, and social inequality.

9. BLUEPRINTS FOR THE FUTURE

Poverty in the Lower Rio Grande Valley of Texas is more than an economic problem. Solutions to it must not neglect the entrenched political and socio-cultural arrangements. To ignore relationships of class and race destines any solution, however well intended, to failure. Attempts to ameliorate poverty should, in short, reflect the complexities of the region.

ELITE SOLUTIONS TO POVERTY

Solutions proposed by the Valley business elite and their elected representatives reflect traditional approaches to the elimination of poverty: poverty is defined strictly in economic terms and stereotypes about the poor prevail. Business elites actively seek to attract maquiladoras to the Valley, promoting the cheap labor supply that is available. In this development scenario new plants create new jobs to hire the unemployed and the underemployed; this investment of capital stimulates demand within local economies which then generates more jobs. Thus the poor also receive the "trickle down" benefits of a growing economy.

Another related strategy, suggested by both those in and out of power, is that the state and federal governments provide massive funding programs similar to the post–World War II Marshall Plan. Such a plan would erect an economic infrastructure in the Valley which would include roads, energy sources for new industries, improved water resources, educational facilities, etc. The Valley under this plan would be brought into the twentieth century in a decade or less, ready to economically compete with other Texas regions. This infrastructure would attract a diversity

161

of large corporations to the Valley which would create jobs for the poor.

The booming of maquiladoras will provide limited benefits to some of the poor. It is better to have a job that pays the minimum wage than no job at all. Maquiladoras probably do help to stimulate local economies, although far less so than their supporters suggest. The negative impact of these new plants, a topic already addressed in previous chapters, also requires serious consideration. Maquiladoras will do little, in the long run, to eradicate the poverty in this region.

The Valley desperately requires capital to create an infrastructure which can begin to attract a wide range of industries. A Marshall Plan for the Valley would improve the quality of life among some of the poor who would become employed in such construction; no doubt many more would benefit from the stimulation of the regional economy.

But neither hundreds of new maquiladoras nor vast infrastructural improvements will do much in the long run to ameliorate local poverty. More twin plants will provide a poverty-level wage to more poor people, while large amounts of capital from state and federal agencies will reinforce the domination of elites over the poor. The solutions proposed will guarantee that the rich will get even richer and the ever-increasing number of poor will remain powerless. This region requires much more than minimum wage jobs and capital investment in the economic infrastructure.

ELECTORAL POLITICS

Electoral politics is at the root of all fundamental change in the Valley.[1] The real problems that Valley poverty creates can only be addressed if the systems of political spoils are replaced by a plurality of interests representing all classes, especially the poor majority. Only when residents can freely and openly participate in the political system in an informed manner without fear of intimidation and retribution is there a chance to create long-term solutions to Valley poverty.

A first step toward this end is the registration of all eligible voters. At the same time, a massive voters' education project is required that is culturally sensitive to the local population. Oversight of voter registration by a task force of state and federal officials would minimize abuses.

Grass-roots community organizations representing the needs of the poor majority and the middle class are essential. Grass-root organizations focusing on specific community and neighborhood issues can do much to reshape the priorities of the political patronage systems that are in power. The history of the Valley clearly demonstrates that individuals who speak out stand little chance of affecting real change and a good probability of being personally destroyed. On the other hand, organizations can better protect their members from the pressures of Valley elites.

Such organizations require limited start-up and maintenance funding. Their major source of money and labor soon becomes their membership; an executive director and a handful of full and part-time staff are all the personnel who are needed. Initial funds can be solicited from private national foundations which are change-oriented, from religious and voluntary organizations, and from other successful grass-roots organizations. Valley Interfaith can easily serve as a model for these community organizations. Valley Interfaith has already enjoyed limited success in its brief existence; it also has confronted some of the problems that new community organizations would soon face.

Essential changes in the Valley's political structure are feasible to the extent that the new majority of voters is both educated in its own best interests and protected from traditional forms of intimidation and control. Voluntary participation in grass-roots neighborhood and community groups can provide an important part of this political education. Residents will become less apathetic when they begin to see their first small victories. A modest reallocation of existing city funds to provide limited improvements in their neighborhoods is one example. Voter apathy, bred by many years of political and economic impotence, will begin to dissipate; it will, however, remain a crucial problem to overcome.

Leadership among the Valley poor, as suggested earlier in a discussion of Valley Interfaith, is also a real problem. Community leadership programs in several Valley cities currently train younger members of the elite to carry on in the footsteps of their elders. Similar programs could be initiated for the poor. As well, the new grass-roots organizations could identify and encourage potential leaders within their own membership. Leadership among the poor has to be developed; it will take time, but is essential to real political change in this region.

The existing machines will attempt to subvert these legitimate changes in the political process. They will seek to discredit organizations representing the interests of the poor at the same time that they use their existing resources to manipulate the electoral process. They will use the broadcast and print media in their own best interests; they will regularly distort the goals and the victories of those who would legitimately wrest political power from them. Finally, they will use litigation, and the threat of litigation, to limit the political power of the poor. A modest increase in funding to Texas Rural Legal Aid, or any other agency which targets the legal needs of the Valley poor, would do much to limit these excesses.

ADDITIONAL NO COST AND LOW COST SOLUTIONS

There are a number of other solutions to Valley poverty which do not require expensive planning grants, teams of experts, and large capital expenditures. These solutions take into consideration the complexities of the region while focusing on the political rearrangement of existing human and material resources.

The Valley's governmental sector, one of the largest sources of employment in the region, is a case in point. Removing traditional elites from city, county, state, and federal programs and agencies located in the Valley will take some time. During this period in which political machines are dismembered, citizen watch-dog committees can be set up to monitor the hiring, firing and promotion of public employees. Cleaning the governmental sector of political cronies will not only provide for better management and operation of public services in the Valley, services that have historically discriminated against the poor, but open up new jobs to those who qualify.

Too often in the Valley formal education requirements and previous job experience are waived in favor of hiring a political crony. Supervisors can be encouraged to hire only those who meet the job requirements. Adherence to the formal requirements for positions will guarantee that some of the grosser hiring practices will not reoccur.

Whistle blowing, an almost unheard of phenomenon in the Valley, can be encouraged and rewarded with cash bonuses and public fanfare in order to reduce political favoritism, inefficiency, and corruption. At the same time, the legal rights of whistle blowers can be carefully protected from the arm of boss politics.

Contract and bid practices are another area of the political patronage system which demands closer public scrutiny. The linkages between those who sit on city councils, county commissions, and agency boards and those vendors who submit bids for goods and services can be studied by oversight committees and grassroots organizations and appropriate action taken when needed.

An improved system of public education could do much to indirectly reduce poverty in the Valley.[2] Additional funding is crucial, but of equal importance is the wise utilization of existing resources. Again, changes in the electoral process are fundamental. A minority of voters in Valley communities continue to elect school boards which then select unqualified superintendents who are a part of the spoils systems.

Communities which hire qualified superintendents can expect them to hire and promote district staff and school principals based upon merit rather than bossism. Communities which fairly evaluate their superintendents and other key staff on an annual basis can expect better schools. A school district should no longer be considered successful based solely on the win-loss record of its high school football team. Scores of students on state tests can be one of the most important criteria by which to judge the effectiveness of district systems.

Teachers, one of the best-educated segments of the Valley's middle class, can make a tremendous contribution to the improvement of public education. They can provide the concrete ideas for educational changes in the classroom and they can alert their communities to particular abuses of public education. By unionizing, they can see to their own best interests on the job.

By participation in neighborhood and community grass-roots organizations, they can themselves become future leaders.

At the same time, Valley legislators can be urged to lobby
long and hard for a fair share of state and federal funds for
education. It is not by chance that the nearest professional schools
are hundreds of miles from the Valley. The Valley's only professional school, the newly founded Reynaldo Garza Law School,
remains poorly funded and unaccredited. Pan American University, Texas Southmost College, and Texas State Technical Institute
are all regularly short-changed at budget time in favor of other
state institutions.

Higher education in the Valley can serve as a resource for
the improvement of school districts. PAU and, to a lesser extent,
TSC, can provide staff to upgrade the professional skills of Valley
public school teachers and administrators as well as provide direction for programs that would solve some of the problems in
secondary education. Model curriculums designed to meet the
specific needs of the Valley's school-aged children can be developed. A partial list of such efforts would focus on retention
programs for dropouts, drug and sex education, and courses designed for those with learning disabilities. One successful, low
cost program is already in practice at TSC. Junior high school
students are introduced to campus life through a series of courses
offered by regular college staff during the summer. These classes
provide potential college students with a taste of college life, and,
at the same time, promote good college-community relations.

An informed electorate can greatly influence health care in
this region. Recent advances in the health status of the Valley's
population should not be forsaken because of local, state, and
national politics. The Valley's fair share of state and federal funds
can be better assured through the hard lobbying of public officials
backed by organizations representing the interests of the poor. At
the state and federal levels sufficient funds to develop programs
to solve binational health problems are long overdue. At the in-
sistence of well-organized grass-roots groups, city and county level
budgets can be reprioritized to fund health care programs and/
or to match state and federal dollars for such programs.

The special health needs of those who live in the colonias
and the poorest of the barrios can be addressed through small,

cost-effective health programs. Many of their maladies are a direct result of living conditions—unsafe drinking water, inadequate drainage, the use of privies, and exposure to pesticides and herbicides. Greater use of physician-assistants and public health educators can contribute to a marked improvement in the health status of those who are most impoverished.

This region's birth rate is among the highest in the nation. A lower birth rate, assuming migration from south of the Rio Grande can be regulated, would ultimately mean a higher quality of life for all Valley residents. Fewer jobs would need to be created for those entering the labor market, fewer classrooms erected, pressures on social services would diminish, and limited natural resources could be stretched further. The poor in the Valley have large families, in comparison to the rest of the United States, in part because of cultural and religious beliefs and values which find strong support in the Catholic Church. The poor also have large families to insure economic security; the more children one has, the more potential income earners.

The availability of contraceptives to the poor, as well as basic education about human reproduction, also play important roles in determining family size among the poor. Many Valley women either cannot afford contraceptives or have certain misconceptions about them. One way to decrease family size in the Valley is to make contraceptives easily available to all who would choose to use them.

Sex education in the public schools is another closely related issue that should be addressed if the birth rate is to fall. It should be taken out of the hands of the football or basketball coach and placed under the control of qualified personnel. While the Catholic Church cannot be expected to support most forms of contraception, it can be enlisted to help with sex education. Parish classes which focus on sexuality can be initiated for children and adults, again at a very modest cost.

CHANGES IN PUBLIC POLICY

Other changes can be initiated that require limited funds but will directly improve the lives of the poor. Among the most important is closing the border to undocumented workers. While recent changes in the immigration laws have attempted to control illegal immigration to this country from Mexico and Central America, their impact on the Valley has been less than effective. New legislation is a first step that should be followed by extensive enforcement and additional legislation that meets the Valley's needs.

The INS has not been particularly successful in offering amnesty to those in the Valley who have resided here illegally. In effect, the INS is asking those who have long evaded the border patrol to suddenly trust them and turn themselves in. Those same individuals who have lived in the Valley for many years and have carefully developed ways around the existing legal structure must now show exacting documentation of their fraud.

Wages in the Valley will remain dismally low as long as Valley industries and businesses, including agriculture, can depend on a steady supply of undocumented workers and/or continually use the existence of such a labor supply as a threat to their workforce. Such wages, often below the federal minimum wage, guarantee that many of the poor in the Valley will be the working poor. Ways can be found to provide amnesty to those who remain in hiding at the same time stricter and more comprehensive enforcement of the law are brought against those who employ illegal workers. Those who knowingly hire the undocumented must be punished and aliens who seek work with false documents must be similarly discouraged.

Bilateral economic programs can do much to assist the Valley and Mexico; well-conceived programs that can create good jobs in Mexico, in contrast to the Border Industrialization Program, can in part help to reduce the number of undocumented workers coming to this country. The importance of our neighbor to the south only now seems to be recognized by our nation's leaders. While several federal programs have poured funds into drug enforcement along the border, there has been little national interest in developing model bilateral economic and social programs which would address Mexico's economic problems and U.S. border problems as interdependent and self-sustaining. It is ultimately cheaper to develop programs which would help Mexican workers on Mexican soil than it is to solve the problems of undocumented workers once they have crossed the Rio Grande.

The basis for cooperation exists between officials in most Valley cities which border the Rio Grande and their Mexican counterparts.[3] In such communities binational problems are typically handled from one day to the next through informal, personal arrangements since it has often been the case that conflicts exponentially expand when officials in Mexico City and Washington get involved.[4]

Washington can do much now, with a very limited commitment of funds, to build upon these informal bilateral relationships. It can actively support problem-solving task forces composed not just of "national experts," but of a generous representation of those in the community with knowledge and contacts on the other side of the river. For example, police officials in McAllen can be encouraged to promote informal ties with their counterparts in Reynosa. They may wish to pick a problem that is relatively noncontroversial, but solvable, as their first objective.

THE VALLEY ECONOMY

In many ways the Valley resembles an internal economic colony. Agricultural products are one example of Valley resources which are shipped to other regions for final processing before entering the retail market. It is these non-Valley processors which receive the lion's share of the retail price; local processors most often simply grade, clean, and package the product for shipment to the north. If local processing was encouraged, then the region's economy and workers would directly benefit; more jobs would be created and more dollars would be fed into the local economy.

The Valley cattle industry must reconsider its economic future. As beef prices continue their fall only those operations that are the most cost-effective will survive. Cattle ranchers should consider new and productive ways to use the vast range lands of Willacy and Starr counties and the northern parts of Cameron and Hidalgo counties. Recent unsuccessful attempts by the King Ranch to turn part of its extensive holdings into shrimp mari-

culture ponds demonstrate the necessity of prudent planning before capital is invested. State agricultural research centers can be
pressed to develop feasible alternatives to traditional uses of South
Texas lands.

The gulf shrimping industry is another case in point. More
Americans each year are eating less beef and more chicken and
fish. Valley shrimp trawlers can be easily transformed into vessels
which harvest additional species of fish in the Gulf of Mexico.
Such attempts were made several years ago, but trawler owners
found no local market for their fish; in several instances the fish
literally rotted at the dock for want of a buyer. Gulf species that
could be utilized more extensively are red snapper, drum, croaker,
flounder, sea bass, grouper, and shark, among others. Fish and
shrimp processing plants erected in Port Isabel, Port Brownsville,
and Port Mansfield could sell directly to retail markets in San
Antonio, Dallas, and Houston providing jobs to the regional
economy.

Valley banks export massive amounts of capital out of the
Valley with little benefit to the local economy. Grass-roots organizations representing the poor can ask that local banks commit
a greater percentage of their loans to local small businesses. Consumer boycotts have been effective in persuading banks in other
regions to better serve their communities. It is also not unrea-
sonable for Valley banks to commit a percentage of their profits
from Mexican investors to the future of this region. It is time to
closely scrutinize the banking practices and policies of Valley
banks and how these practices directly impact the regional
economy.

The development of coastal lands has not been prudent and,
in the long run, the Valley tourist industry will be adversely
affected. Like the rest of the state, the region has no overall
management plan nor governmental entity which supervises the
use of coastal resources for the greatest public good. Instead,
local coastal lands have been developed along the lines of the
"Houston model," which is to say there has been no planning at
all, little consideration of the limited resources that are available,
and widespread displacement of the poor.[5] Destruction of the very
resources which draw tourists to the Valley has already taken
place.

Business development and destruction of the environment are not synonymous. Local governments can begin to limit the excesses of some developers as they seek to use the Valley's natural resources most wisely. In this light, the attempt to turn the mouth of the Rio Grande into a gigantic, upper-class beach resort must be closely examined. Will the Playa del Rio project benefit the majority of the public in the long run? Is the trade-off between permanent jobs that will be created and destruction of the environment a fair one? These kinds of questions should be fully answered before the citizens of the Valley lend their support to any new projects.

THE CATHOLIC CHURCH

Electoral politics fueled by grass-roots organizations is at the root of any possibilities for fundamental political, economic, and social change in this region. It is only the Catholic Church, however, that can support the initial fragile transformation of this region from a system of political patronage to a democracy. The Church has actively helped the poor in many ways by its social service programs, in particular its support of Su Clinica Familiar, its sponsorship of Valley Interfaith and, more recently, its takeover of a failing educational television station. But much more is required of this religious institution if real change is to take place.

The leadership of the Church is crucial to eradicating poverty in this region. The Church can lend its full weight to social change only after it has reevaluated its own priorities and reorganized its human and material resources. For example, it has been particularly ineffective at responding to criticism by Valley elites. It has shunned press conferences, sometimes acted in a secretive manner, and constantly turned the other political cheek, refusing to take the offensive.

Those who would argue that religious institutions should not be involved in politics ignore American history as well as contemporary movements around the world. The poorest of Americans will not succeed without the full support of the Catholic Church.[6]

A POSSIBLE SCENARIO

What will happen if basic changes do not occur in the Valley? The scenario is unattractive, but one that should be seriously considered. As the Valley's population continues to grow from a high birth rate and immigration from Mexico and Central America, the conditions for poverty will exponentially increase. Unemployment will soar as the number of young adults entering the job market dwarfs the number of available jobs. Wages will remain at or below minimum wage, contributing to increasing numbers of those who are employed full time but, nevertheless, earn a poverty income. The quality of public education will decline, overburdened by pressures of ever-expanding enrollments on available resources. The health status of the poor will decline as funds to provide services are stretched beyond reasonable limits. The Valley's population will reflect demographic characteristics similar to those of Third World countries.

Public services and facilities within the Valley's largest cities, already inadequate, will deteriorate rapidly given this scenario. Police and fire protection, already problematic to the poor, will rapidly decline. Crime will rapidly increase, even as more police are hired. As the quality of life for the majority of Mexican Americans declines, both elected and nontraditional leaders will offer easy answers to complex questions. Political bossism will grow in proportion to the increasing number of poor and the decreasing quality of life; the worse off the population, the greater the value of favors offered through patronage. Leaders will make a strong appeal to those who cannot look forward to a better future. Race will provide ideological fuel for new leaders who will thrive on graft and corruption even as they preach a new moralistic and political order. Such leadership will seem far more attractive then grass-roots organizations which offer few promises, but require long hours of work and unflinching commitment.

The Valley will export this poverty to the rest of Texas and the nation. Larger and larger numbers of men, women, and children will leave the Valley in search of a better life. The major metropolitan areas of Texas will be most affected by this exportation of poverty, but other regions in the country will not be immune. Poverty in San Antonio, Dallas, and Houston will be increasingly influenced by the thousands of Valley poor in search of jobs.

There are now about one quarter of a million poor people in the Valley and an additional one hundred thousand who would be considered poor by the standards of most Americans. The problems of these people are a state and a national problem. The nature of this poverty and its solutions, only a few of which have been suggested, are concerns that can be actively debated both in Austin and in Washington.[8] In this public debate the complexities of this region should be squarely addressed; money alone is not enough. It is long past time to seriously consider ways in which these poorest of Americans may be helped and may help themselves.

NOTES

1. HOW POOR?

1. See Michael V. Miller and Robet Lee Maril, "Poverty in the Lower Rio Grande Valley of Texas: Contemporary and Historical Dimensions," Texas Agricultural Experiment Station, Technical Report Number 78–2, College Station, 1979.

2. See, in particular, L. Beeghley, "Illusion and Reality in the Measurement of Poverty," *Social Problems* 31 (1984): 322–333, and S. Danziger and P. Gottschalk, "The Measurement of Poverty," *American Behavioral Scientist* 26 (1983): 739–756, for discussions of this problem.

3. See the definition of poverty in U.S. *Department of Commerce, General Social and Economic Characteristics, Part 45, Texas* (1983): 3–4. See also, Robert Sheak, "Poverty Estimates: Political Implications and Other Issues," *Sociological Spectrum* 8 (no. 4, 1988).

4. These data are directly from *General Social and Economic Characteristics, Part 45, Texas,* three volumes (1960, 1970, 1983).

5. See *Poverty in Texas* (Austin, Texas: Office of Economic Opportunity, 1974).

6. From Miller and Maril, "Poverty in the Lower Rio Grande Valley," and *General Social and Economic Characteristics, Part 45, Texas.*

7. As cited in *USA Today,* May 10, 1988, p. 1.

8. Data from 1980 are from Texas Employment Commission, "Cameron County SDA," "Hidalgo and Willacy Counties SDA," and "South Texas SDA," Planning Information PY 1986, Austin, 1986. I would like to thank the Texas Employment Commission staff in Cameron, Hidalgo, Starr, and Willacy Counties for their help as well as the Staff Statisticians at the Texas Employment Commission in Austin, Texas. Data from 1960 and 1970 are from Bureau of the Census, *County and City Data Book.*

The figures for Starr County misrepresent the actual incidence of poverty. Unreported income, the majority of which is earned from

175

trafficking in illegal drugs, brings annual earnings in Starr County more into line with that of the other three counties. This fact (discussed further in chapter four) does not undermine the seriousness of poverty in this county; it only serves to qualify census data.

9. Data are taken directly from *County and City Data Book*.

10. See Michael V. Miller, "Poverty, Development, and the Quality of Life in a Texas Border City," Ph.D. dissertation, Texas A&M University, College Station, 1981.

11. Data are estimates from "Cameron County SDA," and "Willacy County SDA." Data do not include Starr County.

12. For a complete discussion of how occupational distribution differentially impacts Anglos and Mexican Americans, see D. L. Poston et al., "Earning Differences Between Anglo and Mexican-American Male Workers in 1960 and 1970: Changes in the Cost of Being Mexican-American" *Social Science Quarterly* 57 (1976): 618–632. See also T. D. Kane, "Structural Change and Chicano Employment in the Southwest, 1950–1970: Some Preliminary Observations," *Aztlan* 4 (1974): 383–390.

13. Data from "Cameron County SDA" and "Hidalgo and Willacy Counties SDA."

14. See Cary Davis, "U.S. Hispanics: Changing the Face of America," Population Reference Bureau, no. 3 (1983): 37–40.

15. See Ellwyn R. Stoddard, "Patterns of Poverty Along the U.S.–Mexico Border," Center for Inter-American Studies, University of Texas at El Paso and Organization of U.S. Border Cities and Counties, 1978. See also, Ellwyn R. Stoddard and John Hedderson, "Trends and Patterns of Poverty Along the U.S.–Mexico Border," Borderlands Research Monograph Series no. 3, New Mexico State University, Las Cruces, 1987.

16. See Refugio I. Rochin and Nicole Ballenger, "Labor and Labor Markets," in *Borderlands Sourcebook*, ed. Ellwyn R. Stoddard et al. (Norman, Okla: University of Oklahoma Press, 1983).

17. See various issues of the Texas Employment Commission's "Labor Market Review," especially those concerning their revised unemployment estimates since 1976. For national unemployment trends, see various issues of the Council of Economic Advisers, "Economic Indicators," U.S. Government Printing Office, Washington, D.C.

18. Data are directly from various issues of Texas Employment Commission, "Labor Market Review"; Heather Ball and J. Michael Patrick, "The Jobs of South Texas: Still Frozen," Texas Department

of Agriculture, Austin, 1985; and Miller and Maril, "Poverty in the Lower Rio Grande Valley."

19. For a discussion of the psychological problems which the unemployed must confront, see J. M. Borrero, "Psychological and Emotional Impact of Unemployment," *Journal of Sociology and Social Welfare* 7 (1980): 916–934. See the debate on the oil bust in Texas in *Texas in Transition*, ed. Michael L. Gillette (Austin, Texas: Lyndon Baines Johnson Library and Lyndon Baines Johnson School of Public Affairs, 1986).

20. For a discussion of how American poverty especially impacts women, see Barbara Ehrenreich and Frances Fox Piven, "The Feminization of Poverty," *Dissent* 31 (1984): 162–170. There is a clear presentation of the ways in which Mexican-American women are victimized by poverty in *Twice a Minority: Mexican-American Women*, ed. M. B. Melville (St. Louis, Mo.: C. V. Mosby, 1980). For a discussion of the impact of poverty on women and the young, see Ruth Sidel, *Women and Children Last* (New York: Penguin Books, 1986).

21. Data collected from the staff of the Texas Department of Human Services, Austin, Texas, February 1987.

22. For a brief history of federal support of the food stamp program, see M. MacDonald, "Food Stamps: An Analytical History," *Social Service Review* 51 (1977): 642–648. For a critique of the program, see N. Amidei, "Food Stamps: The Irony of Success," *Public Welfare* 39 (1981): 15–21. See also, Spencer Rich, "Census Bureau Tells Where Noncash Benefits Go," *Washington Post*, March 8, 1987.

23. See Robert Lee Maril, *Texas Shrimpers: Community, Capitalism and the Sea* (College Station, Texas: Texas A&M University Press, 1983).

24. See Texas Employment Commission, "Cameron County SDA," and "Hidalgo and Willacy Counties SDA."

25. In doing this, the Valley poor are no different than many other American poor. See N. C. Wyers, "Shame and Public Dependency: A Literature Review," *Journal of Sociology and Social Welfare* 4 (1977): 955–966.

26. Data from telephone communication with staff of Women's, Infants', and Children's Nutrition Program, Austin, Texas, March 1986.

27. Data from in-house documents of Texas State Department of Human Services, Brownsville, Texas. For a general discussion of problems with the AFDC program, see W. Bell and D. M. Bushe,

"The Economic Efficiency of AFDC," *Social Service Review* (1975): 175–190.

28. Data are from *General Social and Economic Characteristics, Part 45, Texas* and *County and City Data Book.*

29. This same point is discussed in greater detail in Miller and Maril, "Poverty in the Lower Rio Grande Valley."

30. Lower Rio Grande Valley Development Council, "Regional Housing Plan for Lower Rio Grande Valley," McAllen, 1978; Lower Rio Grande Valley Development Council, "Housing Data for the Lower Rio Grande Valley, 1970," McAllen, 1973; and Lower Rio Grande Valley Development Council, "Resources Handbook of the Lower Rio Grande Valley," McAllen, 1977.

31. U.S. Department of Commerce, *Census of the Population and Housing, 1983.*

32. See Lyndon Baines Johnson School of Public Affairs, "Colonias in the Lower Rio Grande Valley of South Texas," Policy Research Project no. 18, Austin, 1977.

33. Peggy Fikac, "Homes Rated Least Affordable" in *Brownsville Herald,* June 7, 1986.

34. Lower Rio Grande Valley Development Council, "Regional Housing Plan."

35. See J. Michael Patrick, "A Social and Economic Portrait of Colonia Residents: Living Outside of the Mainstream of American Life," Pan American University, August 1988.

36. See Lower Rio Grande Valley Development Council, "Assessment of Rural Sewage Disposal Practices / Management," McAllen, 1985.

37. Interview with J. Michael Patrick, Pan American University, Edinburg, Texas, July 1985.

38. Basilio Hernandez, *Brownsville Herald,* June 1, 1987.

39. Data from *County and City Data Book.* See Michael V. Miller, "The Impact of the 1982 Peso Devaluation on Crime in Texas Border Cities," *Journal of Borderland Studies* 1, no. 2 (1986): 1–23.

40. Michael V. Miller, "Vehicle Theft Along the Texas-Mexico Border," *Journal of Borderland Studies* 2, no. 2 (1987): 12–32.

2. BLOOD AND CASTE: FROM SPANISH COLONIZATION TO THE TWENTIETH CENTURY

1. See the work of Thomas R. Hester which includes "Tradition and Diversity Among the Prehistoric Hunters and Gatherers of

Southern Texas," *Plains Anthropologist* (1981): 119–128; "A Chronological Overview of Prehistoric Southern and South-Central Texas," in *Papers on the Prehistory of Northeastern Mexico and Adjacent Texas*, ed. Epstein, Hester, and Graves (San Antonio, Texas: Center for Archaeological Research, University of Texas at San Antonio, 1980); "Early Populations in Prehistoric Texas," *Archaeology* 32 (1979): 26–33; "The Archaeology of the Lower Rio Grande Valley of Texas," in *Proceedings, An Exploration of a Common Legacy: Conference on Border Architecture* (Austin, Texas: Texas Historical Commission, 1978), 66–77; "Hunters and Gatherers of the Rio Grande Plain and the Lower Coast of Texas" (San Antonio, Texas: Center for Archaeological Research, University of Texas at San Antonio, 1976); "Late Prehistoric Cultural Patterns Along the Rio Grande of Texas," in *Bulletin of the Texas Archaeological Research*, Special Report 1, University of Texas at San Antonio, San Antonio, 1975. See also W. W. Newcomb, Jr., *The Indians of Texas* (Austin, Texas: University of Texas Press, 1961). For an overview of the Indians who lived along the Rio Grande, see Paul Horgan, *Great River* (Austin, Texas: Texas Monthly Press, 1984).

2. See Hester, "Hunters and Gatherers."

3. See R. J. Mallouf et al., "A Predictive Assessment of Cultural Resources in Hidalgo and Willacy Counties, Texas," Office of the State Archaeologist, Archaeological Survey Report 23, Austin, 1977.

4. See M. B. Newton, "The Distribution and Character of Sites, Arroyo Los Olmos, Starr County, Texas," *Bulletin of the Texas Archaeological Society* 38 (1968): 18–24.

5. See Gene J. Paull, "Climatic Variations in the Lower Rio Grande Valley," *South Texas Journal of Research and the Humanities* 1 (1977): 6–28, for a complete discussion of weather in the Valley.

6. Much of the discussion of José de Escandon and the early Spanish explorers relies on Carlos E. Castaneda, *Our Catholic Heritage in Texas*, 7 vols. (Austin, Texas: Von Boekman Jones, 1936). See also Oakah L. Jones, Jr., *Los Paisanos: Spanish Settlers on the Northern Frontier of New Spain* (Norman, Okla.: University of Oklahoma Press, 1979); Lyle N. McAlister, *Spain and Portugal in the New World, 1492–1700,* (Minneapolis, Minn.: University of Minnesota Press, 1984); David J. Weber (ed.), *New Spain's Far Northern Frontier: Essays on Spain in the American West, 1540–1821* (Albuquerque, N.M.: University of New Mexico Press, 1979); and Robert S. Weddle, *Spanish Sea: The Gulf of Mexico in North American Discovery, 1500–1685* (College Station, Texas: Texas A&M University Press, 1985). Less helpful, but still of some interest are

Frank C. Pierce, *A Brief History of the Lower Rio Grande Valley* (Menasha, Wisc.: George Banta, 1917); J. Lee Stambaugh and Lillian J. Stambaugh, *The Lower Rio Grande Valley of Texas* (Austin, Texas: University of Texas Press, 1954), and Brian Robertson, *Wild Horse Desert* (Edinburg, Texas: New Santander Press, 1985).

7. Among others, see Jones, *Los Paisanos*, 65–82.

8. See, for instance, Jack Jackson, *Los Mesteños: Spanish Ranching in Texas, 1721–1820* (College Station, Texas: Texas A&M University Press, 1986).

9. This material is covered in detail in Jones, *Los Paisanos*, 68–69.

10. For a summary of how this system worked along the border, see Clark S. Knowlton, "Land Grants," in *Borderlands Sourcebook*, ed. Ellwyn R. Stoddard et al. (Norman, Okla.: University of Oklahoma Press, 1983), 111–116. See also Jackson, *Los Mesteños*, 443.

11. See the discussion of the adventures of Emmanuel Domenech in Horgan, *Great River*, 793–799.

12. Leroy P. Graf's comments are particularly illustrative in "The Economic History of the Lower Rio Grande Valley, 1820–1875," Ph.D. dissertation, Harvard University, 1942, as are the insights of Hester, "Late Prehistoric Cultural Patterns," and "Early Populations."

13. See Florence Johnson Scott, *Historical Heritage of the Lower Rio Grande* (San Antonio, Texas: Naylor, 1937); Sandra L. Myres, *The Ranch in Spanish Texas, 1691–1800* (El Paso, Texas: Texas Western Press, 1969); and Herbert Eugene Bolton, *Texas in the Middle Eighteenth Century* (Berkeley, Calif.: University of California Press, 1915).

14. The discussion of Indian attacks is based upon Myres, *Ranch in Spanish Texas*; Stambaugh and Stambaugh, *Lower Rio Grande Valley*; Pierce, *Brief History*; Bolton, *Texas in Middle Eighteenth Century*; Paul S. Taylor, *An American-Mexican Frontier: Nueces County, Texas* (Chapel Hill, N.C.: University of North Carolina Press, 1934); Emilia Schunior Ramierez, *Ranch Life in Hidalgo County After 1850* (Edinburg, Texas: New Santander Press, 1963); and Scott, *Historical Heritage*.

15. See, among others, Manuel A. Machado, *Listen Chicano: An Informal History of the Mexican American* (Chicago: Nelan-Hall, 1978); Matt S. Meier and Feliciano Rivera, *The Chicanos: A History of Mexican Americans* (New York: Hill and Wang, 1972); and Rodolfo Acuna, *Occupied America: The Chicano Struggle Toward Liberation* (San Francisco: Canfield Press, 1972). See also W. H. Chatfield, *The Twin Cities of the Border* (Edinburg, Texas: Hidalgo County Historical

Museum, 1982); Oscar J. Martinez, *Border Boom Town* (Austin, Texas: University of Texas Press, 1978); and Robert J. Casey, *The Texas Border* (Indianapolis: Bobbs-Merrill, 1950).

16. See Taylor, *American-Mexican Frontier*, and Evan Anders, *Boss Rule in South Texas* (Austin, Texas: University of Texas Press, 1979).

17. See Taylor, *American-Mexican Frontier*.

18. Ibid.

19. See James A. Irby, *Backdoor at Bagdad: The Civil War on the Rio Grande* (El Paso, Texas: Texas Western Press, 1977).

20. See T.R. Fehrenbach. *Lone Star* (New York: Macmillan, 1975).

21. Much of this discussion relies on Fehrenbach, *Lone Star*, 507–534.

22. See Horgan, *Great River*, 789.

23. See Anders, *Boss Rule*; Stambaugh and Stambaugh, *Lower Rio Grande Valley*; Casey, *Texas Border*; Taylor, *American-Mexican Frontier*; and Pierce, *Brief History*, among others.

24. There is currently a small effort in Brownsville to rename the city Cortinaville in honor of Cortina.

25. See Graf, "Economic History," 436.

26. See the introduction to Anders, *Boss Rule*; Fehrenbach, *Lone Star*; Graf, "Economic History," 450; and Taylor, *American-Mexican Frontier*.

27. See Ramirez, *Ranch Life in Hidalgo County*.

28. See Anders, *Boss Rule*, and Fehrenbach, *Lone Star*.

29. See Anders, *Boss Rule*, 6.

30. The discussion on bossism relies heavily on Anders, *Boss Rule*.

31. See Graf, "Economic History," especially 450–457.

32. Jovita Gonzales describes these social affairs in detail in "Social Life in Cameron, Starr, and Zapata Counties," Masters Thesis, University of Texas, 1930, 50–62.

3. ECONOMIC DEVELOPMENT, RACISM, AND THE GROWTH OF POVERTY

1. There have been few, if any, American political systems which totally dominated a population. See, for instance, George Rawick, *The American Slave: A Composite Biography* (Westport, Conn.: Glenwood, 1972).

2. Much of this discussion is based upon interviews with two of the original Valley land developers.

3. See Graf, "Economic History."

4. See, among others, John R. Peavey, *Echoes from the Rio Grande* (Brownsville, Texas: Springman-King, 1963).

5. From oral histories taken by Maria B. Longoria and Jesus Garcia under the supervision of Manuel Medrano.

6. From an oral history taken by Jesus Garcia.

7. Ibid.

8. Ibid.

9. See examples of those who were able, in spite of considerable constraints, to improve their economic status in Douglas E. Foley et al., "From Peones to Politicos: Ethnic Relations in a South Texas Town, 1900 to 1977" (Austin, Texas: University of Texas Center for Mexican American Studies, Monograph no. 3, 1977). However, these exceptions do not disprove the rule, rather they document in some detail the difficulties that all Mexican and Mexican-American workers faced at that time, not just from Anglos, but from the small affluent Hispanic elite.

10. Paul S. Taylor, *Mexican Labor in the U.S.: Dimitt County, Winter Garden District, South Texas* (Berkeley, Calif.: University of California Press, 1930).

11. John D. Weaver, *The Brownsville Raid* (New York: W.W. Norton, 1970).

12. See Evan Anders, *Boss Rule.*

13. Ibid.

14. The relationship between the Valley agricultural elite, private water corporations, and the development of Valley lands is a rich area for future research. Such an effort would necessarily explore the role of the Valley's Watermaster.

15. Peavy, *Echoes from the Rio Grande.*

16. See Julian Samora, *Gunpowder Justice: A Reassessment of the Texas Rangers* (Notre Dame, Ind.: University of Notre Dame Press, 1978). For a contrasting view, see autobiographical works such as Peavy, *Echoes from the Rio Grande.* See also Fehrenbach, *Lone Star.*

17. See Juan Gomez-Quinones, "Plan de San Diego Reviewed," *Aztlan* (Spring 1970): 124–132, and Charles C. Cumberland, "Border Raids in the Rio Grande Valley, 1915," *Southwestern Historical Quarterly* (January 1954).

18. Anders, *Boss Rule,* 225.

19. J. Gonzales, "Social Life in Cameron, Starr, and Zapata Counties," 108–109.

20. It has not been unusual in the history of American law enforcement to employ minority law enforcement officers to oppress their own racial or ethnic group.

21. Taylor, *American-Mexican Frontier*.

22. See Carey McWilliams, *North From Mexico* (New York: Greenwood, 1968), 87.

23. See Arthur J. Rubel, *Across the Tracks* (Austin, Texas: University of Texas Press, 1966).

24. Gonzales, "Social Life in Cameron, Starr, and Zapata Counties," 98–99.

25. Ibid.

26. See Stuart Jamieson, "Labor Unionism in American Agriculture," Bureau of Labor Statistics Bulletin No. 836, U.S. Government Printing Office, Washington, D.C., 1945.

27. See discussions in Taylor, *Mexican Labor in the U.S.*, and *American-Mexican Frontier*; O. D. Week, "The Texas-Mexican and the Politics of South Texas," *American Political Science Review* (August 1930): 606–627; McWilliams, *North from Mexico*; Leo Grebler et al., *The Mexican-American People: The Nation's Second Largest Minority* (New York: Free Press, 1970); David Montejano, "Race, Labor Repression, and Capitalistic Agriculture: Notes from South Texas, 1920–30," Institute for the Study of Social Change, Berkeley, Calif., 1970; Samora, *Gunpowder Justice*; and Anders, *Boss Rule*.

28. See chapter five for a detailed discussion of this landmark case. Also see *Allee v. Medrano* in *United States Reports*, vol. 416, "Cases Adjudged in the Supreme Court at October Term, 1973" (Washington, D.C.: U.S. Government Printing Office, 1975). A detailed history of the Valley's farm labor movement from the 1920s to the present is seriously needed.

29. For a more general description, see Ellwyn R. Stoddard, *Mexican Americans* (New York: Random House, 1973).

30. This discussion is based in part upon information from interviews with three Cameron County politicians.

31. This topic is further discussed in chapter four.

32. See Miller and Maril, "Poverty in the Lower Rio Grande Valley."

33. See John McBride, *The Vanishing Bracero: Valley Revolution* (San Antonio, Texas: Naylor, 1963). See also *Mexican Workers in the United States: Historical and Political Perspectives*, ed. George C.

Kiser and Martha Woody Kiser (Albuquerque, N.M.: University of New Mexico Press, 1979).

34. See Ernesto Galarza's *Merchants of Labor: The Mexican Bracero Story* (Santa Barbara, Calif.: McNally and Lofton, 1964) and his *Spiders in the House and Workers in the Fields* (Notre Dame, Ind.: University of Notre Dame Press, 1970).

35. See Stoddard, "Patterns of Poverty," and Miller and Maril, "Poverty in the Lower Rio Grande Valley."

36. For the most recent comprehensive treatment, see Ellwyn R. Stoddard, *Maquila.* (El Paso, Texas: Texas Western Press, 1987).

37. See Michael V. Miller and James D. Preston, "Vertical Ties and the Redistribution of Power in Crystal City," *Social Science Quarterly* 53 (1973): 772–784, and Michael V. Miller, "Chicano Community Control in South Texas," *Journal of Ethnic Studies,* no. 3, (1975): 70–89.

38. See the film documentary "Strangers in Their Own Land: The Chicanos," written and directed by Hope Ryan, produced by ABC News, and narrated by the late Frank Reynolds.

39. Alonzo Lopez and Efrain Fernandez were both college-educated Hispanics involved in voter registration drives in Pharr and surrounding Hidalgo County cities. Alonzo Lopez, a teacher corpsman with no previous criminal record, was quickly tried by a predominantly Anglo jury which found him guilty as charged, and received a five year prison sentence. His sentence was later changed to five years of closely supervised probation. Efrain Fernandez was tried six months later, after the Anglo hysteria subsided. He was found not guilty.

The Anglo deputy sheriff who shot and killed the bystander was no-billed by a grand jury and, since that time, has been active in Valley law enforcement. The long-time Hidalgo County prosecutor who handled the case that resulted in a conviction against Alonzo Lopez was, a decade later, charged with conspiring to kill his girl-friend's ex-husband. He was fired from his position as County Prosecutor, disbarred, but later regained his license to practice law and ran again for the position of Hidalgo County District Attorney. He lost, but he did garner considerable support in the election.

The city of Pharr has never been the same. The Anglo mayor was not re-elected after the police riot. A Mexican-American majority gained control of the Pharr city government for the first time in the history of the community (Pharr is 87 percent Mexican-American). The police chief, a Mexican American, who made crucial decisions during the riot, was fired and a Mexican American who represented the interests of the majority of Hispanics took his place.

40. There is evidence to suggest that Valley Hispanics who migrate to other regions of the United States achieve less upward mobility than other Hispanics in the same urban areas. See Lyle W. Shannon, *Minority Migrants in the Urban Community*, (Beverly Hills, Calif.: Sage Publications, 1973).

4. INDUSTRY, RESOURCES, AND THE LABOR FORCE: THE VALLEY AS AN INTERNAL COLONY

1. From Rio Grande Valley Chamber of Commerce, "Valley 2000," Rio Grande Valley Chamber of Commerce, Weslaco, July 1985, p. 19.

2. Ball and Patrick, "Jobs of South Texas."

3. See Texas Crop and Livestock Reporting Service (TCLRS), "1984 Texas County Statistics," Texas Department of Agricultural and U.S. Department of Agriculture, Austin, 1985, for a general overview. For specific information on particular crops, see TCLRS, "1984 Texas Vegetable Statistics," TDA and USDA, Austin, 1985; TCLRS, "1984 Field Crop Statistics," TDA and USDA, Austin, 1985; and TCLRS, "1985 Texas Small Grains Statistics," TDA and USDA, Austin, 1986. I would like to thank the staff at the Texas A&M Extension Service in Weslaco for their help.

4. Data from Rio Grande Valley Chamber of Commerce, "Valley 2000."

5. See TCLRS, "1984 Field Crop Statistics."

6. TCLRS, "1984 Texas Fruit and Pecan Statistics," TDA and USDA, Austin, 1985.

7. Ball and Patrick, "Jobs of South Texas."

8. See TCLRS, "1984 Field Crop Statistics."

9. See Rio Grande Valley Chamber of Commerce, "Valley 2000," 34.

10. See TCLRS, "1984 Texas Livestock, Dairy, and Poultry Statistics," TDA and USDA, Austin, 1985. See, also, Texas Agricultural Experiment Station, "Integrated Brush Management Systems for South Texas: Development and Implementation," Texas Agricultural Experiment Station, Texas A&M University, College Station, no date of publication.

11. Ball and Patrick, "Jobs of South Texas," 13–18.

12. These comments are based upon interviews with Valley bankers, farmers, and Valley agricultural experts. A precise analysis of the ownership of Valley agriculture is needed.

13. Ball and Patrick, "Jobs of South Texas," 13–14. Foreign investors comprise a majority of these grove owners.

14. David Caplovitz, *The Poor Pay More: Consumer Practices of Low Income Families* (New York, MacMillan, 1963).

15. Rio Grande Valley Chamber of Commerce, "Valley 2000," 28.

16. See Texas Employment Commission, "Cameron County SDA."

17. Rio Grande Valley Chamber of Commerce, 1985, 30.

18. To what extent the Valley's wholesale trade is directly tied to the Mexican economy in the 1980s remains more a matter of conjecture than analysis. Future research should explore this topic in depth.

19. See Robert Lee Maril, *Cannibals and Condos: Texans and Texas Along the Gulf Coast* (College Station, Texas: Texas A&M Press, 1986), 99–106, and Robert Lee Maril, "Continuity and Change in a South Texas Fishing Community," unpublished paper, Department of Behavioral Science, Texas Southmost College, 1982.

20. See Maril, *Texas Shrimpers,* 75–97.

21. For a history of Port Brownsville, see Henry Ferguson, *The Port of Brownsville* (Brownsville, Texas: Springman King Press, 1976).

22. See Miller and Maril, "Poverty in the Lower Rio Grande Valley," 10–18.

23. See table 4, "Covered Employment by Valley Labor Force, 1980, 1984," in Texas Employment Commission, 1986.

24. See Economic Development Council, "The McAllen 1985–1986 Annual Economic Report," McAllen Chamber of Commerce, McAllen, 1985, p. 16.

25. For a complete discussion of this issue, see S. A. Levitan and R. S. Belous, *More than Subsistence: Minimum Wages for the Working Poor* (Baltimore, Md.: Johns Hopkins University Press, 1979).

26. Interview with James Herrman, attorney, on lawsuits stemming from the impact of pesticides and herbicides on Valley farm workers.

27. Since 1980 the number and quality of studies on the Border Industrialization Program have substantially increased. See Stoddard, *Maquilla;* Maria Patricia Fernandez-Kelly, *For We Are Sold, I and My People: Women in Mexico's Frontier* (Albany, N.Y.: State University of New York Press, 1983); C. Daniel Dillman, "Border Industrialization," in *Borderlands Sourcebook,* ed. Ellwyn R. Stoddard et al. (Norman, Okla.: University of Oklahoma Press, 1983); and

Niles Hansen, *The Border Economy: Regional Development in the Southwest* (Austin, Texas: University of Texas Press, 1981).

28. For a discussion of the historical development of maquiladoras along the border, see Stoddard, *Maquilla* 1–26.

29. R. Daniel Cavazos, "Official Warns Maquiladora Battle Not Over Yet," *Brownsville Herald,* July 19, 1987.

30. At this writing a study by the International Trade Commission on the impact of tariff breaks to maquiladoras upon American employment and production is underway. The findings of the study may do much to clarify the economic impact of the maquiladora. Still, the specific impacts of maquiladoras on the Valley's poverty economy require examination.

31. See Stoddard, *Maquilla,* 42–66.

32. Cavazos' most recent demands for his union were met when he threatened a strike for December 15, 1987. See Tony Vindell, "Matamoras Labor Leaders Threaten to Go On Strike," *Brownsville Herald,* November 30, 1987.

33. See Stoddard, *Maquilla,* 51–52, and Anthony N. Zavaleta, "A Study of the Unique Factors Affecting Quality of Work Life in the Bicultural Environment at RIMIR, S.A. de C.V. Matamoros, Tamaulipas," United States-Mexico Border Research Associates, Brownsville, 1981. A visit in April of 1985 to the General Motors plant in Matamoros lends support to Stoddard's assertions. The plant, only a few years old, was very clean; safety and working conditions, at least to the untrained eye, seemed reasonable. The work that this shift of 800 women was involved in provided an income which was vital for their livelihood. While the workers were either repeatedly soldering electronic components or assembling them, Stoddard and others have found in their surveys of Mexican workers that there is very little worker dissatisfaction.

However, I have no way of knowing how typical this plant was of other plants in the region. I have been told by local businessmen that this plant is the best of the local maquiladoras. Access to other plants is restricted.

34. See Stoddard, *Maquilla,* 51–52.

35. The Mexican Census is traditionally unreliable. Estimates of the current population in Matamoros and Reynosa are from interviews with Brownsville and McAllen city planners.

36. These observations are based in part upon approximately forty interviews with undocumented Mexicans working on Texas shrimp trawlers in Port Isabel and Port Brownsville in 1979. See Maril, *Texas Shrimpers,* 39. Since 1979 I have monitored this work

force. See also Alejandro Portes and Robert L. Bach, *Latin Journey: Cuban and Mexican Immigrants in the United States* (Berkeley, Calif.: University of California Press, 1985); Vernon M. Briggs et al., *The Chicano Worker* (Austin, Texas: University of Texas Press, 1977); and Michael J. Piore, *Birds of Passage: Migrant Labor and Industrial Societies* (New York: Cambridge University Press, 1979).

37. On a rare visit to Matamoros and Reynosa on July 9, 1987, Mexican President Miguel de la Madrid stated, "We can't talk about an economic crisis along the border anymore." See Hector F. Garza-Trejo, "De la Madrid Says Maquillas Help Border," *Brownsville Herald,* July 10, 1987.

38. Allan G. King et al., "The Effects of Hispanic Immigrants on the Earnings of Native Hispanic Americans," *Social Science Quarterly* 67 (1986): 673–689, argues to the contrary. Their data, however, are based upon the 1970 Census and do not identify specific regions which would, I assert, show a greater diversity of impacts than suggested. A number of others have discussed the impact of Mexican undocumented workers on unionization, wage levels, and a variety of other issues. Among those are Lamar B. Jones, "Mexican American Labor Problems in Texas," Ph.D. dissertation, University of Texas, Austin, 1965; Vernon M. Briggs, *Chicanos and Rural Poverty* (Baltimore, Md.: Johns Hopkins University Press, 1973), and F. Ray Marshall, "Economic Factors Influencing the International Migration of Workers," in *Views Across the Border: The United States and Mexico,* ed. Stanley R. Ross (Albuquerque, N.M.: University of New Mexico Press, 1978). Also see Barton Smith and Robert Newman, "Depressed Wages Along the U.S.-Mexico Border: An Empirical Analysis," in *Economic Inquiry,* January 1977.

39. See Economic Development Council, "McAllen Annual Report," 14.

40. See Louis Dubose, "Toxic Cloud in Texas City," *Texas Observer,* December 18, 1987.

41. Tony Videll, "Matamoros Landfill May Contaminate Area," *Brownsville Herald,* March 4, 1988.

42. In November 1983 Scott Lind, a reporter for the *McAllen Monitor,* was arrested in a Reynosa restaurant where he was having dinner with a few friends. Lind had that same day been covering the arrests by Reynosa municipal police of workers protesting the low wages paid at the Zenith plant, one of the many maquiladoras in the border city. The hunger strikers were carried or dragged to waiting ambulances as Lind watched and made notes. After his arrest, Lind was blindfolded, handcuffed, and tortured at the police station.

"During four hours of interrogation, I received electric shocks to my neck, the groin area, and my legs...They would periodically strike me on the ears and on the side of the face while asking me who I had talked to that day. The faceless interrogator told me... 'if you cooperate with us, you will be crossing the bridge within thirty minutes back to the United States. But if you don't, something very bad will happen to you. You'll be swimming face down in the river. Your hands will be tied behind your back. Your legs will be tied with rope. No one will ever see you again. They think you're already back in the United States. No one knows you're here.'" In order to get released, Lind signed a forced confession. (As cited in *The Progressive,* November 1984, p. 15, and from an interview with staff at the *McAllen Monitor,* January 4, 1989.)

43. Valley business leaders have formed an organization, the Border Trade Alliance, to boost the image of border maquiladoras. They also are concerned that Congress will pass legislation unfavorable to the maquiladoras.

44. See Maril, "Continuity and Change in Fishing Community."

45. See Martinez, *Border Boom Town,* for an excellent discussion of the impact of American tourism on Juarez, Mexico.

46. Since the mid-1970s William Rush at Pan American University, Edinburg, has been studying Valley winter tourists. See William Rush, "A Study of Winter Tourists," Business Research Institute, Pan American University at Edinburg, 1977. See also Rio Grande Chamber of Commerce, "Valley 2000."

47. Maril, "Continuity and Change in Fishing Community," and *Texas Shrimpers.*

48. Data from South Padre Island Chamber of Commerce.

49. See U.S. Army Corps of Engineers, "Galveston District and Texas Water Commission, Public Notice SWGCO-RP, Permit Application 17714 (Revised)," for a complete description of the planned project.

50. Personal communication with Donald Hockaday, Pan American University Coastal Lab, South Padre Island, June 17, 1987.

51. Data from Economic Development Council, "McAllen Annual Report."

52. See chapter seven for a more detailed discussion of this topic.

53. Tourism also drives up the costs of food and other consumer items in the Valley. I cannot statistically demonstrate the validity of this observation; it awaits further research efforts.

54. Maril, "Cannibals and Condos."

55. See Rio Grande Valley Chamber of Commerce, "Valley 2000." A part of this decrease in tourism could be attributed to Mexican tourists adversely affected by the peso devaluations.

56. See Maril, *Texas Shrimpers,* for an elaboration of this discussion.

57. National Marine Fisheries Services, "Fisheries of the United States, 1984," U.S. Department of Commerce, National Oceanic and Atmospheric Administration, Washington, D.C., 1985.

58. Since 1979 I have collected a sample of annual wages from shrimpers at Port Isabel and Port Brownsville.

59. Maril, *Texas Shrimpers.*

60. Ibid., 53–71.

61. Ibid., 186–198.

62. Robert Lee Maril, "The Arbitrary Enforcement of the Lacey Act," a paper presented at the annual meeting of the Rural Sociology Society, College Station, Texas, 1984, and Ben M. Crouch and T. Mark Miller, "Lacey Act Enforcement in the Texas Gulf: A Sociological Analysis," draft of an unpublished paper, Department of Sociology, Texas A&M University, College Station, 1987.

63. Maril, *Texas Shrimpers,* 54.

64. Ibid., 63.

65. I worked as a consultant on this project.

66. See especially William Madsen, *The Mexican Americans of South Texas* (New York: Holt, Rinehart, Winston, 1964) and Rubel, *Across the Tracks.* In contrast, see William P. Kuvlesky et al., "Status Projections and Ethnicity: A Comparision of Mexican American, Negro, and Anglo Youth," *Journal of Vocational Behavior* (April 1971), and William Kuvlesky and Rumaldo Z. Juarez, "Mexican-American Youth and the American Dream," in *Career Behavior of Special Groups,* ed. J. Steven Picou and Robert E. Campbell (Columbus, Ohio: Charles E. Merrill, 1975). Also see Michael V. Miller, "Variations in Mexican-American Family Life: A Review Synthesis of Empirical Research," *Aztlan* (Spring 1977).

67. See William Ryan, *Blaming the Victim* (New York: Random House, 1971).

68. Data from R. Daniel Cavazos, "Officials to Investigate High Gas Prices," *Brownsville Herald,* January 18, 1987. An historical survey of Valley gas prices compared to state and national prices should be done.

69. See Rio Grande Chamber of Commerce, "Valley 2000," p. 16.

70. See Texas Employment Commission, "Cameron County SDA."

71. See Mike Swartz, "Valley Banks Below Average Lending," *Brownsville Herald,* April 8, 1986.

72. This information is based in part upon an interview with a Valley banker who wished to remain anonymous. A detailed study of the loan practices of Valley banks is seriously needed.

73. See Texas Employment Commission, "Cameron County SDA."

74. See Antonio N. Zavaleta, "Federal Assistance and Mexican-American Health Status in Texas," *Health* (Jan.-Feb. 1981): 19–25.

75. I am not suggesting that anyone who is affluent in Starr County is associated with illegal drugs, but that much of the affluence in this poverty-stricken county has been and is directly or indirectly associated with illegal drugs and/or smuggling.

76. Graf, "Economic History."

77. "The Rio Grande Valley may have replaced Florida as the no. 1 entry point into the United States for illegal drugs, local officials say" (Jennifer Dixon, "Valley's Border Area Top Smuggling Point," *Brownsville Herald,* January 11, 1987). See also "Dope Economy Providing Jobs," *Brownsville Herald,* February 16, 1987, which estimates that the illegal drug industry employs 10,000 people in South and West Texas.

78. See Mario Barrera, *Race and Class in the Southwest* (Notre Dame, Ind.: University of Notre Dame Press, 1979).

5. "LIKE ALWAYS, EDDIE, LIKE ALWAYS": POLITICS, JOBS, AND LIVES

1. From an oral history taken by Jesus Garcia.

2. For a general discussion of American elites and representative government, see G. William Domhoff, *Who Really Rules?* (Santa Monica, Calif.: Goodyear Publishing Co., 1978) and C. Wright Mills, *The Power Elite* (New York: Oxford University Press, 1956). For a contrasting view, see Arnold M. Rose, *The Power Structure* (London: Oxford University Press, 1967). For discussions of the difficulties Mexican Americans have faced in participating in politics, see Rudolph O. de la Garza, "Voting Patterns in Bi-cultural El Paso," *Aztlan* 5 (1974): 235–260; Donald M. Freeman, "Party, Vote, and the Mexican American in South Tucson," in *La Causa Politica,* ed. F. Chris Garcia (Notre Dame, Ind.: University of Notre Dame Press, 1974), 55–66;

and John Staples Shockley, *Chicano Revolt in a Texas Town* (Notre Dame, Ind.: University of Notre Dame, 1974). For a more general discussion of this same topic, see McWilliams, *North From Mexico*. Relevant community studies include Oscar J. Martinez, *The Chicanos of El Paso* (El Paso, Texas: Texas Western Press, 1986); S. Achor, *Mexican Americans in a Dallas Barrio* (Tucson, Ariz.: University of Arizona Press, 1978); R. Horowitz, *Honor and the American Dream: Culture and Identity in a Chicano Community* (New Brunswick, N.J.: Rutgers University Press, 1983); Miller, "Poverty, Development, and Quality of Life," and Benjamin Marquez, *Power and Politics in a Chicano Barrio* (New York: University Press of America, 1985).

3. The manipulation of the Mexican-American vote is not unique to the Valley. For general discussions of Mexican-American voting patterns, see Maurilio Vigil, *Chicano Politics* (Washington D.C.: University Press of America, 1977) and Rudolph Gomez, "The Politics of the Mexican-United States Border," in *Views Across the Border: The United States and Mexico,* ed. Stanley R. Ross (Albuquerque, N.M.: University of New Mexico Press, 1978), 386–389. For a discussion of the ways in which Mexican Americans have been systematically disenfranchised, see Clifton McCleskey and Bruce Merrill, "Mexican-American Political Behavior in Texas," *Social Science Quarterly* 53 (1973): 785–799 and Dan Nimmo and Clifton McCleskey, "Impact of the Poll Tax on Voter Participation: The Houston Metropolitan Area in 1966," *Journal of Politics* 31 (1969): 682–699. Roberto E. Villarreal contributes an excellent overview of Mexican-American voting with his "Political Activity and Voting," in *Borderlands Sourcebook,* ed. Ellwyn R. Stoddard et al. (Norman, Okla.: University of Oklahoma Press, 1983), 224–227.

4. Compare Samora, *Gunpowder Justice,* to the view of Walter Prescott Webb, *The Texas Rangers: A Century of Frontier Defense* (Austin, Texas: University of Texas Press, 1965). See also Clifford Alan Perkins and C.L. Sonnichesen, *Border Patrol* (El Paso, Texas: Texas Western Press, 1978). Marshall Carter's essay "Law Enforcement," in *Borderlands Sourcebook,* 214–216, presents an excellent overview of law enforcement along the border.

5. For recent voting data of Texas border counties, see Armando Gutierrez, "The Politics of the Texas Border: An Historical Overview and Some Contemporary Directions," in *Views Across the Border,* ed. Stanley R. Ross (Albuquerque, N.M.: University of New Mexico Press, 1978), 117–137.

6. See Lyle W. Shannon, *Minority Migrants in the Urban Community* (Beverly Hills, Calif.: Sage, 1973).

7. According to Armando Guttierrez, "Politics of the Texas Border," from one-half to three-quarters of all eligible voters in 1970 in Texas border counties were not registered. Registered voters in Cameron, Hidalgo, and Starr Counties accounted for 34, 34, and 46 percent, respectively, of the total population. Of those few who registered in Cameron County, 46 percent actually voted, as compared to 48 percent in Hidalgo and 66 percent in Starr. See also Nimmo and McCleskey, "Impact of Poll Tax on Voter Participation," and Clifton McCleskey and Dan Nimmo, "Differences Between Potential Registered and Actual Voters: The Houston Metropolitan Area in 1969," *Social Science Quarterly* 49 (1968): 103–114.

8. For a more detailed discussion of this topic, see Robert Lee Maril, "Towards a Media Theory of the Lower Rio Grande Valley," *South Texas Journal of Research and the Humanities,* 1, (Fall 1976): 32–41.

9. In 1975, I worked at the *Valley Morning Star* in Harlingen. For three days I stood at the AP and UPI wire machines, rolled the news onto a little spool, and carried it to the editor's desk. The editor fed this computer tape directly to the printer. The front page of the paper was always, word for word, news as reported by the wire services. The back page was "local news," which consisted of announcements of meetings and other local events. The rest of the newspaper, except for large sports and social events sections, was filler and ads. I finally asked the editor when I was going to write a story. I was told that their reporters did not write stories unless they covered the high school sports beat. One reporter with two years experience was allowed to phone City Hall regularly and report the news that the public information officer gave to him.

10. Maril, "Towards a Media Theory."

11. See Stuart L. Hills, *Demystifying Social Deviance* (New York: McGraw-Hill, 1980) for a complete discussion of this topic. Also helpful is Ronald L. Akers et al., "Social Learning and Deviant Behavior," *American Sociological Review* 44 (1979): 635–655.

12. In 1978 I co-authored a preliminary study of poverty in the Valley. I received considerable negative feedback about the study, not only from the general public but from some friends and colleagues as well. I found myself in arguments with peers about whether poverty in the Valley was, in fact, a serious problem. Gradually I began to question the results of my study. Maybe the data were wrong; maybe the census materials and other secondary data were based upon biased questions. The power of peer pressure to bring a potential "troublemaker" into line should not be underemphasized.

13. See Miguel David Tirado, "Mexican-American Community Political Organizations: The Key to Chicano Political Power," in *La Causa Politica*, ed. F. Chris Garcia (Notre Dame, Ind.: University of Notre Dame Press, 1974), 105–127.

14. Much of this discussion is based upon interviews with farm workers who participated in the strike or those who represented their legal interests. See also David Montejano, "The Demise of Jim Crow," *Texas Observer* 79 (1987): 8–13.

15. For a historical discussion of the Church's involvement with social concerns in South Texas, see Grebler et al., *Mexican-American People,* 449–485.

16. United States Government Printing Office, *The United States Reports*, vol. 416, 806–808, Washington, D.C., 1975.

17. For a discussion of the Brown Berets, see Grebler et al., *Mexican-American People,* 553–554.

18. See Gutierrez, "Politics of the Texas Border," 128.

19. See Saul Alinsky, *Rules for Radicals* (New York: Vintage Books, 1972).

20. See Maril, *Cannibals and Condos*, 80–89.

21. For a discussion of Mexican-American elites see, among others, Julian Samora, "Minority Leadership in a Bi-racial Cultural Community," Ph.D. dissertation, University Microfilm, Ann Arbor, Michigan, 1953; John R. Martinez, "Leadership and Politics," in *La Raza: Forgotten Americans*, ed. Julian Samora (Notre Dame, Ind: University of Notre Dame Press, 1966); and Juan Ramos, "Spanish-Speaking Leadership in Two Southwestern Cities: A Descriptive Study," Ph.D. dissertation, Brandeis University, 1968.

6. THE MISEDUCATION OF THE POOR

1. The education of Valley Mexican Americans compares unfavorably to other Texas Mexican Americans. For a discussion of how Mexican Americans have fared in education throughout Texas, see U.S. Commission on Civil Rights, Report 4, "Mexican-American Education in Texas: A Function of Wealth," Mexican-American Education Study, 1973. For a national perspective, see Thomas P. Carter and Roberto D. Segura, *Mexican Americans in School: A Decade of Change* (New York: College Entrance Examination Board, 1979); *Educating the Mexican American*, ed. Henry S. Johnson and William J. Hernandez-M. (Valley Forge, Penn.: Judson Press, 1970); and Grebler et al., *Mexican-American People*, 102–103.

2. Bureau of the Census, *Statistical Abstracts of the United States, 1985*, p. 443. See also G. D. Squires, *Education and Jobs: The Imbalance of the Social Machinery* (New Brunswick, N.J.: Transaction Books, 1979).

3. See Christopher Jencks et al., *Inequality* (New York: Basic Books, 1972).

4. See Jules Henry, *Culture Against Man*, (New York: Random House, 1965), 181–182.

5. Much of the discussion on education in Cameron County prior to 1900 relies on J. Gonzales, "Social Life in Cameron, Starr, and Zapata Counties," and Peter Gawenda, "Brownsville's Public Schools One Century Ago, 1875–1905," in *Studies in Brownsville History*, ed. Milo Kearney (Brownsville, Texas: Pan American University at Brownsville, 1986), 190–200.

6. See W. H. Chatfield, *Twin Cities of the Border*, for comments on early problems with education in Brownsville.

7. Gawenda, "Brownsville's Public Schools, 1875–1905."

8. Ibid., 192.

9. See the collection of "The Palmetto" in the Hunter Room of Texas Southmost College Library, Brownsville.

10. See Rubel, *Across the Tracks*.

11. See Anders, *Boss Rule*, 14–15.

12. Gawenda, "Brownsville's Public Schools, 1875–1905."

13. Mark Williams, "Mechanic Teachers Frustrated by TECAT," in *Brownsville Herald*, August 28, 1986.

14. Peggy Fikac, "Report Shows PAU Graduates Did Worse in EXCET," in *Brownsville Herald*, December 17, 1986.

15. A student is defined as "mastering" the mathematics section of the test in 1986 if he correctly answers only 50 percent or more of the questions. To master the language arts section, including parts which test one's ability in reading and writing skills, the student need answer correctly 62 percent of the questions.

16. See Robert R. Galvan, *Bilingualism As It Relates to Intelligence Test Scores and School Achievement Among Culturally-deprived Spanish-American Children* (New York: Arno Press, 1978). TEAMS tests probably still retain some cultural bias against low-income Mexican-American students in the Valley. Valley students, however, score low on these tests because they do not have the skills, including skills at taking tests, that other students have obtained. See also, Meyer Weinberg, *A Chance to Learn: A History of Race and Education in the United States* (Cambridge: Cambridge University Press, 1977). At my own school, which operated in Brownsville from 1981 to 1984,

Mexican-American students often scored substantially higher than previously on standardized tests after only one year of preparation by competent teachers in classes of twenty or less.

17. BISD and other Valley school systems are not the only reason that the young lack the necessary skills to thrive in their communities, but the public school system is one of the most crucial problems. One must also examine the kinds of family support that students receive. I am aware of only one Valley school system that has taken any serious steps to involve families in the education of their children.

18. See Celestino Fernandez, "Education," in *Borderlands Sourcebook*, ed. Ellwyn Stoddard et al. (Norman, Okla.: University of Oklahoma Press, 1983), 257–258. This essay provides an excellent review of the literature on education along the U.S.-Mexico border.

19. There is an extensive literature on bilingual education. See D. E. Lopez, "The Social Consequences of Chicano Home/School Bilingualism," *Social Problems* 24 (1976): 234–246; and Guadalupe San Miguel, Jr., "Conflict and Controversy in the Evolution of Bilingual Education in the United States," in *The Mexican American Experience*, ed. Rudolph O. de la Garza et al. (Austin, Texas: University of Texas Press, 1985). Also see George Borjas and Maria Tienda, *Hispanics in the U.S. Economy* (New York: Academic Press, 1985).

20. Many BISD bilingual teachers who speak Spanish fluently are unable to teach students how to read or write well in Spanish. It is not unusual for these same teachers to lack similar skills in English. Some of BISD's best bilingual teachers have been lured to other school districts in Dallas and Houston by higher salaries. Not surprisingly, BISD administrators show no interest in the results of studies of their bilingual program by independent social scientists.

21. For a discussion of this topic, see S. L. Lightfoot, *Worlds Apart: Relationships Between Families and Schools* (New York: Basic Books, 1978).

22. See F. Chris Garcia, *Political Socialization of Chicano Children: A Comparative Study with Anglos in California Schools* (New York: Praeger, 1972).

23. For a discussion of the impact of the tracking system upon minorities, see T. J. Cottle, "What Tracking Did to Ollie Taylor," *Social Science* 5(1974): 21–24.

24. The most significant protest in 1987 against school officials at BISD occurred when about 100 students at one of the high schools walked out of their afternoon classes. Students said they were mad

because their spring vacation was not scheduled in conjunction with a rock concert at South Padre Island. The students returned to class the next day.

25. See Drop-Out Task Force Number 2, "Subcommittee on School Climate Status Quo Report," March 1987, Brownsville Independent School District, Brownsville, Texas.

26. See Litte Chow, "School Drop-Outs Increasing Problem," in *Valley Morning Star,* June 1, 1986. Also, see Mark Williams, "School Officials Looking for Disappearing Students," in *Brownsville Herald,* June 1, 1986. BISD has never had any way to accurately document the number of students who quit school, nor have the majority of other school systems. By its own admission, BISD's records are not reliable.

27. Reasons for staying in school vary with each individual student. My foster son, for example, viewed school as a place to demonstrate his maturity by fighting and by socializing with friends. Education per se, the substance of the classes he attended, or the opportunities which education might eventually provide, were not primary to his staying in school.

28. See Kuvlesky et al., "Status Projections and Ethnicity"; "Ethnicity and Aspirations for Upward Mobility"; and "Mexican American Youth and the American Dream." Also see Johnson and Hernandez-M., *Educating the Mexican American,* and Celia Stopnika Heller, *Mexican-American Youth: Forgotten Youth at the Crossroads* (New York: Random House, 1966).

29. The impact of reforms in this school system and the local community response to the reforms are topics which would benefit from future research.

30. Unfortunately this same researcher quit his job in 1987 and the position was not filled by as competent a researcher. One result is that BISD has very little idea of either its educational accomplishments or failures.

31. See Mark Williams, "BISD Approves Criteria Reduction," in *Brownsville Herald,* April 2, 1986.

32. Most recently a wave of criminal indictments has hit the BISD system with charges of mismanagement of funds in several different programs. Nevertheless, the BISD board has considered lengthening the five year contract of its long-time superintendent.

33. This discussion is based on interviews with teachers, administrators, and students at Texas Southmost College. The staff of the developmental reading program was particularly helpful in providing data as was the staff of the TSC's Department of Institutional Research.

Enrollment figures were provided along with the results of a recent survey of the college alumni. Finally, historical data were gathered from an analysis of college yearbooks from 1940 to 1987.

34. C. Fernandez, "Education."

35. I have taught courses in sociology in the Department of Behavioral Sciences at TSC for more than twelve years. Probably 15 percent of my students have been functionally illiterate. The majority enter with seventh grade reading levels; only 30 percent are able to read the textbook which is written at the eleventh grade level with a maximum of comprehension. The first dilemma teachers at TSC face is whether to continue to pass students along who, based upon their level of academic skills, should not be in college in the first place, despite their A or B average in high school.

36. The vocational-technical division of TSC, for instance, received a federal grant to initiate a training program for aquaculture technicians. However, there never was a market demand for the graduates and the program folded after two years.

7. NO MONEY, NO DOCTOR

1. See especially Charles H. Teller, "Physical Health Status and Health Care Utilization in the Texas Borderlands," in *Views Across the Border,* ed. Stanley R. Ross (Albuquerque, N.M.: University of New Mexico Press, 1978), 256–279. See also Miller, "Poverty, Development, and Quality of Life"; Miller and Maril, "Poverty in the Lower Rio Grande Valley"; and Antonio N. Zavaleta, Gorgiana Coray, and Carlos Rubinstein, "Health Needs Assessment Survey" (Brownsville, Texas: City of Brownsville, 1985).

2. This is a problem along the entire U.S.-Mexico border. See Ellwyn R. Stoddard and Gustavo M. Quesada, "Health and Health Care," in *Borderland Sourcebook,* ed. Ellwyn R. Stoddard et al. (Norman, Okla.: University of Oklahoma Press, 1983), 248–251.

3. See the two studies by William Madsen, *The Mexican Americans of South Texas,* and *Society and Health in the Lower Rio Grande Valley* (Austin, Texas: Hogg Foundation for Mental Health, 1968). See also Rubel, *Across the Tracks.* Similar studies done in other parts of the borderlands include Margaret Clark, *A Community Study: Health in the Mexican-American Culture* (Los Angeles: University of California Press, 1959) and Ari Kiev, *Curanderismo: Mexican-American Folk Psychiatry* (New York: Free Press, 1968).

4. U.S. Bureau of the Census, *County and City Data Book,* 1983.

5. See Miller and Maril, "Poverty in the Lower Rio Grande Valley," 20–22.

6. See Teller, "Physical Health Status and Heath Care Utilization," 262.

7. See M. Richard Leopold, "Report on the Public Health Significance of the Midwife Training Program in Brownsville, Texas," *South Texas Journal of Research and the Humanities*, (Spring 1977): 45–52.

8. See Center for Disease Control, "Ten State Nutrition Survey, 1968–1970," (Washington, D.C.: U.S. Department of Health, Education, and Welfare, Health Service and Mental Health Administration, 1972), and "Health Services for Domestic Agricultural Workers, (Washington, D.C.: Government Printing Office, 1972).

9. Testimony of Dr. Raymond Wheeler before the U.S. Senate Subcommittee on Migratory Labor of the Committee on Labor and Public Welfare, July 20, 1970, as cited in *Poverty in Texas,* Office of Economic Opportunity, Texas Department of Community Affairs, 1974, p. 161.

10. Miller and Maril, "Poverty in the Lower Rio Grande Valley."

11. See J. C. Smith et al., "The U.S.-Mexico Border: Contraceptive Use and Maternal Health Care in Perspective," United States and Mexico Border Health Association, El Paso, 1979.

12. This observation is from an interview with a Valley genetics counselor who described the difficulty of working with parents of limited education.

13. This point was made particularly well in Miller, "Poverty, Development, and Quality of Life," 256–282. Miller cites the suggestive work of Reuel H. Waldrop and John G. Bruhn, "Health Manpower and Health Professions Education in South Texas" (Galveston, Texas: University of Texas Medical Branch, 1975).

14. See Miller, "Poverty, Development, and Quality of Life."

15. For a recent description of this problem, see Frank Gibney, Jr., "In Texas, a Grim New Appalachia," in *Newsweek,* June 8, 1987, 27–28.

16. See Robert Lee Maril and Anthony N. Zaveleta, "Drinking Patterns of Lower-Income Mexican-American Women," *Journal of Studies on Alcohol* 40 (1979): 480–485, and Robert T. Trotter and Jan Antonio Chavira, *Curanderismo: Mexican-American Folk Healing* (Athens, Ga.: University of Georgia Press, 1981).

17. Access to decent health care is not a problem unique to the Valley, but one common to Mexican Americans all along the U.S-Mexican border. See Marvin Karno and Robert B. Edgerton, "Perception of Mental Illness in a Mexican-American Community," *Archives of General Psychiatry* 20 (1969): 233–238, and Emile J. Farge, "A Review of Findings from Three Generations of Chicano Health Care Behavior," *Social Science Quarterly* 58 (1977): 407–411. See also Rachel E. Spector, "The Utilization of Parteras as a Source of Maternal Care Along the U.S.-Mexico Border," Lyndon B. Johnson School of Public Affairs, Working Paper No. 23, University of Texas, Austin, 1983.

18. A student in one of my classes recently became a licensed partera. She paid a small fee, filled out a brief form, and is now legally qualified to deliver babies. In 1987, within the span of one week, two infants delivered by Brownsville parteras died during childbirth. As always there was a brief public reaction calling for reforms. See Lisa Baker, "Baby Deaths Spark Outcry Against Midwives," *Brownsville Herald,* August 13, 1987.

19. See Miller, "Poverty, Development, and Quality of Life."

20. This is particularly true in Brownsville, Harlingen, and McAllen as evidenced in a review of the composition of school boards and membership on city councils.

21. This discussion is based upon interviews with Valley doctors, political leaders, and bankers.

22. This point is based upon my experience as the owner of a private school in Brownsville.

23. A review of the membership records of the Cameron County Medical Association demonstrates this point. For many years there were more foreign-born doctors than Mexican-American.

24. From interviews with former doctors and staff members of Su Clinica Familiar.

25. From interviews with the major participants in the dispute.

26. This discussion is based in part on my work from 1978–1985 with a Valley health clinic that served the poor.

27. See Zavaleta, "Federal Assistance and Mexican-American Health Status."

28. Ibid. See also Zavaleta et al., "Health Needs Assessment Survey," and Miller, "Poverty, Development, and Quality of Life," 5. Research on drug abuse among adolescents is particularly needed. See Eligio R. Padilla and Amado M. Padilla, "Inhalant, Marijuana, and Alcohol Abuse among Barrio Children and Adolescents," Occasional

Paper No. 4, University of Southern California at Los Angeles, Los Angeles, 1977.

29. For an overview of how this legislation impacts Hispanics, see Clara Ana Gonzales, "Indigent Health Care for Hispanics in Texas," *Texas Journal of Rural Health* Summer (1987): 5–10.

30. See A. Taher Moustafa and Gertrud Weiss, "Health Status and Practices of Mexican Americans," Mexican-American Study Project, Advance Report no. 2, University of Southern California at Los Angeles, 1968; Jerry L. Weaver, "Mexican-American Health Care Behavior: A Critical Review of the Literature," *Social Science Quarterly* 54 (1973): 85–102; and *Modern Medicine and Medical Anthropology in the United States-Mexico Border Population*, ed. Boris Velimirovic, (Washington, D.C.: Pan American Health Organization, 1978). See also Herbert K. Abrams, "Occupational and Environmental Problems Along the U.S.-Mexico Border," *Southwest Economy and Society* 40 (1979): 3–17, and "Mexican-American Health Status: Selected Topics from the Borderlands," *Borderlands Journal* 4 (1980). At this writing Phil Gramm, Republican Senator from Texas, is submitting legislation to Congress to help clean up the Rio Grande. He describes the Rio Grande as, ". . . rapidly evolving into an open sewer. 12 to 15 billion tons of raw sewage are annually dumped into the river, the majority south of Laredo where the bacteria levels exceed accepted safety margins by several thousand percent" ("Gramm Unveils Plan to Fight River Pollution," in *Brownsville Herald*, August 17, 1987).

31. See Stoddard and Quesada, "Health and Health Care."

8. IGNORING THE OBVIOUS

1. See for instance Albert Szymanski, *Class Structure: A Critical Perspective* (New York: Praeger, 1983).

2. See Richard L. Cole, Ann C. Smith, and Delbert A. Taebel, *Urban Life in Texas* (Austin, Texas: University of Texas Press, 1986).

3. For an example of the journalistic treatment of the Valley by national media in the mid-1970s, see Kenneth R. Sheets, "Poorest Area in America Begins to Fight Its Way Up," in *U.S. News and World Report*, October 7, 1974, 45–48.

4. See Frank Gibney Jr., "In Texas, A Grim New Appalachia," in *Newsweek*, June 8, 1987, 27–28.

5. Kaye Northcott has done an excellent job of summarizing the attitude of many Texans towards poverty in Texas in "In Texas

Ain't No Such Thing as Free Barbecue" in *Mother Jones*, Feb.–March 1978, 59–64.

6. This point was suggested in Miller and Maril, "Poverty in the Lower Rio Grande Valley," and in Miller, "Poverty, Development, and Quality of Life."

7. In contrast, see Michael V. Miller and Avelardo Valdez, "Immigration and Perceptions of Economic Deprivation Among Working-Class Mexican-American Men," *Social Science Quarterly* 65 (1984): 455–464.

8. This observation comes in part from conversations with Anthony N. Zavaleta.

9. This point is more fully discussed in Miller, "Poverty, Development, and Quality of Life."

10. In this respect the Valley affluent are not necessarily different than any other classes in other regions.

11. This point was strongly supported in the interviews I conducted.

12. This is true not only of Valley physicians and staff. See the comments of Stoddard and Quesada, "Health and Health Care," 248–251.

13. See Paul Fussell, *Class: A Guide Through the American Status System* (New York: Summit, 1983).

14. For a more detailed discussion, see Robert Lee Maril, "Condos and the Poor: The Texas Coast in the 1990's," unpublished paper, Department of Behavioral Sciences, Texas Southmost College, Brownsville, 1983.

15. My own experience in serving for seven years on the board of a non-profit health agency supports these generalizations. Colleagues often found it difficult to justify to themselves and their families the time and energy required for board membership. Once they understood the nature of the need for their particular services, and the status of the women in poverty who required the services, many were likely to become less, rather than more, involved in the agency. This withdrawal was heightened by the constant financial constraints. Turnover on this board and other community boards is quite high.

9. BLUEPRINTS FOR THE FUTURE

1. See F. F. Piven and R. A. Cloward, *Poor People's Movements: Why They Succeed, How They Fail* (New York: Vintage Books, 1979); S. Danziger and R. Plotnik, "Can Welfare Reform Eliminate

Poverty?" *Social Service Review* 53 (1979): 244–260; H. J. Gans, "What Can Be Done About Poverty?" *Dissent* 28 (1981): 40–46; and S. R. Cox, "Why Eradicating Urban Poverty Requires a Long-Term Multi-Purpose War: A Review of Anti-Poverty Strategies for the Needs of the Late 1970's," *American Journal of Economics and Sociology* 34 (1975): 249–265.

2. See a most recent example in Cathy Corman, "Deadline Error could Rob Valley Schools of $709,590 in Funds," *Brownsville Herald*, September 23, 1987.

3. See Jonathan P. West, "Public Administration and Local Coordination," in *Borderlands Sourcebook*, ed. Ellwyn R. Stoddard et al. (Norman, Okla.: University of Oklahoma Press, 1983), 195–203.

4. One example is binational car theft. See Michael V. Miller, "Vehicle Theft Along the Texas-Mexico Border," *Journal of Borderlands Studies* 2, no. 2 (1987): 12–33.

5. See Maril, *Cannibals and Condos*.

6. See J.L. Roach and J.K. Roach, "Organizing the Poor: Road to a Dead End," *Social Problems* 26 (1978): 160–171.

7. A virtual flood of new poor from Central America have, at this writing, added to the Valley's considerable problems. The Immigration and Naturalization Service changed its policy in the spring of 1988 and no longer allows those seeking asylum to travel to other destinations after registering with the INS. The immediate result of the new policy was that thousands of applicants were stranded in Valley cities, quickly overtaxing the limited services for the poor. On January 9, 1989, U.S. District Judge Filemon Vela issued a temporary restraining order against the new INS policy. The INS is now attempting to determine the status of refugees more quickly.

8. Congressman Solomon Ortiz, Democrat from Corpus Christi, recently introduced the Colonia Water and Sewage Act. This bill would provide a total of $45 million in federal grants and loans to improve water systems in colonias. Similar legislation has just been introduced in the Texas State Legislature.

BIBLIOGRAPHY

Abrams, Herbert K. 1979. "Occupational and Environmental Problems Along the U.S.-Mexico Border." *Southwest Economy and Review* 4 (no.3): 3–17.

Achor, S. 1978. *Mexican Americans in a Dallas Barrio*. Tucson, Ariz.: University of Arizona Press.

Acuna, Rodolfo. 1972. *Occupied America: The Chicano's Struggle Toward Liberation*. San Francisco: Canfield Press.

———. 1981. *Occupied America: A History of Chicanos*. New York: Harper.

Agee, James, and Walker Evans. 1960. *Let Us Now Praise Famous Men*. Boston: Houghton Mifflin Co.

Akers, Ronald L., et al. 1979. "Social Learning and Deviant Behavior." *American Sociological Review* 44 (1979): 635–655.

Alinsky, Saul. 1972. *Rules for Radicals*. New York: Vintage Books.

Amidei, N. "Food Stamps: The Irony of Success." 1981 *Public Welfare* 39 (no. 2): 15–21.

Anders, Evan. 1986. *Boss Rule in South Texas*. Austin: University of Texas Press.

Anderson, James G., and William H. Johnson. 1971. "Stability and Change Among Three Generations of Mexican Americans: Factors Affecting Achievement." *American Educational Research Journal* 8: 285–308.

Anti-Hunger Coalition of Texas. 1982. "Hunger in Texas: A State Need." Austin, Texas: Anti-Hunger Coalition of Texas.

Ball, Heather, and J. Michael Patrick. 1985. "The Jobs of South Texas." Austin, Texas: Texas Department of Agriculture.

Barrera, Mario. 1979. *Race and Class in the Southwest: A Theory of Racial Inequality*. Notre Dame, Ind.: University of Notre Dame Press.

Beeghley, Leonard. 1984. "Illusion and Reality in the Measurement of Poverty." *Social Problems* 31: 322–333.

Bell, W., and D. M. Bushe. 1975. "The Economic Efficiency of AFDC." *Social Service Review* 47: 175–190.

205

Bienen, Henry. 1968. *Violence and Social Change*. Chicago: University of Chicago Press.

Block, Fred, et al. 1987. *The Mean Season*. New York: Pantheon Books.

Blumberg, Paul. 1980. *Inequality in an Age of Decline*. New York: Oxford University Press.

Bolton, Herbert Eugene. 1915. *Texas in the Middle Eighteenth Century. Studies in Spanish Colonia History and Administration*. 1915. Berkeley: University of California Press.

Borchart, Kurt. 1970. *Structure and Performance in the U.S. Communications Industry*. Boston: Harvard University Press.

The Borderlands Journal. 1980. Special Issue on Mexican American Health Status: Selected Topics from the Borderlands. 4 (no. 1).

———. 1985. Special Issue on Business and Economic Opportunities. 8 (no. 2).

Borjas, George, and Maria Tienda. 1985. *Hispanics in the U.S. Economy*. New York: Academic Press.

Borrero, I. M. 1980. "Psychological and Emotional Impact of Unemployment." *Journal of Sociology and Social Welfare* 7 (no. 6): 916–934.

Boucher, Stanley W. (ed.) 1970. *Mexican-American Mental Health Issues: Present Realities and Future Strategies*. Boulder, Col.: Western Interstate Commission for Higher Education.

Bridgeland, W. 1975. "War on Poverty: Its Conflicts and Collapse." *Urban Life* 4 (no.1): 79–98.

Briggs, Vernon M., Jr. 1973. *Chicanos and Rural Poverty*. Baltimore, Md.: Johns Hopkins University Press.

Briggs, Vernon M., Walter Fogel, and Fred H. Schmidt. 1977. *The Chicano Worker*. Austin, Texas: University of Texas Press.

Brown, George H. 1980. "The Condition of Education for Hispanic Americans." Washington, D.C.: U.S. Government Printing Office.

Burma, John H. 1970. *Mexican Americans in the United States: A Reader*. New York: Harper and Row.

Cameron County, Texas. 1985. "Proposal for the Location of a Surface Action Group Homeport in the Brownsville Ship Channel." Brownsville, Texas: Cameron County, Texas.

Campbell, Angus, et al. 1960. *The American Voter*. New York: John Wiley and Sons.

Caplovitz, David. 1963. *The Poor Pay More: Consumer Practices of Low Income Families*. New York: MacMillan Co.

Carter, Thomas P., and Roberto D. Segura. 1979. *Mexican Americans in School: A Decade of Change.* New York: College Entrance Examination Board.

Casey, Robert . 1950. *The Texas Border.* Indianapolis: Bobbs-Merrill Co.

Cassety, J. H., and R. McRoy. 1983. "Gender, Race, and the Shrinking Welfare Dollar," *Public Welfare* 41 (no. 3): 36–39.

Castaneda, Carlos E. 1936. *Our Catholic Heritage in Texas.* Vol. 1–7. Austin, Texas: Von Boekman Jones, Co.

Center for Disease Control. 1972. "Ten State Nutrition Survey, 1968–1970." U.S. Department of Health, Education, and Welfare. Publication No. (HSM) 72–8131. Washington, D.C.: U.S. Government Printing Office.

Chalfant, H. Paul. 1985. *Sociology of Poverty in the United States: An Annotated Bibliography.* Westport, Conn.: Greenwood Press.

Chatfield, W. H. 1982. *The Twin Cities of the Border.* Edinburg, Texas: Hidalgo County Historical Museum.

City of Brownsville. 1979. "The State of the City." Brownsville, Texas: City of Brownsville.

Clark, Margaret. 1959. *A Community Study: Health in the Mexican-American Culture.* Los Angeles: University of California Press.

Cole, Richard L., Ann C. Smith, and Delbert A. Taebel. 1986. *Urban Life in Texas.* Austin, Texas: University of Texas Press.

Community Development. 1984. "Brownsville 1980 to 2000 Population Data." Brownsville, Texas: City of Brownsville.

Cosby, Arthur G., and Ivan Charner (eds.) 1978. *Education and Work in Rural America: The Social Context of Early Career Decision and Achievement.* Houston, Texas: Stafford-Lowdon.

Costin, Lela B., and Charles A. Rapp. 1984. *Child Welfare Policies and Practices.* New York: McGraw-Hill, Inc.

Cottle, T.J. 1974. "What Tracking Did to Ollie Taylor." *Social Policy* 5 (no. 2): 21–24.

Council of Economic Advisors. 1988. "Economic Indicators." Various issues. Washington, D.C.: U.S. Government Printing Office.

Cox, S. R. 1975. "Why Eradicating Urban Poverty Requires a Long-Term Multi-Program War: A Review of Anti-Poverty Strategies for the Needs of the Late 1970s." *American Journal of Economics and Sociology* 34 (no. 3): 249–265.

Craig, Richard B. 1980a. "Human Rights and Mexico's Antidrug Campaign." *Social Science Quarterly* 60 (no. 4): 691–701.

————1980b. "Operation Intercept: The International Politics of Pressure." *The Review of Politics* 42 (no. 4).

Crouch, Ben M., and T. Mark Miller. 1987. "Lacey Act Enforcement in the Texas Gulf: A Sociological Analysis." Unpublished paper. Department of Sociology, Texas A&M University.

Cumberland, Charles C. 1954. "Border Raids in the Lower Rio Grande Valley, 1915." *The Southwestern Historical Quarterly* (January).

Dahrendorf, Ralf. 1959. *Class and Class Conflict in Industrial Society.* Stanford, Calif.: Stanford University Press.

————. 1968. *Essays in the Theory of Society.* Stanford, Calif.: Stanford University Press.

D'Antonio, William V., and William H. Form. 1965. *Influentials in Two Border Cities.* Notre Dame, Ind.: Notre Dame University Press.

Danziger, S., and R. Plotnick. 1979. "Can Welfare Reform Eliminate Poverty?" *Social Service Review* 53 (no. 2): 244–260.

Danziger, S., and P. Gottschalk. 1983. "The Measurement of Poverty." *American Behavioral Scientist* 26 (no. 6): 739–756.

Davis, Cary, Carl Haub, and Jo Anne Willette. 1983. "U.S. Hispanics Changing the Face of America." Population Reference Bureau, Inc., Washington, D.C. 38 (no. 3).

de la Garza, Rudolph O. 1974. "Voting Patterns in Bi-Cultural El Paso." *Aztlan* 5 (nos. 1, 2): 235–260.

Department of Agriculture. 1984. "Pesticide Safety for Texas" Austin, Texas: Department of Agriculture.

Dillman, C. Daniel. 1968. "The Functions of Brownsville, Texas, and Matamoros, Tamaulipas: Twin Cities of the Lower Rio Grande." Ph.D. Dissertation, University of Michigan.

Domhoff, G. William. 1970. *The Higher Circles.* New York: Random House.

————. 1978. *Who Really Rules?* Santa Monica, Calif.: Goodyear Publishing Co.

————. 1983. *Who Rules America Now? A View for the 80s.* Englewood Cliffs, N.J.: Prentice-Hall.

Donovan, John C. 1967. *The Politics of Poverty.* New York: Pegasus.

Drop-Out Task Force Number 2. 1987. "Subcommittee on School Climate Status Quo Report." Brownsville Independent School District, Brownsville, Texas.

Dunbar, Tony. 1969. *Our Land Too.* New York: Vintage Books.

Duncan, Greg J., et al. 1984. *Years of Poverty, Years of Plenty: The Changing Economic Fortunes of American Workers and Families.* Ann Arbor, Mich.: Institute for Social Research.

Duncan, Hugh. 1962. *Communication and the Social Order.* New York: Bedmister Press.

Dutton, D. 1982. "Re-blaming the Victim." *American Sociological Review* 47 (no. 7): 557–61.

Economic Development Council. 1985. "The McAllen 1985–1986 Annual Economic Report." McAllen, Texas: McAllen Chamber of Commerce.

Ehrenreich, Barbara, and Frances Fox Piven. 1984. "The Feminization of Poverty." *Dissent* 31: 162–170.

Elman, Richard M. 1968. *The Poorhouse State.* New York: Dell Publishing Co., Inc.

Elo, Irma T., and Calvin L. Beale. 1986. "Natural Resources and Rural Poverty: An Overview." Washington, D.C.: National Center for Food and Agricultural Policy.

Farge, Emile J. 1977. "A Review of Findings from Three Generations of Chicano Health Care Behavior." *Social Science Quarterly* 58: 407–411.

Fehrenbach, T. R. 1973. *Fire and Blood.* New York: MacMillan Publishing Co., Inc.

————. 1975. *Lone Star.* New York: MacMillan Publishing Co. Inc.

Ferguson, Henry N. 1976. *The Port of Brownsville.* Brownsville, Texas: Springman King Press.

Fernandez, Raul A. 1977. *The United States-Mexico Border.* Notre Dame, Ind.: University of Notre Dame Press.

Fernandez-Kelly, Maria Patricia. 1983. *For We Are Sold, I and My People: Women in Mexico's Frontier.* Albany, N.Y.: State University of New York Press.

Foscue, Edwin J. 1934. "Agricultural History of the Lower Rio Grande Valley Region." *Agricultural History* 8 (no. 3): 124–137.

Foster, David William (ed.) 1982. "Sourcebook of Hispanic Culture in the United States." Chicago: American Library Association.

Frantz, Joe B. 1976. *Texas: A Bicentennial History.* New York: W. W. Norton & Co.

Freeman, Donald M. 1974. "Party, Vote, and the Mexican American in South Texas." In *La Causa Politica,* ed. Chris Garcia, pp. 55–60. Notre Dame, Ind.: University of Notre Dame Press.

Furlong, W. L. 1972. "Peruvian and Northern Mexican Municipalities: A Comparative Analysis of Two Political Subsystems." *Comparative Political Studies,* 59–83.

Fussell, Paul. 1983. *Class: A Guide Through the American Status System.* New York: Summit.

Galarza, Ernesto, 1964. *Merchants of Labor: The Mexican Bracero Story.* Santa Barbara, Calif.: McNally & Loftin.

————. 1970. *Spiders in the House and Workers in the Field.* Notre Dame, Ind.: University of Notre Dame Press.

Galvan, Robert R. 1978. *Bilingualism as It Relates to Intelligence Test Scores and School Achievement Among Culturally-Deprived Spanish-American Children.* New York: Arno Press.

Gans, H. J. 1981. "What Can Be Done About Poverty." *Dissent,* 28 (no. 1): 40–41.

Garcia, F. Chris. 1972. *Political Socialization of Chicano Children: A Comparative Study with Anglos in California Schools.* New York: Praeger Publishers.

Garcia, F. Chris, and Rudolph de la Garza. 1978. *The Chicano Political Experience.* North Scituate, R.I.: Duxbury Press.

Garson, Barbara. 1977. *All the Livelong Day.* New York: Penguin Books.

Gerking, Shelby D., and John H. Mutti. 1980. "Costs and Benefits of Illegal Immigration: Key Issues for Government Policy." *Social Science Quarterly* 61 (no. 1), 1980: 71–85.

Gilder, George. 1981. *Wealth and Poverty.* New York: Basic Books.

Gillette, Michael L. (ed.). 1986. *Texas in Transition.* Austin, Texas: Lyndon Baines Johnson Library & Lyndon Baines Johnson School of Public Affairs.

Gomez, Joseph R., Jr. (ed.). 1981. "Proceedings of Invitational Symposium on Hispanic-American Diversity." Michigan State University, East Lansing, Michigan.

Gomez-Quinones, Juan. 1970. "Plan de San Diego Reviewed." *Aztlan* (Spring): 124–132.

Gonzales, Clara Ana. 1987. "Indigent Health Care: Hispanics in Texas." *Texas Journal of Rural Health* (Summer).

Gonzales, Jovita. 1930. "Social Life in Cameron, Starr, and Zapata Counties." Masters Thesis. University of Texas.

Goodman, Paul. 1962. *Compulsory Mis-education and the Community of Scholars.* New York: Vintage Books.

Graf, Leroy P. 1942. "The Economic History of the Lower Rio Grande Valley, 1820–1875." Ph.D. Dissertation. Harvard University.

Graham, Hugh Davis, and Ted Robert Gurr. 1969. *Violence in America.* Washington, D.C.: U.S. Government Printing Office.

Greater South Texas Cultural Basin Commission. 1979. "Accelerating Development in South Texas: A Report to the Governor and 66th Legislature." Office of the Governor, Austin, Texas.

————. 1977. "Developing South Texas." Office of the Governor, Austin, Texas.

Grebler, Leo, Joan W. Moore, and Ralph C. Guzman. 1970. *The Mexican-American People: The Nation's Second Largest Minority.* New York: Free Press.

Grubb, W. N. and M. Lazerson. 1982. *Broken Promises.* New York: Basic Books.

Hansen, Niles. 1981. *The Border Economy: Regional Development in the Southwest.* Austin, Texas: University of Texas Press.

Harper, Douglas A. 1982. *Good Company.* Chicago: University of Chicago Press.

Harrington, Michael. 1962. *The Other America.* New York: Penguin Books.

————. 1985. *The New American Poverty.* New York: Penguin Books.

Haupt, Arthur, and Thomas T. Kane. 1985. "Population Handbook." 2nd ed. Washington, D.C.: Population Reference Bureau, Inc.

Heller, Celia Stopnika. 1966. *Mexican-American Youth: Forgotten Youth at the Crossroads.* New York: Random House.

Henry, Jules. 1965. *Culture Against Man.* New York: Random House, Inc.

Hernandez, Norma G. 1973. "Variables Affecting Achievement of Middle School Mexican-American Students." *Review of Educational Research* 43: 1–39.

Hess, Beth B. (ed.) 1980. *Growing Old in America.* New York: Transaction, Inc.

Hester, Thomas R. 1969. "The Floyd Morris and Ayala Sites: A Discussion of Burial Practices in the Rio Grande Valley and the Lower Texas Coast." *Bulletin of the Texas Archaeological Society* 40: 157–166.

————. 1975. "Late Prehistoric Cultural Patterns Along the Rio Grande of Texas." *Bulletin of the Texas Archaeological Society* 46: 106–125.

————. 1976. "Hunters and Gatherers of the Rio Grande Plain and the Lower Coast of Texas." San Antonio, Texas: Center for Archaeological Research.

————. 1978. "The Archaeology of the Lower Rio Grande Valley of Texas." *Proceedings: An Exploration of a Common Legacy: Conference on Border Architecture,* pp. 66–74. Austin, Texas: Texas Historical Commission.

————. 1979. "Early Populations in Prehistoric Texas." *Archaeology* 3 (no. 6): 26–33.

———. 1981. "Tradition and Diversity Among the Prehistoric Hunters and Gatherers of Southern Texas." *Plains Anthropologist,* pp. 119–128.

Hester, Thomas R., and T. C. Hill, Jr. 1975. "Some Aspects of Late Prehistoric and Protohistoric Archaeology in Southern Texas." Special Report 1. San Antonio, Texas: Center for Archaeological Research.

Hills, Stuart L. 1980. *Demystifying Social Deviance.* New York: McGraw-Hill Book Co.

Hinojosa-Smith, Rolando. 1983. *The Valley.* Ypsilanti, Mich.: Bilingual Press.

Horgan, Paul. 1984. *Great River.* Austin, Texas: Texas Monthly Press.

Horowitz, Ruth. 1983. *Honor and the American Dream: Culture and Identity in a Chicano Community.* New Brunswick, N.J.: Rutgers University Press.

Irby, James A. 1977. *Backdoor at Bagdad: The Civil War on the Rio Grande.* El Paso, Texas: Texas Western Press.

Jackson, Jack. 1986. *Los Mesteños: Spanish Ranching in Texas, 1721–1821.* College Station, Texas: Texas A&M University Press.

Jamail, Milton H. 1980. *The United States–Mexico Border: A Guide to Institutions, Organizations, and Scholars.* Tucson, Ariz.: University of Arizona Latin America Area Center.

Jamieson, Stuart, 1945. "Labor Unionism in American Agriculture." *Bureau of Labor Statistics Bulletin,* No. 836. Washington, D.C.: U.S. Government Printing Office.

Jaramillo, Phillip. 1981. "Hispanic Health Research Bibliography." U.S. Department of Health and Human Services. Washington, D.C.: U.S. Government Printing Office.

Jencks, Christopher, et al. 1972. *Inequality.* New York: Basic Books.

Jessor, Richard, Theodore D. Graves, Robert Hansom, and Shirley L. Jessor. 1968. *Society, Personality, and Deviant Behavior.* New York: Holt, Rinehart, and Winston, Inc.

John, Elizabeth A. H. 1975. *Storms Brewed in Other Men's Worlds: The Confrontation of Indians, Spanish, and French in the Southwest, 1540–1795.* Lincoln, Neb.: University of Nebraska Press.

Johnson, Henry S.,Wiliam J. Hernandez-M. (eds.) 1970. *Educating the Mexican American.* Valley Forge, Penn.: Judson Press.

Johnson, Lyndon Baines, School of Public Affairs. 1977. "Colonias in the Lower Rio Grande Valley of South Texas: A Summary Report." Policy Research Project No. 18. Austin, Texas: Lyndon Baines Johnson School of Public Affairs.

————. 1979. "The Health of Mexican Americans in South Texas." Mexican-American Policy Research Project. Austin, Texas: Lyndon Baines Johnson School of Public Affairs.

Jones, Lamar B. 1965. "Mexican-American Labor Problems in Texas." Ph.D. Dissertation, University of Texas.

Jones, Lamar B., and C. R. Rice. 1980. "Agricultural Labor in the Southwest: The Post-Bracero Years." *Social Science Quarterly* 61 (no. 1): 86–94.

Jones, Oakah L., Jr. 1979. *Los Paisanos: Spanish Settlers on the Northern Frontier of New Spain*. Norman, Okla.: University of Oklahoma Press.

Kahn, Kathy. 1974. *Hillbilly Women*. New York: Avon.

Kane, T. D. 1974. "Structural Change and Chicano Employment in the Southwest, 1950–1970: Some Preliminary Observations." *Aztlan* 4: 383–390.

Karno, Marvin, and Robert B. Edgerton. 1969. "Perception of Mental Illness in a Mexican-American Community." *Archives of General Psychiatry* 20: 233–238.

Key, V. O. 1966. *The Responsible Electorate*. Cambridge, Mass.: Harvard University Press.

Kiev, Ari. 1968. *Curanderismo: Mexican-American Folk Psychiatry*. New York: Free Press.

King, Allen G., B. Lindsay Lowell, and Frank D. Bean. 1986. "The Effects of Hispanic Immigrants on the Earnings of Native Hispanic Americans." *Social Science Quarterly* 67 (no. 4): 673–689.

King, W. A. 1964. *Rattling Yours*. Brownsville, Texas: Springman-King.

Kiser, George C., and Martha Woody Kiser. 1979. *Mexican Workers in the United States: Historical and Political Perspectives*. Albuquerque, N.M.: University of New Mexico Press.

Klapp, Orrin E., and L. Vincent Padgett. 1960. "Power Structure and Decision-Making in a Mexican Border City." *American Journal of Sociology* 65: 400–406.

Klapper, Joseph, and Elmo Roper. 1960. *The Effects of Communication*. Glencoe, Ill.: The Free Press.

Kuvlesky, William P., David E. Wright, and Rumaldo Z. Juarez. 1971. "Status Projections and Ethnicity: A Comparison of Mexican American, Negro, and Anglo Youth." *Journal of Vocational Behavior* 1: 137–151.

Kuvlesky, William P., and Victoria M. Patella. 1971. "Degree of Ethnicity and Aspirations for Upward Social Mobility Among

Mexican-American Youth." *Journal of Vocational Behavior* 13: 231–244.

Kuvlesky, William P., and Rumaldo Z. Juarez. 1975. "Mexican-American Youth and the American Dream." In *Career Behavior of Special Groups,* ed. J. Steven Picou and Robert E. Campbell. Columbus, Ohio: Charles E. Merrill Publishing Co.

Lamare, James. 1982. *Texas Politics: Economics, Power, and Politics.* St. Paul, Minn.: West Publishing Co.

Larner, Jeremy, and Irving Howe (eds.). 1968. *Poverty: Views from the Left.* New York: William Morrow & Co., Inc.

Lea, Tom. 1957. *The King Ranch,* 2 vol. Boston: Little Brown and Company.

LeBlanc, Donna Marie. 1983. "The Quality of Maternity Care in Rural Texas." Houston, Texas: University of Texas.

Leopold, Richard M. 1977. "Report on the Public Health Significance of the Midwife Training Program in Brownsville, Texas." *South Texas Journal of Research and the Humanities* (Spring).

Levey, Mark R. 1974. "Patterns of Chicano Voting Behavior." In *La Causa Politica,* ed. F. Chris Garcia. Notre Dame, Ind.: University of Notre Dame Press.

Levitan, S. A., and R. S. Belous. 1979. *More Than Subsistence: Minimum Wages for the Working Poor.* Baltimore, Md.: Johns Hopkins University Press.

Levitan, S. A., and Isaac Shapiro. 1988. *Working But Poor.* Baltimore, Md.: Johns Hopkins University Press.

Lightfoot, S. L. 1978. *Worlds Apart: Relationships Between Families and Schools.* New York: Basic Books.

Livingstone, D. W. 1983. *Class Ideologies and Educational Futures.* Barcombe, Lewes: Palmer Press.

Lopez, D. E. 1976. "The Social Consequences of Chicano Home/School Bilingualism." *Social Problems* 24 (no. 2): 234–246.

Lower Rio Grande Development Council. 1973. "Housing Data for the Lower Rio Grande Valley, 1970." McAllen, Texas: Lower Rio Grande Valley Development Council.

———. 1977. "Resources Handbook of the Lower Rio Grande Valley." McAllen, Texas: Lower Rio Grande Valley Development Council.

———. 1978. "Regional Housing Plan for Lower Rio Grande Valley." McAllen, Texas: Lower Rio Grande Valley Development Council.

———. 1985. "Assessment of Rural Sewage Disposal Practices/Management." McAllen, Texas: Lower Rio Grande Valley Development Council.

Lurie, H. J., and G. L. Lawrence. 1972. "Communication Problems Between Rural Mexican-American Patients and Their Physicians: Description of a Solution." *American Journal of Orthopsychiatry* 42 (no. 5): 777–783.

McAlister, Lyle N. 1984. *Spain and Portugal in the New World, 1492–1700.* Minneapolis, Minn.: University of Minnesota Press.

McBride, John. 1963. *The Vanishing Bracero: Valley Revolution.* San Antonio: Naylor.

McCleskey, Clifton, and Dan Nimmo. 1968. "Differences Between Potential Registered and Actual Voters: The Houston Metropolitan Areas in 1964." *Social Science Quarterly,* 49 (June): 103–114.

McCleskey, Clifton, and Bruce Merrill. 1973. "Mexican-American Political Behavior in Texas." *Social Science Quarterly* 53 (March): 785–799.

McDonald, M. "Food Stamps: An Analytical History." *Social Service Review* 51 (no. 4): 642–648.

MacLachlan, Colin M., and Jaime E. Rodriguez O. 1980. *The Forging of the Cosmic Race: A Reinterpretation of Colonial Mexico.* Berkeley, Calif.: University of California Press.

McLemore, S. Dale. 1973. "The Origins of Mexican-American Subordination in Texas." *Social Science Quarterly* (March).

McManus, Elaine. 1982. "The Impact of Selected Federal Health Programs on Rural Texas." Austin, Texas: The Texas Rural Health Field Services Program.

McWilliams, Carey. 1968. *North From Mexico.* New York: Greenwood Press.

Machado, Manuel A., Jr. *Listen Chicano: An Informal History of the Mexican American.* Chicago: Nelan-Hall Publishers.

Madsen, William. 1964. *The Mexican Americans of South Texas.* New York: Holt, Rinehart, Winston.

———. 1968. *Society and Health in the Lower Rio Grande Valley.* Austin, Texas: Hogg Foundation for Mental Health.

Mallouf, R. J., B. J. Baskin, and K. L. Killen. 1977. "A Predictive Assessment of Cultural Resources in Hidalgo and Willacy Counties, Texas." Survey Report 23. Austin, Texas: Office of the State Archaeologist.

Maril, Robert Lee. 1976. "Towards a Media Theory of the Lower Rio Grande Valley." *South Texas Journal of Research and the Humanities* 1 (no. 1): 32–41.

———. 1982. "Continuity and Change in a South Texas Fishing Community." Paper presented at the annual meeting of the American Anthropology Association, Washington, D.C.

——. 1983a. *Texas Shrimpers: Community, Capitalism, and the Sea.* College Station, Texas: Texas A&M University Press.

——. 1983b. "Condos and the Poor: The Texas Coast in the 1990s." Unpublished paper, Texas Southmost College.

——. 1984. "They Follwed Us With Jets and My Own Country Arrested Us: The Arbitrary Enforcement of the Lacey Act." Paper presented at the annual meeting of the Rural Sociological Society, College Station, Texas.

——. 1986. *Cannibals and Condos: Texans and Texas Along the Gulf Coast.* College Station, Texas: Texas A&M University Press.

Maril, Robert Lee, and Anthony N. Zavaleta. 1979. "Drinking Patterns of Low-Income Mexican-American Women." *Journal of Studies in Alcohol* 40 (no. 5): 480–485.

Marquez, Benjamin. 1985. *Power and Politics in a Chicano Barrio.* New York: University Press of America.

Martinez, John R. 1966. "Leadership and Politics." In *La Raza: Forgotten Americans,* ed. Julian Samora. Notre Dame, Ind.: University of Notre Dame Press.

Martinez, Oscar J. 1978. *Border Boom Town.* Austin, Texas: University of Texas Press.

——. 1986. *The Chicanos of El Paso.* El Paso, Texas: Texas Western Press.

Meier, Matt S., and Feliciano Rivera. 1972. *The Chicanos: A History of Mexican Americans.* New York: Hill and Wang.

Melville, M. B. (ed.) 1980. *Twice a Minority: Mexican-American Women.* St. Louis, Mo.: C. V. Mosby.

Mexican American Research Center, Inc. 1984. "Brownsville Downtown Study." Austin, Texas: Mexican American Research Center, Inc.

Milburn, Lonna, Mary Walker, and Yvonne D. Knudson. 1985. "Acute Health Delivery, Energy Impact, and Rural Texas." Austin, Texas: Texas Rural Health Fields Service Program.

Miller, Michael V. 1974. "Variations in Mexican-American Family Life: A Review Synthesis of Empirical Research." *Aztlan* (Spring).

——. 1975a. "Chicano Community Control in South Texas: Problems and Prospects." *Journal of Ethnic Studies* (Fall).

——. 1975b. "Mexican-American and Mexican National Farm Workers: A Literature Review." Paper presented at the annual meeting of the Rural Sociological Society, San Francisco.

——. 1981. "Poverty, Development, and the Quality of Life in a Texas Border City." Ph.D. Dissertation, Texas A&M University.

——. 1982. "Economic Growth and Change Along the U.S.-Mexico Border." Austin, Texas: Bureau of Business Research.

———. 1987. "Vehicle Theft Along the Texas-Mexico Border." *Journal of Borderland Studies* 2 (no. 2): 12–32.

Miller, Michael V., et al. 1986. "The Impact of the 1982 Peso Devaluations on Crime in Texas Border Cities." *Journal of Borderland Studies* 1 (no. 2): 1–23.

Miller, Michael V., and William P. Kuvlesky. 1975. "The Farm Labor Movement in South Texas: Historical Development, Current Status, and Implications for Change." Department of Rural Sociology, Texas A&M University.

Miller, Michael V., and Robert Lee Maril. 1979. "Poverty in the Lower Rio Grande Valley of Texas: Historical and Contemporary Dimensions." Technical Report No. 78–2. College Station, Texas: Texas Agricultural Experiment Station.

Miller, Michael V., and James D. Preston. 1973. "Vertical Ties and the Redistribution of Power in Crystal City." *Social Science Quarterly* 53 (March): 771–784.

Mills, C. Wright. 1956. *The Power Elite*. New York: Oxford University Press.

———. 1959. *The Sociological Imagination*. New York: Oxford University Press.

Montejano, David. 1977. "Race, Labor Repression, and Capitalistic Agriculture: Notes from South Texas, 1920–30." Berkeley, Calif.: Institute for the Study of Social Change.

Montiel, Miguel. 1970. "The Social Science Myth of the Mexican-American Family." *El Grito* 3 (Summer): 56–63.

Mountain, Karen, et al. 1984. "The Rural Texas Environment: A Profile of Stressors." Austin, Texas: Texas Rural Health Field Services Program.

Moustafa, A. Taher, and Gertrud Weiss. 1968. "Health Status and Practices of Mexican Americans." Mexican-American Study Project Advance Report No. 11. Los Angeles: University of California at Los Angeles.

Myres, Sandra L. 1969. *The Ranch in Spanish Texas, 1691–1800*. El Paso, Texas: Texas Western Press.

National Marine Fisheries Service. 1985. "Fisheries of the United States, 1984." Washington, D.C.: U.S. Government Printing Office.

Neavel, Celia, et al. 1982. "Rural Medicine in Texas: A Study." Austin, Texas: Texas Rural Health Field Services Program.

Neubeck, K. J. and J. L. Roach. 1981. "Income Maintenance Experiments, Politics, and the Perpetuation of Poverty." *Social Problems* 28 (no. 3): 309–320.

Newcomb, W. W., Jr. 1961. *The Indians of Texas*. Austin, Texas: University of Texas Press.

Newton, M. B. 1968. "The Distribution and Character of Sites, Arroyo Los Olmos, Starr County, Texas." *Bulletin of the Texas Archaeological Society* 38: 18–24.

Nimmo, Dan, and Clifton McCleskey. 1969. "Impact of the Poll Tax Voter Participation: The Houston Metropolitan Area in 1966." *Journal of Politics* (August): 682–699.

Northcott, Kaye. 1977. "All Roads Lead From Roma." *Texas Monthly* 5 (April): 82–87, 180–188.

———. 1978. "In Texas Ain't No Such Thing as a Free Barbecue." *Mother Jones* (Feb.-March): 59–64.

Office of Economic Opportunity. 1974. *Poverty in Texas*. Austin, Texas: Office of Economic Affairs.

O'Hare, William P. 1985. "Poverty in America: Trends and New Patterns." Vol. 40, No. 3. Washington, D.C.: Population Reference Bureau, Inc.

Padilla, Eligio R., and Amado M. Padilla. "Inhalant, Marihuana and Alcohol Abuse Among Barrio Children and Adolescents." Occasional Paper No. 4. Los Angeles: University of Southern California.

Paredes, Americo. 1958. *With a Pistol in His Hand: A Border Ballad and Its Hero*. Austin, Texas: University of Texas Press.

Paull, Gene J. 1977. "Climatic Variations in the Lower Rio Grande Valley." *South Texas Journal of Research and the Humanities* 1 (no. 1): 6–28.

Peavy, John R. 1963. *Echoes From Rio Grande*. Brownsville, Texas: Springman-King.

Perkins, Clifford Alan, and C. L. Sonnichsen. 1978. *Border Patrol*. El Paso, Texas: Texas Western Press.

Pettigrew, Thomas F. (ed.) 1975. *Racial Discrimination in the United States*. New York: Harper & Row.

Physician Task Force on Hunger in America. 1985. *Hunger in America: The Growing Epidemic*. Boston: Harvard University School of Public Health.

Pierce Frank C. 1917. *A Brief History of the Lower Rio Grande Valley*. Menasha, Wisc.: George Banta Publishing Co.

Piore, Michael J. 1979. *Birds of Passage: Migrant Labor and Industrial Societies*. New York: Cambridge University Press.

Piven, Frances Fox, and Richard A. Cloward. 1971. *Regulating the Poor*. New York: Pantheon Books.

Piven, Frances Fox, and Richard A. Cloward. 1979. *Poor People's Movements: Why They Succeed, How They Fail*. New York: Vintage Books.

Portes, Alexandro, and Robert L. Bach. 1985. *Latin Journey: Cuban and Mexican Immigrants in the United States*. Berkeley, Calif.: University of California Press.

Poston, D. L., D. Alvirez, and M. Tienda. 1976. "Earning Differences Between Anglo and Mexican-American Male Workers in 1960 and 1970: Changes in the Cost of Being Mexican American." *Social Science Quarterly* 57 (no. 3): 618–632.

Price, John A. 1973. *Tijuana: Urbanization in a Border Culture*. Notre Dame, Ind.: University of Notre Dame Press.

Purcell, Susan K., and John F. H. Purcell. 1974. "Community Power and Benefits from the Nation: The Case of Mexico." In *Latin American Urban Research,* ed. F. Rabinovitz and F. Trueblood, pp. 49–76. Beverly Hills, Calif.: Sage Publications.

Pye, Lucian. 1963. *Communications and Political Development*. Princeton, N.J.: Princeton University Press.

Ramirez, Emilia Schunior. 1971. *Ranch Life in Hidalgo County After 1850*. Edinburg, Texas: New Santander Press.

Ramos, Juan. 1968. "Spanish-Speaking Leadership in Two Southwestern Cities: A Descriptive Study." Ph.D. Dissertation, Brandeis University.

Ratcliff, Richard E., Mary Elizabeth Gallagher, and Kathryn Strother Ratcliff. 1979. "The Civic Involvement of Business Leaders: An Analysis of the Influence of Economic Power and Social Prominence in the Command of Civic Policy Positions." *Social Problems* (February).

Rawick, George P. 1972. *The American Slave: A Composite Biography*. Westport, Conn.: Glenwood Publishing Co.

Richardson, Russell C. 1987. *A Citizen's Guide to Government and Politics in Brownsville*. Valencia, Calif.: Blue Moon Publishing.

Riding, Alan. 1985. *Distant Neighbors*. New York: Alfred A. Knopf.

Rio Grande Valley Chamber of Commerce. 1985. "Valley 2000." Revised edition. Weslaco, Texas: Rio Grande Valley Chamber of Commerce.

Rips, Geoffrey. 1985. "A New Spirit Flows Along the Rio Grande." *In These Times* 12 (no. 25, May): 12–13.

Roach, J. L., and J. K. Roach. 1978. "Organizing the Poor: Road to a Dead End." *Social Problems* 26 (no. 2): 160–171.

Robertson, Brian. 1985. *Wild Horse Desert*. Edinburg, Texas: New Santander Press.

Rose, Arnold M. 1967. *The Power Structure*. London: Oxford University Press.

Ross, Stanley R. (ed.) 1978. *Views Across the Border: The United States and Mexico*. Albuquerque, N.M.: University of New Mexico.

Rubel, Arthur J. 1966. *Across the Tracks*. Austin, Texas: University of Texas Press.

Ryan, William. 1971. *Blaming the Victim*. New York: Random House.

Samora, Julian. 1971. *Los Mojados: The Wetback Story*. Notre Dame, Ind.: University of Notre Dame Press.

————. 1978. *Gunpowder Justice: A Reassessment of the Texas Rangers*. Notre Dame, Ind.: University of Notre Dame Press.

Sanders, Marion K. 1965. *The Professional Radical: Conversations with Saul Alinsky*. Evanston, Ill.: Harper and Row, Publishers.

Scott, Florence Johnson. 1937. *Historical Heritage of the Lower Rio Grande*. San Antonio, Texas: Naylor Co.

Scott, Oran Randolph. 1937. "History of Hidalgo County 1749–1852." Masters Thesis, Texas Christian University.

Segalman, R., and A. Basu. 1981. *Poverty in America: The Welfare Dilemma*. Westport, Conn.: Greenwood Press.

Shannon, Lyle W. 1973. *Minority Migrants in the Urban Community*. Beverly Hills, Calif.: Sage Publications.

Sheak, Robert. 1989. "Poverty Estimates: Political Implications and Other Issues." *Sociological Spectrum* (Forthcoming).

Shelton, Edgar G. 1946. "Political Conditions Among Texas Mexicans Along the Rio Grande." Masters Thesis, University of Texas.

Shockley, John Staples. 1974. *Chicano Revolt in a Texas Town*. Notre Dame, Ind.: University of Notre Dame Press.

Sidel, Ruth. 1986. *Women and Children Last*. New York: Penguin Books.

Simmons, Ozzie G. 1952. "Anglo Americans and Mexican Americans in South Texas: A Study of Dominant-Subordinate Group Relations." Ph.D. Dissertation, Harvard University.

Sissons, Peter L. 1985. "The Hispanic Experience of Criminal Justice." Monograph No. 3, Hispanic Research Letter. Bronx, N.Y.: Fordham University.

Sloan, John W. and Jonathan P. West. 1977. "The Role of Informal Policy-Making in U.S. Mexico Border Cities." *Social Science Quarterly* 58 (September): 270–282.

Smith, Barton, and Robert Newman. "Depressed Wages Along the U.S.-Mexico Border: An Empirical Analysis." *Economic Inquiry* (January): 51–66.

Smith, J. C., et al. 1979. "The U.S.-Mexico Border: Contraceptive Use and Maternal Health Care in Perspective." El Paso, Texas: United States and Mexico Border Health Association.

Social Science Quarterly. 1984. Special Issue on the Mexican Origin Experience in the United States. Austin, Texas: University of Texas Press.

Spector, Rachel E. 1983. "The Utilization of Parteras as a Source of Maternal Care Along the U.S.-Mexico Border." Lyndon Baines Johnson School of Public Affairs, Working Paper Series No. 23. Austin, Texas: University of Texas.

Squires, G. D. 1979. *Education and Jobs: The Imbalance of the Social Machinery.* New Brunswick, N.J.: Transaction Books.

Stambaugh, J. Lee. (No date). "History of Hidalgo County Elected Officials, 1852–1963." Pharr, Texas: Pharr Press.

Stambaugh, J. Lee, and Lillian J. Stambaugh. 1954. *The Lower Rio Grande Valley of Texas.* Austin, Texas: The University of Texas Press.

Steiner, Stan. 1969. *The Mexican Americans.* New York: Harper & Row.

Stoddard, Ellwyn R. 1973. *Mexican Americans.* New York: Random House.

———. 1978. "Patterns of Poverty Along the U.S.-Mexico Border." El Paso, Texas: Center for Inter-American Studies, University of Texas at El Paso, and the Organization of U.S. Border Cities and Counties.

Stoddard, Ellwyn R., and John Hedderson. 1987. "Trends and Patterns of Poverty Along the U.S.-Mexico Border." Borderlands Research Monograph Series No. 3. Las Cruces, N.M.: New Mexico State University.

Stoddard, Ellwyn R., Richard L. Nostrand, and Jonathan P. West. (eds.) 1983. *Borderlands Sourcebook.* Norman, Okla.: University of Oklahoma Press.

———. 1987. *Maquilla.* El Paso, Texas: Texas Western Press.

Szymanaski, Albert. 1983. *Class Structure: A Critical Perspective.* New York: Praeger.

Taylor, Paul S. 1930. *Mexican Labor in the United States: Dimmitt County, Winter Garden District, South Texas.* Berkeley, Calif.: University of California Press.

Texas Employment Commission. 1986. "Cameron County SDA, Planning Information PY 1986." Austin: Texas Employment Commission.

Texas Rural Legal Aid, Inc. 1982. "Texas State Plan for Farmworkers." Farmworker Policy Impact Project. Austin, Texas: Texas Rural Legal Aid, Inc.

Texas Southmost College. 1983. "Improving the Employment Opportunities of Hispanic Women in the Brownsville Border Area." Brownsville, Texas: Texas Southmost College.

Theobald, Robert. 1968. *An Alternative Future for America.* Chicago: Swallow Press, Inc.

Tienda, M. 1983. "Marketing Characteristics and Hispanic Earnings: A Comparison of Natives and Immigrants." *Social Problems* 31 (no. 1): 59–72.

Tirado, Miguel David. "Mexican-American Community Political Organizations: The Key to Chicano Political Power." In *La Causa Politica,* ed. F. Chris Garcia, 105–127. Notre Dame, Ind.: Notre Dame University Press.

Trattner, Walter I. 1984. *From Poor Law to Welfare State: A History of Social Welfare in America.* New York: The Free Press.

Trotter, Robert T. 1982. "Ethnic Patterns of Alcohol Use: Anglo and Mexican-American College Students." *Adolescence Journal* 17 (Summer): 305–325.

Trotter, Robert T., and Juan Antonio Chavira. 1981. *Cuaranderismo: Mexican-American Folk Healing.* Athens, Ga.: University of Georgia Press.

Ugalde, Antonio. 1970. *Power and Conflict in a Mexican Community.* Albuquerque, N.M.: University of New Mexico Press.

———. 1974. "The Urbanization Process of a Poor Mexican Neighborhood." Austin, Texas: Institute of Latin American Studies.

U.S. Army Corps of Engineers, Galveston District, and Texas Water Commission. 1986. "Public Notice SWGCO-RP. Permit Application-17714 (Revised)." Dec. 23, 1986.

U.S. Bureau of the Census. 1982. "Characteristics of the Population Below the Poverty Level: 1980." Washington, D.C.: U.S. Government Printing Office.

———. 1983a. *General Social and Economic Characteristics, Part 45, Texas.* Washington, D.C.: U.S. Government Printing Office.

———. 1983b. *County and City Data Book.* Washington, D.C.: U.S. Government Printing Office.

———. 1983c. *Detailed Population Characteristics, Texas.* 2 vols. Washington, D.C.; U.S. Government Printing Office.

U.S. Government Printing Office. 1972. *Health Services for Domestic Agricultural Workers.* Washington, D.C.: U.S. Government Printing Office.

————. 1975. *The United States Reports*. Vol 416. Washington, D.C.: U.S. Government Printing Office.

Vassberg, David E. 1966. "The Use of Mexicans and Mexican-Americans in the Agricultural Work Force in the Lower Rio Grande Valley of Texas." Masters Thesis, University of Texas.

Velimirovic, Boris (ed.) 1978. *Modern Medicine and Medical Anthropology in the United States–Mexico Border Population*. Washington, D.C.: Pan American Health Organization.

Vigil, Maurilio, 1977. *Chicano Politics*. Washington, D.C.: University Press of America.

Waldrop, Revel H., and John G. Bruhn. 1975. "Health Management and Health Professions Education in South Texas." Galveston, Texas: University of Texas Medical Branch.

Ward, Richard A. 1975. *The Economics of Health Resources*. Reading, Mass.: Addison-Wesley Publishing Company.

Weaver, Jerry L. 1973. "Mexican-American Health Care Behavior: A Critical Review of the Literature." *Social Science Quarterly* 54 (June): 85–102.

Weaver, John D. 1970. *The Brownsville Raid*. New York: W. W. Norton.

Webb, Walter Prescott (ed.) 1952. *The Handbook of Texas*. Austin, Texas: Texas State Historical Association.

————. 1965. *The Texas Rangers: A Century of Frontier Defense*. Austin, Texas: University of Texas Press.

Weber, David J. (ed.) 1979. *New Spain's Far Northern Frontier: Essays on Spain in the American West, 1540–1821*. Albuquerque, N.M.: University of New Mexico Press.

Weddle, Robert S. 1985. *Spanish Sea: The Gulf of Mexico in North American Discovery, 1500–1685*. College Station, Texas: Texas A&M University Press.

Week, O. D. 1930. "The Texas-Mexican and the Politics of South Texas." *American Political Science Review* (August): 606–627.

Weinberg, Meyer. 1977. *A Chance to Learn: A History of Race and Education in the United States*. Cambridge: Cambridge University Press.

Weisbrod, Burton A. (ed.) 1965. *The Economics of Poverty*. Englewood Cliffs, N.J.: Prentice-Hall, Inc.

Williams, William Appleman. 1966. *The Contours of American History*. Chicago: Quadrangle Books.

Wilson, William Julius. 1987. *The Truly Disadvantaged*. Chicago: University of Chicago Press.

Zavaleta, Antonio N. 1981. "Federal Assistance and Mexican-American Health Status in Texas." *Health* (January): 43–49.

Zavaleta, Antonio N., Gorgiana Coray, and Carlos Rubinstein. 1985. "Health Needs Assessment Survey." Brownsville, Texas: City of Brownsville.

Zeitlin, Irving M. 1972. *Capitalism and Imperialism*. Chicago: Markham Publishing Company.

NEWSPAPERS:

Brownsville Herald (Brownsville, Texas)
Labor Market Review (Texas Employment Commission)
McAllen Monitor (McAllen, Texas)
Port Isabel Press (Port Isabel, Texas)
Valley Morning Star (Harlingen, Texas)

INDEX

POOREST OF AMERICANS

OTHER BOOKS BY ROBERT LEE MARIL

Texas Shrimpers: Community, Capitalism, and the Sea (1983)
Cannibals and Condos: Texans and Texas Along the Gulf Coast
  (1986)

DATE DUE